Problem-Oriented Policing
and Crime Prevention

Problem-Oriented Policing and Crime Prevention

Second Edition

Anthony A. Braga

LYNNE
RIENNER
PUBLISHERS

BOULDER
LONDON

In memory of Joshua D. Christian —
a good friend, brother, son and uncle

Published in the United States of America in 2010 by
Lynne Rienner Publishers, Inc.
1800 30th Street, Boulder, Colorado 80301
www.rienner.com

and in the United Kingdom by
Lynne Rienner Publishers, Inc.
3 Henrietta Street, Covent Garden, London WC2E 8LU

ISBN: 978-1-881798-78-1 (pb : alk. paper)

First published in 2008 by Criminal Justice Press.
Reprinted here from the original edition.

Permissions: Figure 1-1 and Table 5-1 are reprinted under provisions of Her Majesty's
Stationery Office core license C02W0005902. Figures 3-1 and 3-2 are reprinted with permission
from Sage Publications, Inc. Figure 6-4 is reprinted with permission from the Police Executive
Research Forum.

Printed and bound in the United States of America

∞ The paper used in this publication meets the requirements
of the American National Standard for Permanence of
Paper for Printed Library Materials Z39.48-1992.

5   4   3   2   1

CONTENTS

LIST OF FIGURES AND TABLES

ABOUT THE AUTHOR

Anthony A. Braga is a Senior Research Associate in the Program in Criminal Justice Policy and Management at Harvard University's John F. Kennedy School of Government, and in the Berkeley Center for Criminal Justice at the University of California, Berkeley's Boalt Hall Law School. His research focuses on developing problem-oriented policing strategies to prevent gang violence, disrupt illegal gun markets, and address violent crime hot spots. Dr. Braga currently serves as the Chief Policy Advisor to the Commissioner of the Boston Police Department. He has also served as a consultant on these issues to many large police departments–including the Baltimore Police Department, Los Angeles Police Department, New York Police Department, Minneapolis Police Department, Milwaukee Police Department, Oakland Police Department, and San Francisco Police Department–as well as the U.S. Department of Justice, the U.S. Department of the Treasury, the U.S. National Academy of Sciences, and the Bureau of Alcohol, Tobacco, Firearms, and Explosives. Dr. Braga was a Visiting Fellow at the U.S. National Institute of Justice and teaches in the Police Executive Research Forum's Senior Management Institute for Police. He received his M.P.A. degree from Harvard University and a Ph.D. in Criminal Justice from Rutgers University.

FOREWORD TO THE SECOND EDITION

In his introduction, Anthony Braga describes this book as "a modest attempt to enrich the practice of problem-oriented policing" – but it is the author that is modest, not the book, which in fact is quite ambitious. The first edition published six years ago was the first systematic attempt to spell out the relevance of environmental criminology to the practice of problem-oriented policing. Unlike most other branches of criminology, environmental criminology focuses on studying crime not criminals, and its literature contains a wealth of findings about the highly specific forms of crime and disorder that comprise the core business of policing. It helps police understand the ways that offenders set about their business and the choices they must make in committing and getting away with their crimes. It explains why crime is heavily concentrated at particular "hot spots" and on certain kinds of "repeat victims," and why it ebbs and flows with the hour of the day, day of the week, and season of the year. This information, together with the mapping and other analytic techniques that environmental criminologists have helped to develop is of great assistance to police who undertake problem-oriented policing.

Though an academic field, environmental criminology is ultimately concerned with identifying and removing the situational conditions that give rise to specific crime problems. One of its branches, situational crime prevention, is explicitly focused on this objective – the same one that is served by problem-oriented policing. However, because situational prevention was developed by the British Home Office Research and Planning Unit, a policy research department, its evidence-base is more extensive than that of problem-oriented policing. In particular, its literature contains many case studies in which situational temptations and opportunities have been deliberately reduced and the results have been evaluated, including examination of so-called displacement effects. Anthony Braga was one of the first to recognize that this body of research was of direct relevance to problem-oriented policing and to understand that the different enterprises of the two groups – police and environmental criminologist – could be enriched by greater collaboration and understanding between them. It was no accident that he recognized this. He was exposed early in his career to environmental criminology and he made good use of this knowledge in his dissertation research, which was concerned with policing of violent hot spots in Jersey City. Subsequently, he became a core member of the team responsible for the Boston Gun Project, one of the best known and most successful police crime prevention efforts. He now straddles the worlds of academia and policing. He is a senior research associate in Harvard University's Program in Criminal Justice Management and in the University of California's Berkeley Center for Criminal Justice, and he serves as the Chief Policy Advisor to the Boston Police Commissioner.

The first edition of this book was published comparatively recently and one might question whether the small worlds of problem-oriented policing and environmental criminology have developed sufficiently in the interim to justify a new edition. This concern is quickly dispelled by a close look at the book. It is considerably longer than the first edition, though thankfully it is written in the same clear style. It covers some topics addressed only briefly or not at all in the first edition (including disrupting illegal firearms markets, analyzing criminal networks and identifying "near repeat" victimization), and it includes about 40 percent more references than the more than 300 references in the first edition.

Even if longer than the first edition, the book is still comparatively short, which is in keeping with its main purpose: to have provided anything more than an introduction to environmental criminology would have required a much longer work. For example, while it includes some case studies, the book does not attempt to summarize the wealth of studies on specific kinds of crimes and disorder, the details of which are only likely to be of interest to police officers when they are dealing with the crimes in question. To fill this need, the Center for Problem-Oriented Policing, with the support of funds from the Office of Community-Oriented Police Services (COPS), is now producing individual "Problem-Specific Guides" that summarize the research on specific problems and on efforts to control the problems. Some 50 of these guides are available on the Center's web site, *www.popcenter.org*, the three most recent of which deal with bank robbery, robbery of convenience stores, and traffic congestion around schools. Some specially written guides on common police responses to problems, such as crackdowns and street closures, and some problem solving "Tool Guides" on topics such as analyzing repeat victimization and interviewing offenders, can also be found on the web site. Other sections of the web site include a repository of several hundred submissions for the Goldstein and Tilley problem-oriented policing awards, an extensive library of publications relating to problem-oriented policing, and a "learning center" that includes a model college curriculum for a course on problem-oriented policing. The first edition of this book is the only recommended text for all modules of the curriculum, and surely the second edition will replace it.

As a founding member of the Center for Problem-oriented Policing, I find it particularly gratifying that much of the material for this new edition book is drawn from the Center's web site, which was designed specially for the police. Indeed, this serves one other purpose of the book, which Braga identifies at the end of his Introduction: to "help theoretical criminologists think about what concepts are useful for police at the practical level." This shows how the traffic in ideas and influence is not simply one way: just as environmental criminology can assist practical policing, so can the practice of policing help criminological theorizing to become more rooted in reality.

Ronald V. Clarke
Rutgers University, Newark
October 29, 2007

FOREWORD TO THE FIRST EDITION

From among the many developments in the past two decades relating to the improvement of policing and, more broadly, the prevention of crime and disorder, two clusters of activity hold special promise. One is the movement within policing to analyze the specific behavioral problems that the police are called on to handle in the community, and to use the results of these analyses as a basis for developing more effective responses to those problems. The other is the progress made by researchers, almost all of whom are located outside police agencies, in gaining new insights into the nature of crime and disorder and in producing findings about the effectiveness of different preventive strategies.

The two developments are obviously interrelated. They are, in many respects, interdependent. But in practice, they are not sufficiently connected. The major contribution of this book is in the effort the author makes to strengthen that connection; to build bridges between the initiatives of the police and the work of the researchers.

Much of the effort within policing has been accomplished under the umbrella of problem-oriented policing. That concept calls for the police to examine, anew and in-depth, groups of similar incidents to which they most likely have responded in a generic, routine manner in the past; to explore alternatives for responding to these grouped incidents or problems (with a priority on preventive action); and to test the relative value of these new responses. We now have a substantial collection of work, largely the product of individual police officers, that demonstrates the value of adopting this inquiring posture. But fuller development of the concept has been limited by a number of factors. Chief among these has been our failure to build an institutional capacity within policing to engage in in-depth research that could then be used to inform police practices. Part of that effort would require that the police become more knowledgeable about relevant research, much of which has not been easily accessible to them.

In the research field, the relevant development has been in the emerging field of environmental criminology. Building on routine activity theory, rational choice theory, and situational crime prevention, researchers have produced a substantial body of findings – not previously available – that are relevant to the police. These studies provide new insights into common problems of crime and disorder and evaluate the effectiveness of various preventive strategies. But while the volume, quality, and relevance of this research has increased rapidly, the studies are rarely used by the police. Moreover, further advances in this type of research – in both volume and refinement – require a greater number of people with the requisite research skills. They also require closer collaboration between researchers and the police. Researchers need to take advantage of the untapped insights of operating police personnel and the vast amount of data that they acquire.

Thus, while the accomplishments to date with regard to both developments – the initiatives of the police and those of the researchers – are significant and substantial, they are just evolving. They are uneven in their quality. And they are relatively small compared to the ultimate need and, excitedly, the potential. Speeding them up will require a greater investment of resources and skills, and an intensified commitment of both police practitioners and researchers. But progress also requires connecting the two developments – especially by making already available research findings accessible and comprehensible to police personnel. It is to that need that the author of this volume has addressed himself.

Having completed a comprehensive review of the relevant literature, Anthony Braga synthesizes that literature in a way that communicates clearly to police practitioners and to other interested parties. He is well positioned to bridge the existing gap. Braga has an in-depth understanding of problem-oriented policing. He is thoroughly familiar with recent developments in criminology – enabling him to explain clearly how each research effort is grounded in current criminological theories. He knows the literature on crime prevention. And he has the direct experience of having had a key role in one of the most ambitious efforts to bring police practitioners and academic researchers together in an extended collaboration aimed at addressing a specific problem – youth gun violence in Boston.

Given the substantial accumulation of research, the author faced a major challenge in deciding on how best to organize his synthesis of it. He neatly solved this problem by grouping his descriptions of relevant research findings under the three dominant focuses that have emerged in that research: (1) preventing crime at *problem places*; (2) controlling high-activity *offenders*; and (3) protecting *repeat victims*. His three central chapters – the essence of the book – correspond to this grouping. Each of the three terms – and the research findings and methods they embrace – will have meaning to the police. Presenting the material in this way itself has the potential for positively advancing the way in which police think about their work.

The more police practitioners and researchers can join in thinking productively about the specific problems that constitute police business and the more they join in testing the value of different preventive strategies, the greater is the likelihood that they will acquire the evidence to support good practice. And ultimately, it is such evidence that will enable the police to resist being pressured to resort to traditional, but questionable methods of operating; to resist being buffeted about by trends and fads. They will have a more solid basis on which to appeal for a more enlightened form of policing – a form of policing that is effective, and also achievable within democratic constraints.

Herman Goldstein
University of Wisconsin, Madison
August 15, 2002

ACKNOWLEDGMENTS

The research for the first edition of this book was supported under award number 1999-IJ-CX-0023 from the National Institute of Justice, Office of Justice Programs, U.S. Department of Justice. The original project was ably monitored by Lois Mock and well supported by former NIJ Director Jeremy Travis. The second edition of the book was supported by intramural funds from the Program in Criminal Justice Policy and Management at Harvard University's John F. Kennedy School of Government. Points of view in this document are those of the author and do not necessarily represent the official position of the U.S. Department of Justice or Harvard University.

I would like to thank Herman Goldstein, Mark Moore, David Kennedy, Frank Hartmann, and Michael Scott for their helpful comments in the preparation of the manuscript. Each played important roles in challenging and stimulating my thinking on effective crime prevention practices. Special thanks are due to Ronald Clarke, who strongly supported this project from the outset and was a constant source of encouragement and positive feedback. If this book proves useful to practitioners, it was his direction that made it so. I am particularly grateful to Rich Allinson of the Criminal Justice Press for knowing when to be patient when certain deadlines were missed due to unforeseeable life challenges and knowing when to apply gentle pressure when the writing of the text had stalled due to dubious competing interests. Phyllis Schultze, also known as the world's greatest librarian, deserves special mention for her generosity and indefatigable willingness to locate obscure references located deep in the stacks of Rutgers University's Criminal Justice Library. My long-time companion Cassie provided much needed kindness and support throughout the production of this manuscript. Finally, I would like to thank the police officers and civilian staff from the many law enforcement agencies that I've been fortunate enough to work with over the years. I learned much from you.

Anthony A. Braga

1. INTRODUCTION

Society has long looked to police departments to deal effectively with crime. Our ideas about how the police should go about dealing with crime have evolved over time. For a long time the public was content with police departments whose primary role was to apprehend offenders, so society could hold law breakers accountable for their crimes (Wilson and McLaren, 1977). Their primary technologies to fulfill this goal were preventive patrol, rapid response, and retrospective investigations (Sparrow et al., 1990). As the limits of these approaches are by now well known, the police became more interested in preventing crime through more aggressive preventive tactics and hoped this thicker response would deter crime.[1] These aggressive tactics included directed patrols and patrols targeting particular individuals (Pate et al., 1976), field interrogations and searches (Moore, 1980), decoy operations (Moore, 1983a), and sting operations (Klockars, 1980; Marx, 1988). Although these differed from past tactics – in other words, the new tactics were now focused on anticipating crimes rather than simply reacting to crime – they were primarily intended to produce deterrent effects through arrests.

Recently, police departments have been experimenting with a much broader idea of crime prevention. Proactive efforts to prevent crime were advanced by the publication of Herman Goldstein's seminal article on problem-oriented policing (Goldstein, 1979). He argued that police departments were much too focused on how they were organized to do their work rather than on the crime problems they needed to solve. Goldstein further suggested that greater operational effectiveness could be accomplished through detailed analyses of crime problems and the development of appropriate solutions, rather than by effecting improvements in organization and management. The problem-solving process requires "identifying these problems in more precise terms, researching each problem, documenting the nature of the current police response, assessing the adequacy of existing authority and resources, engaging in a broad exploration of alternatives to present responses; weighing the merits of these alternatives, and choosing from among them" (Goldstein, 1979: 236). Since Goldstein's article, many police departments have experimented with this "problem-oriented" approach, and the available evaluation research suggests that problem-oriented policing is effective in dealing with a wide range of crime problems, including thefts and burglary (Eck and Spelman, 1987), street-level drug markets (Kennedy, 1993; Hope, 1994), and violent crime hot spots (Braga et al, 1999). Another example is in Boston, where an inter-agency working group crafted a problem-oriented strategy that has shown much promise in reducing a seemingly intractable problem – youth gun homicide (Kennedy et al., 1996a; Braga et al., 2001).

This book represents a modest attempt to enrich the practice of problem-oriented policing. As others observe (e.g., Read and Tilley, 2000; Eck, 2000; Clarke 1998), there are many avenues through which the practice of problem-oriented policing can be improved. These include creating better classification systems for problems, improving the capacity of police departments to analyze data on problems, and developing response guides that reveal the conditions that are necessary for interventions to be successful. This book attempts to contribute to improving practice by a) systematically assembling research and experience on successful problem-oriented policing and "situational crime prevention"[2] projects; b) linking the crime prevention mechanisms at work in these projects to theoretical concepts; and c) drawing out the lessons to be learned from these experiences so these insights can be more easily incorporated into the everyday practice of problem-oriented policing.

This book is also based on the idea that one often gets more inspiration and more useful ideas from looking at concrete examples of problem-oriented policing and situational crime prevention than from understanding the general principles of these processes. The development of effective crime prevention techniques depends on a great deal of creativity and imagination from police practitioners. The need for creativity may be partly due to the fact that the field has not developed an adequate knowledge of prevention methods. But it also could be true that the work of problem-oriented policing will never be entirely routinized. It is quite possible that even after we have had long experience with the techniques of problem-oriented policing, developed a high degree of self-consciousness about the methods, and even learned about how particular kinds of problems are best solved generally, effective crime prevention may still require a great deal of imagination and creativity to deal with the peculiarities of a new situation (Kennedy and Moore, 1995). As such, this book should be regarded not as a cookbook on effective crime prevention, but, hopefully, as a text that will help inspire creativity in dealing with real world crime problems.

Organization of This Book

The chapters in this book are organized around the well known problem analysis triangle (Figure 1-1), which breaks crime down into the features of places, features of offenders, and features of victims (see, e.g., Hough and Tilley, 1998; Leigh et al., 1996). This analytic device was intended to help analysts visualize crime problems and understand relationships among the three elements. Moreover, research suggests that crime tends to cluster among a few places, offenders, and victims. Spelman and Eck (1989) examined several studies and estimated that 10 percent of the victims in the United States are involved in 40 percent of victimizations, 10 percent of offenders are involved in over 50 percent of crimes, and 10 percent of places are the sites of about 60 percent of crimes. As such, these broad categories of crime problems are useful ways to think about focusing limited police resources. In practice, the underlying conditions that give rise to

Figure 1-1. Problem Analysis Triangle.
Source: Hough and Tilley (1998: 23). Reprinted with permission.

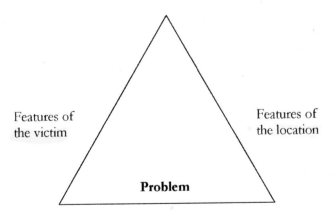

Features of
the victim

Features of
the location

Problem

Features of the offender

crime problems – and the resulting interventions to alleviate crime problems – are likely to overlap these areas and, quite possibly, not fit neatly into the three areas. For example, analysis of a gang violence problem may well reveal that much gang violence is retaliatory in nature (Decker, 1996) and that today's offenders are tomorrow's victims and vice versa. Analysis may also reveal that gang violence tends to cluster at particular places in the city (Block and Block, 1993; Kennedy et al., 1996a). As such, the resulting problem-oriented interventions to reduce gang violence may well address relevant features of places, offenders, and victims. Nonetheless, the crime triangle provides an easy-to-understand framework around which to organize examples of effective problem-oriented policing and situational crime prevention efforts.

Chapters 3, 4 and 5 begin with a few examples of effective crime prevention projects, which are followed by a discussion of criminological research and theory that provides some insight on why these measures were effective. Additional interventions and research are also discussed as each chapter unfolds. The final chapter in this book presents a few administrative arrangements in police departments that could facilitate effective problem-oriented policing. Since many of the projects included in this book were not designed explicitly to link particular theories to observed crime prevention gains, the discussions of crime prevention mechanisms at play are based to some extent on speculation. As such, this is not an exercise in theory testing, but an exercise in applying theoretical knowledge to the task of illuminating crime prevention processes that could enrich practice.

Readers who are familiar with the wide range of criminological theories will undoubtedly notice that certain theories and perspectives are privileged over others. Most criminological research focuses on why some people become persistent offenders (Felson and Clarke, 1998). However, as Eck (2000) observed, by the time a problem comes to the attention of the police, the questions of why people offend are no longer relevant. The most pressing concerns are why offenders are committing crimes at particular places, selecting particular targets, and committing crimes at specific times (Eck, 2000). While police officers are important entry points to social services for many people, they are best positioned to prevent crimes by focusing on the situational opportunities for offending rather than attempting to manipulate socio-economic conditions that are the subjects of much criminological inquiry and the primary focus of other governmental agencies. Theories that deal with the "root causes" of crime focus on interventions that are beyond the scope of most problem-oriented policing projects. Theories that deal with opportunities for crime and how likely offenders, potential victims, and others make decisions based on perceived opportunities have greater utility in designing effective problem-oriented policing interventions (Eck, 2000; Felson and Clarke, 1998).

The Police and Crime Prevention: A Brief Historical Overview

The police developed as a mechanism to do justice by apprehending offenders and holding them accountable (Wilson and McLaren, 1977). Since their primary practical goal was to reduce crime victimization, police long believed that they were in the business of crime prevention (President's Commission on Law Enforcement and Administration of Justice, 1967). Police strategists relied upon two ideas to prevent crimes: deterrence and incapacitation. The imminent threat of arrest was their main strategy to generate *general deterrence*, which is the use of threatened punishment to dissuade the general public from contemplating crimes. The police attempted to generate *specific deterrence* by apprehending criminals with the intent of discouraging those particular individuals from committing crimes in the future. The police also believed that arrests would prevent crime by the *incapacitation* of criminals: their removal from the everyday world and subsequent confinement in jail or prison. In particular, the police sought to prevent repeat offenders from continuing their careers through specific deterrence, incapacitation, and, to some degree, *rehabilitation* (a change from illegal to legal behavior patterns as a result of their subsequent incarceration or community supervision). The police were reliant on the other parts of the criminal justice system to pursue these goals, but they could at least start the process by arresting offenders and building credible cases against them. As many observers have pointed out, these police crime prevention efforts were, in reality, reactive (see, e.g., Goldstein, 1979); they only began after a crime was committed.

In addition to preventing crime through deterrence and incapacitation, in U.S. policing circles prior to 1965, the term *prevention* also referred to the work of a unit handling juvenile cases (often referred to as the "crime prevention unit") or a unit of officers assigned to conducting educational "outreach" programs in the schools. These programs were neither department-wide nor large in size, but were significant in that they were often seen as segregating and compartmentalizing the "prevention" work of the police.

Since the early 1990s, the police have become much more interested a broader idea of prevention and the use of a wide range of crime prevention tactics (Roth et al., 2000). The search for greater citizen satisfaction, increased legitimacy, and more effective crime prevention alternatives to the traditional tactics used by most police departments led to the development of problem-oriented policing and "hot spots" policing (see Chapter 3). The operational paradigms of many modern American police departments have steadily evolved from a "professional" model of policing to a community-oriented, problem-solving model (Roth et al., 2000; Greene, 2000). Growing community dissatisfaction and a series of research studies that questioned the effectiveness of the professional model's basic tenets served as catalysts for the shift. Professional policing was, in turn, initiated as a reform of the deplorable policing practices prevalent before the 1930s during the so-called "political era." Corruption, widespread abuse of authority, scandals, and a lack of professional standards were pervasive problems in this earlier period; these considerable shortcomings resulted in a public outcry for better policing.

Criminologists such as August Vollmer – the reform-minded chief in Berkeley, CA from 1905 to 1932 – and O.W. Wilson – the Chicago police chief in the post-World War II period – were pivotal figures in the development of "professional," also known as "reform," policing. These police leaders were the architects of the dominant paradigm, between the 1940s and 1960s, which remained influential through the 1980s. The professional model emphasized military discipline and structure, higher education for police officers, adoption of professional standards by police agencies, separating the police from political influence, and the adoption of technological innovations ranging from strategic management techniques to scientific advances such as two-way radios and fingerprinting.

The corrupt policing practices of the "political era" were slowly eliminated during the 1940s and 1950s as departments changed operational strategies to the reform model. The more rigorous standards and professionalism of the reform model successfully controlled much misbehavior and maintained policing as a viable profession. During the post World War II period, the police officer's role as "crime fighter" was solidified (Walker, 1992). Policing focused itself on preventing serious crimes and advanced three operational strategies to achieve this goal: preventive patrol, rapid response, and investigation of more serious cases by specialized detective units.

During the 1970s, researchers sought to determine how effective these policing strategies actually were in controlling crime. Preventive patrol in radio cars was thought by most police executives to serve as a deterrent to criminal behavior. Contrary to this consensus, an early British experiment concluded that, although crime increases when patrol is completely removed from police beats, the *level* of patrolling in beats makes little difference in crime rates (Bright, 1969). The well known Kansas City Patrol Experiment further examined the effectiveness of varying levels of random preventive patrol in reducing crime. This landmark study revealed that crime rates and citizen satisfaction remained the same no matter what the level of radio car patrol – whether it was absent, doubled, or tripled (Kelling et al., 1974). Replications followed and obtained similar results. In Nashville, Tennessee, a level of 30 times the normal amount of patrol for selected districts was found to be successful in reducing crime at night, but not during the day (Schnelle et al., 1977). However, permanent long-term increased preventive patrol in an entire district is neither cost-effective, economically feasible, nor practical for a department's operations. Other studies revealed that preventive patrol's inefficiency might be due to the fact that many serious crimes occur in locations (homes, alleys, businesses) not easily visible from a passing radio car (see Eck and Spelman, 1987; Skogan and Antunes, 1979).

In addition, police departments have placed a great emphasis on reducing response time in the belief that it would increase the probability of arrest. However, several studies found that rapid response had little effect on clearance rates (e.g., Spelman and Brown, 1984; Kansas City Police Department, 1978). Only about 3 percent of crimes are reported while in progress; thus rapid response to most calls does not increase the probability of arrest (Spelman and Brown, 1984). The problem is that police departments have no control over two key elements between the time a crime is committed and the time a police officer arrives on the scene: the interval between the commission of a crime and the time it is discovered; and the interval between discovery and the time the citizen calls the police (Walker, 1992). Most crimes are discovered after the fact, and even in most "involvement" crimes – i.e., where the victim is present (e.g., assault) – there is some delay between victimization and the subsequent call to the police.

The third component of the professional "crime fighter" model – successful investigations – rests on the reputation of detectives as possessing special skills and crime-solving abilities. However, this image is largely perpetuated and romanticized by the media. Several researchers have described the reality that criminal investigations largely consist of routine, unspecialized work that is often unfruitful (Walker, 1992). Studies by the Rand Corporation (Greenwood et al., 1977) and the Police Executive Research Forum (Eck, 1983) documented that investigations involve mostly paperwork, phone calls, and the interviewing of victims and witnesses. Only 21 percent of all "index (more serious) crimes" are cleared, and patrol officers at the scene of the crime usually make these arrests. In fact, most crimes are solved through the random circumstances of the crime scene, such as the availability of witnesses or the presence of evidence such as fingerprints, rather than by any special follow-up investigations by detectives.

This series of studies, conducted in the 1970s and 1980s, challenged the three basic tenets of the professional model and raised many questions about proper crime control methods. An even more powerful harbinger of change was the growing community dissatisfaction with the activities of the police departments that served them. During the 1940s and 1950s, many reform-era police departments attempted to improve response times and clearance rates by moving police officers from walking beats into radio cars. This practice had the unfortunate effect of distancing the police from their constituencies. During the 1960s and early 70s, police officers were called upon to quell many conflicts that revolved around larger social issues, such as the civil rights movement and the Vietnam War. College students, minorities, and disenfranchised communities clashed with police departments, which symbolized and enforced the norms of a society that did not represent them. The police were viewed as part of the problem and not a solution (Weisburd and Uchida, 1993; U.S. National Advisory Commission on Civil Disorders, 1968; U.S. President's Commission on Law Enforcement and Administration of Criminal Justice, 1967a, 1967b). The tactics used in law enforcement responses were viewed as draconian, and there was a public outcry over police forces that resembled and acted like "occupying armies" rather than civil servants (Kelling and Moore, 1988). Equally important, the crime rate soared and public satisfaction with the police decreased between the late 1960s and early 1970s; thus, the legitimacy of the police was deeply questioned (Kelling and Moore, 1988).

Other research in the 1970s and 1980s pointed the police in promising directions. Frustrated by the shortcomings of the professional model, police administrators tested different strategies designed both to control crime and to bring the police and the public closer together. The Newark Foot

Patrol Experiment revealed that although foot patrol did not affect the rate of serious crime, citizens perceived their environments as safer and their opinions about the police improved (Police Foundation, 1981). In Houston, a multifaceted fear reduction project was implemented. The components of this project included community stations, citizen contact foot patrol, community organizing teams, and a victim re-contact program. The evaluation of the program found generally positive results. Although serious crime did not decrease, communication between police and citizens increased and fear of crime was reduced (Pate et al., 1986).

Another important finding of these projects was that a large gap existed between the serious crime problems that professional departments attacked and the day-to-day concerns of citizens. Frequently, the police officers who staffed these programs were called upon to deal with less serious complaints, such as abandoned cars, raucous neighborhood youth, and barking dogs (Trojanowicz, 1983). Disorder in the community was more of an ongoing concern for the average citizen than the risk of being the victim of a serious crime. Police agencies soon learned that social incivilities (such as unsavory loiterers, loud music, public drinking, and public urination), and physical incivilities (such as trash, vacant lots, graffiti, and abandoned buildings), had a definite impact on the quality of life in communities (Skogan, 1990).

A police focus on controlling disorder has been hypothesized to be an important way to reduce more serious crimes in neighborhoods. Wilson and Kelling's (1982) "broken windows" thesis suggests the link between disorder and serious crime (see Chapter 3). Signs of deterioration in a community indicate that no one in authority cares and that rules no longer apply; disorder signals potential or active criminals that offenses will be tolerated, and thus serious crime rates increase (Wilson and Kelling, 1982). Research has established that incivilities generate fear (LaGrange et al., 1992; Ferraro, 1995) and are correlated with serious crime (Skogan, 1990; but see Sampson and Raudenbush, 1999). Collectively, this body of research suggests that if the police want to be more efficient at controlling crime, police departments should redefine their role to become more involved in communities and improve the neighborhood environment.

Problem-Oriented Policing

The reactive methods of the professional model are often described as "incident-driven policing." Under this model, departments are aimed at resolving individual incidents instead of solving recurring crime problems

(Eck and Spelman, 1987). Officers respond to repeated calls and never look for the underlying conditions that may be causing like groups of incidents. Officers become frustrated because they answer similar calls and seemingly make no real progress. Citizens become dissatisfied because the problems that generate their repeated calls still exist (Eck and Spelman, 1987). In 1979, Herman Goldstein, a respected University of Wisconsin law professor and former aide to Chicago police chief O.W. Wilson, proposed an alternative; he felt that police should go further than answering call after call, that they should search for solutions to recurring problems that generate the repeated calls. Goldstein described this strategy as the "problem-oriented approach" and envisioned it as a department-wide activity.

His proposition was simple and straightforward. Behind every recurring problem there are underlying conditions that create it. Incident-driven policing never addresses these conditions; therefore incidents are likely to recur. Answering calls-for-service is an important task and still must be done, but police officers should respond systematically to recurring calls arising from the same problem (see Figures 1-2 and 1-3). In order for the police to be more efficient and effective, they must gather information about incidents and design an appropriate response based on the nature of the underlying conditions that cause the problem(s). Goldstein (1990) said, as summarized by Eck and Spelman, (1987: xvi):

> Underlying conditions create problems. These conditions might include the characteristics of the people involved (offenders, potential victims, and others), the social setting in which these people interact, the physical environment, and the way the public deals with these conditions. A problem created by these conditions may generate one or more incidents. These incidents, while stemming from a common source, may appear to be different. For example, social and physical conditions in a deteriorated apartment complex may generate burglaries, acts of vandalism, intimidation of pedestrians by rowdy teenagers, and other incidents. These incidents, some of which come to police attention, are symptoms of the problem. The incidents will continue as long as the problem that creates them persists.

And in Goldstein's words (1979: 236), the problem-solving process requires:

> Identifying these problems in more precise terms, researching each problem, documenting the nature of the current police response, assessing its adequacy and the adequacy of existing authority and resources, engaging in a broad exploration of alternatives to present responses, weighing the merits of these alternatives, and choosing among them.

Figures 1-2 and 1-3. Incident-Driven Policing versus Problem-Oriented Policing.

Source: Eck and Spelman (1987: 4).

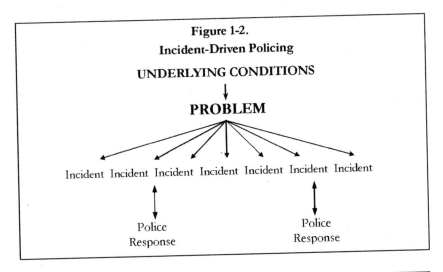

Figure 1-2.
Incident-Driven Policing

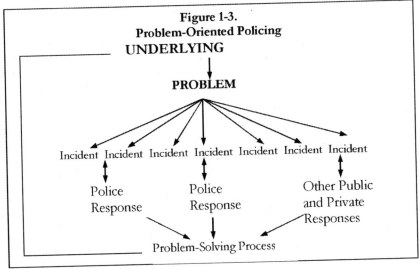

Figure 1-3.
Problem-Oriented Policing

Problem-Oriented Policing and Situational Crime Prevention

The developing field of situational crime prevention has also supported the problem-oriented policing movement since its genesis in the British Government's Home Office Research Unit in the early 1980s (Clarke, 1992). Instead of preventing crime by altering broad social conditions such as poverty and inequality, situational crime prevention advocates changes in local environments to *decrease opportunities* for crimes to be committed. Situational crime prevention techniques comprise "opportunity-reducing measures that (1) are directed at highly specific forms of crime, and that (2) involve the management, design, or manipulation of the immediate environment in as systematic and permanent way as possible so as to (3) increase the effort and risks of crime and reduce the rewards as perceived by a wide range of offenders" (Clarke, 1992: 4). The situational analysis of crime problems follows an action-research model that systematically identifies and examines problems, develops solutions, and evaluates results (Clarke, 1992; Lewin, 1947). The applications of situational crime prevention have shown convincing crime prevention results to a variety of problems ranging from obscene phone callers (Clarke, 1990), to burglary (Pease, 1991), to car radio theft (Braga and Clarke, 1994), among many others. This simple but powerful perspective is applicable to crime problems facing the police, security personnel, business owners, local government officials, and private citizens. Indeed, Goldstein's (1990) formulation of problem-oriented policing shares many similarities to the action-research underpinnings of situational prevention (Clarke, 1992).

Problem-Oriented Policing and Community Policing

During the late 1980s and throughout the 1990s, problem-oriented policing and *community policing* were both heralded as revolutionary alternatives to the professional model of policing. The two terms have become political buzzwords, and scores of books and articles have been written on these new strategic concepts.[3] The terms are sometimes referred to as essentially the same strategy (Walker, 1992; Kennedy and Moore, 1995), however others maintain a distinct separation between the two concepts (Goldstein, 1990; Eck and Spelman, 1987). Problem-oriented policing (POP) is typically defined as focusing police attention on the underlying causes of problems behind a string of crime incidents, while community policing emphasizes the development of strong police-community partnerships in a joint effort to reduce crime and enhance security (Moore, 1992). Indeed, community-oriented police officers use problem solving as a tool, and problem-oriented departments often form partnerships with the community.

The term "problem solving" is often conceptualized as what an officer does to handle small, recurring beat-level problems, and it is distinguished from problem-oriented policing based on its rudimentary analysis of the problem and lack of formal assessment (see, e.g., Cordner, 1998). In short, some observers suggest that the term "problem solving" does not adequately capture the substance of problem-oriented policing as envisioned by Goldstein (1990). Scott (2000) reports that Goldstein himself has been especially careful to avoid the term "problem solving" because many, if not most, problems the police confront are too complex for anything approaching a final solution; reducing harm, alleviating suffering, and/or providing some measure of relief are ambitious enough aims for the police.

Summary. The primary purpose of this book is to understand why problem-oriented policing interventions are effective, and, in doing so, to strengthen and enrich what is happening in practice. While examining promising problem-solving interventions, this book assembles selected theories and research findings in a manner intended to be useful to practitioners. By understanding the theoretical mechanisms at work, practitioners may be able to develop more robust problem-solving interventions when dealing with real-life situations in the field. Also, by linking policy to academic theory, this research review will help theoretical criminologists think about what concepts are useful for police at the practical level.

NOTES

1. See Kelling et al., 1974; Spelman and Brown, 1984; Greenwood et al., 1977).
2. Situational crime prevention is defined on page 12 in this chapter, and further detailed in Chapter 2 (see Table 2-3).
3. For example, Rosenbaum, 1994; Greene and Mastrofski, 1988; Hartmann, 1988; Goldstein, 1990; Toch and Grant, 1991; Trojanowicz and Bucqueroux, 1990, 1994.

2. THE PRACTICE OF PROBLEM-ORIENTED POLICING

The problem-oriented policing approach was given an operational structure in Newport News, Virginia. Researchers from the Police Executive Research Forum (PERF) and a group of officers selected from the various ranks of the Newport News Police Department crystallized the philosophy into a set of steps known as the SARA model (Eck and Spelman, 1987). The SARA model consists of these stages:

- *Scanning* – the identification of an issue and determining whether it is a problem;

- *Analysis* – data collection on the problem to determine its scope, nature, and causes;

- *Response* – the use of the information from the analysis to design an appropriate response, which can involve other agencies outside the normal police arena; and,

- *Assessment* – evaluation of the impact of the response on the problem it was supposed to solve, the results of which can be used to reexamine the problem and change responses or to maintain positive conditions (Eck and Spelman, 1987).

In practice, it is important to recognize that the development and implementation of problem-oriented responses do not always follow the linear, distinct steps of the SARA model (Capowich and Roehl, 1994; Braga and Weisburd, 2006). Rather, depending on the complexity of the problems to be addressed, the process can be characterized as a series of disjointed and often simultaneous activities. A wide variety of issues can cause deviations from the SARA model, including identified problems needing to be reanalyzed because initial responses were ineffective, and implemented responses that sometimes reveal new problems (Braga and Weisburd, 2006). It is also important to remember that the SARA model is only one way of operationalizing problem-oriented policing; as Read and Tilley (2000) remind us, it is not the only way and perhaps may not be the best way for police to address problems. Problem-oriented policing is an analytic approach, not a specific set of technologies (Kennedy and Moore, 1995). Interventions implemented as part of the problem-oriented process can be multiple and may evolve over time if field conditions change or offenders adapt to the original response.

Scanning

Scanning involves the identification of problems that are worth looking at because they are both important and amenable to solution. Herman Goldstein suggested that the definition of problems be at the street-level of analysis and not be restricted by preconceived typologies. As he suggested (1990: 68):

> It is not yet clear what significance, if any, there may be to the way in which problems are naturally defined. Nor is it clear if, for the purposes of analysis, one way of defining problems is preferable to another. It may be that none of this matters: that the primary concern ought to be to define the problem in terms that have meaning to both the community and the police.

Goldstein specified what is meant by a problem as: "a cluster of similar, related, or recurring incidents rather than a single incident; a substantive community concern; or a unit of police business" (1990: 66). Eck (2003: 82) delineated three elements of crime problems:

> First, problems are groups of incidents, not singular events. Second, the elements in this group are connected in some meaningful way, not random or arbitrary. These two elements suggest that the events that make up a problem stem from the same underlying cause. The third element requires that the incidents be disturbing or harmful to members of the public, not just to the police.

Eck and Clarke (2003) identified 6 behaviors and 11 environments to classify common police problems (Table 2-1). The "behaviors" dimension focuses on the way people act, the interactions among participants in a

Table 2-1. A Classification Scheme for Common Problems Facing Local Police[a]

ENVIRONMENTS	Predatory	Consensual	Conflicts	Incivilities	Endangerment	Misuse of Police
Residential						
Recreational			A			
Offices						
Retail		C				B
Industrial						
Agricultural						
Educational						
Human service						
Public ways	G	F		E	D	
Transport						
Open/Transitional				H	H	

Source: Clarke and Eck (2005: Step 15).

[a]*The table above shows the full classification. A problem is classified by putting it in the cell where the appropriate column intersects with the appropriate row. So, for example, the 2001 Tilley Award winner dealt with glass bottle injuries around pubs, a conflict-recreational problem (A). Officers in San Diego had to deal with repeat fraudulent calls of gang member threats at a convenience store (B). Notice how this differs from the 2003 Plano, TX Goldstein award runner-up addressing stores selling alcohol to minors (C). The 2002 Goldstein Award winner dealt with motor vehicle accidents involving migrant farm workers, an endangerment-public ways problem (D). The 1999 Goldstein Award winner dealt with litter and vagrancy, a public way/incivility problem (E). Consider the difference between a problem of street corner drug sales (F) and a robbery-retaliatory shooting problem stemming from drug rip-offs (G). These two problems overlap, but they are not the same.*

problem, and their motivations. The "environments" dimension focuses on who owns the location and has control over people using the environment. Eck (2003) suggested that this classification scheme clarifies common problems by removing vague concerns that can't be located in one of the 66 cells on the grid, such as "neighborhoods" (which often contain problems but are not problems in themselves) and status characteristics such as truancy, where there is no geographic focus or harmful behavior that ought to be the focus of police attention. Removing vague concerns and requiring specificity in problem identification enhances the subsequent steps of problem analysis and response development (Eck, 2003).

While this book mostly focuses on "crime" problems, it is important to note that a great deal of policing relates to non-crime problems, including regulatory problems (e.g., traffic), and very minor criminal matters. Problem-oriented policing, as a concept, is equally applicable to all of the community problems that the community looks to the police to handle. The research on "harder" crime problems described in this book has relevance, in the methodology, to the "softer" problems as well.

There are many ways a problem might be nominated for police attention. A police officer may rely upon his or her informal knowledge of a community to identify a problem that he or she thinks is important to the well-being of the community. Another possibility is to identify problems from the examination of citizen calls-for-service coming into a police department. This approach is implicitly recommended by those who advocate "repeat call analysis" or the identification of "hot spots" (Sherman, 1987; Sherman et al., 1989). The notion is that citizens will let the police know what problems are concerning them by making calls as individuals. By analyzing these calls, and grouping them in ways that point to common causes or common solutions, the police may be able to develop a response that ameliorates the problem that is generating the calls. With the recent proliferation of computerized mapping technology in police departments, there has been a strong movement in police departments to use these techniques in the identification of crime problems (Weisburd and McEwen, 1997).

Problems can also be identified by examining the distribution of crime incidents at specific public or private places such as stores, bars, restaurants, shopping malls, ATM locations, apartment buildings, and other facilities. For example, crime analysts in Chula Vista, California, ranked all parks over two acres from the most crime to the least (Clarke and Eck, 2007). A simple bar graph revealed that three parks had far more crime than the rest, and most parks had very little crime (Figure 2-1). The obvious implication is that the police need to understand why crime is clustering at these three parks so they can develop appropriate crime prevention strategies.

Another approach to identifying problems is through consultation with community groups of different kinds, including other government agencies. This differs from analyzing individual calls-for-service because the demands come from groups, rather than individuals. If the police are interested in forging partnerships with groups as well as individuals, then it is important to open up channels through which groups can express their concerns, such as community advisory councils or regular meetings held by the police to which all members of a community are invited (Skogan and Hartnett, 1997). This approach has the advantage of allowing the community's views about what is important to shape police views about

Figure 2-1. Crime in Chula Vista Parks (over 2 acres).

Source: Clarke and Eck (2007: 9).

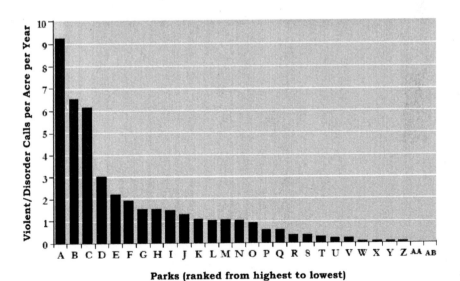

what is important, rather than leaving the nomination of problems to police analysts. Obviously, the best approach to identifying problems would be to combine these efforts.

Analysis

This phase challenges police officers to analyze the causes of problems that lay behind a string of crime incidents or substantive community concern. Once the underlying conditions that give rise to crime problems are known, police officers develop and implement appropriate responses. The challenge to police officers is to go beyond the analysis that naturally occurs to them, which involves finding the places and times where particular offenses are likely to occur, and then identifying the offenders who are likely to be responsible for the crimes. Although these approaches have had some operational success, this type of analysis usually produces directed patrol operations or a focus on repeat offenders. The idea of analysis for problem solving was intended to go beyond this. Goldstein (1990: 98-99) described this as the problem of "ensuring adequate depth" in the analysis, and offers the following as an example of what he means:

> A study of the problem of theft from merchants by shoppers illustrates the need. It is easy, accepting how we have commonly responded to shoplifting to become enmeshed in exploring new ways in which to increase the number of arrests – including more efficient processing by the police. If one digs deeper, however, it becomes apparent that shoplifting is heavily influenced by how the merchandise is displayed and the means used to safeguard it. The police often accept these merchandising decisions as givens and are resigned to processing as many shoplifters as a store chooses to apprehend and deliver into their hands. More in-depth probing raises questions about the effectiveness of arrests as the primary means to reduce shoplifting and the proprietary of delegating to private interests the judgment of who is to be arrested. The police may then focus on ways to curtail theft and on use to be made of arrest, including criteria to be employed in deciding who to arrest. If the analysis of the shoplifting problem had been superficial, limited to exploring ways to increase the number of arrests, the whole purpose of the enterprise would have been lost.

Situational crime prevention has further developed the methodology of analyzing problems, and provided important examples of how crime problems may be closely analyzed. Situational crime prevention measures are tailored to highly specific categories of crime. As Clarke (1997) described, distinctions must be made not between broad crime categories such as burglary and robbery, but between the different kinds of offenses that comprise each of these categories. For example, in their analysis of domestic burglary in a British city, Poyner and Webb (1991) revealed that cash and jewelry burglaries tended to occur in older homes near the city center, while burglaries of electronic goods, such as TVs and VCRs, generally occurred in newer homes in the suburbs. Analysis further revealed that offenders on foot committed cash and jewelry burglaries. In the burglaries of electronic goods, offenders used cars that had to be parked near to the house, but not so close that they would attract attention. The resulting crime prevention strategies differed accordingly. To prevent cash and jewelry burglaries in the city center, Poyner and Webb (1991) recommended improving security and surveillance at the burglar's point of entry; in contrast, to prevent electronic good burglaries in the suburbs, they suggested improving the natural surveillance of parking places and roadways in the area.

In her review of bank robbery problems, Deborah Lamm Weisel (2007) suggested that distinguishing between amateur robbers and professional robbers is critical in selecting crime prevention strategies that are most likely to be effective. Amateur bank robbers are usually solitary offenders who tend to rob banks around midday when branches are full of customers; professionals often work in teams and prefer to operate when there are fewer customers, such as opening time, which increases their control of the crime scene. Lamm Weisel (2007: 14) reported that, " . . . although discouraging an amateur robber is much easier and the approach different than thwarting a team of professionals, the measures that might deter an amateur may well increase the likelihood of violence by professional robbers." In-depth analysis is obviously important in understanding the nature of bank robbery problems and developing an appropriate response that would prevent crime rather than increase the potential for violence. Table 2-2 gives an example of the key elements that an adequate problem analysis would need to consider in distinguishing between professional and amateur bank robbers.

Environmental criminology explores the distribution and interaction of targets, offenders and opportunities across time and space (see Chapter 3). Beyond providing important theoretical and conceptual insights on the dynamics of crime problems, environmental criminology has developed a number of data collection methodologies that can greatly enrich the understanding of crime problems and, in turn, result in more effective responses (Clarke, 1998). Most police agencies usually don't analyze data beyond the information contained in their official systems – typically arrests, crime incidents, and citizen calls-for-service. These alternative data collection methods include (as discussed in Clarke, 1998: 324):

- Victimization surveys, which provide more detail about the impact of the problem on people's everyday lives;

- Crime audits, where interviewers walk around a neighborhood with people who live there or around a park with regular users, and record where they report being afraid; and,

- Structured interviews with offenders to find out more about their motives and their methods of committing crimes.

Police agencies must make investments in developing problem analysis skills, such as training in research methodology, data collection and analysis, and relevant criminological theories, for one or more individuals on their staff (Goldstein, 2003). Improving crime analysis techniques is discussed in greater detail in Chapter 6. The Center for Problem-Oriented Policing (www.popcenter.org) recommends that problem analysis phase should include the following key elements:

- Identifying and understanding the events and conditions that precede and accompany the problem.

- Identifying relevant data to be collected.

- Researching what is known about the problem type.

- Taking inventory of how the problem is currently addressed and the strengths and limitations of the current response.

- Narrowing the scope of the problem as specifically as possible.

- Identifying a variety of resources that may be of assistance in developing a deeper understanding of the problem.

- Developing a working hypothesis about why the problem is occurring.

Response

After a problem has been clearly defined and analyzed, police officers confront the challenge of developing a plausibly effective response. The development of appropriate responses is closely linked with the analysis that is performed. The analysis reveals the potential targets for an intervention, and in turn, ideas about the type of intervention may suggest important

Table 2-2. Distinguishing Professional and Amateur Bank Robbers

	Professional	Amateur
Offenders	• Multiple offenders with division of labor • Shows evidence of planning • May be older • Prior bank robbery convictions • Travels further to rob banks	• Solitary offender • Drug or alcohol use likely • No prior bank crime • Lives near bank target
Violence	• Aggressive takeover, with loud verbal demands • Visible weapons, especially guns • Intimidation, physical or verbal threats	• Note passed to teller or simple verbal demand • Waits in line • No weapon
Defeat Security	• Uses a disguise • Disables or obscures surveillance cameras • Demands that dye packs be left out, alarms not be activated, or police not be called	
Robbery Success	• Hits multiple teller windows • Larger amounts stolen • Lower percentage of money recovered • More successful robberies • Fewer cases directly cleared • Longer time from offense to case clearance	• Single teller window victimized • Lower amounts stolen • Higher percentage of money recovered • More failed robberies • Shorter time from offense to case clearance, including more same-day arrests • Direct case clearance more likely
Robbery Timing	• Targets banks when few customers are present, such as at opening time • Targets banks early in the week	• Targets banks when numerous customers are present, such as around midday • Targets banks near closing or on Friday
Target Selection	• Previous robbery • Busy road near intersection • Multidirectional traffic • Corner locations, multiple vehicle exits	• Previous robbery • Heavy pedestrian traffic or adjacent to dense multifamily residences • Parcels without barriers • Parcels with egress obscured
Getaway	• Via car	• On foot or bicycle

Source: Lamm Weisel (2007: 15).

lines of analysis. For example, the reason police often look at places and times where crimes are committed is that they are already imagining that an effective way to prevent the crimes would be to get officers on the scene through directed patrols. The reason they often look for the likely offender is that they think that the most effective and just response to a crime problem would be to arrest and incapacitate the offender. However, the concept of "problem-oriented policing" as envisioned by Herman Goldstein (1990) calls on the police to make a much more "uninhibited" search for possible responses and not to limit themselves to getting officers in the right places at the right times, or identifying and arresting the offender (although both may be valuable responses). Effective responses often depend on getting other people to take actions that reduce the opportunities for criminal offending, or to mobilize informal social control to drive offenders away from certain locations.

The responses that problem-oriented police officers develop may be close to current police practices or, in some instances, quite different. It is very likely that another police agency may have tried to solve the kind of problem that an officer is addressing and, as such, it is particularly important to search the available literature (in a library or via the Internet) for what other communities with similar problems have done (Clarke and Schultze, 2005). Goldstein (1990: 102-147) offered the following suggestive list of general alternatives police may consider in developing responses to neighborhood crime problems:

- Concentrating attention on those individuals who account for a disproportionate share of the problem;

- Connecting with other government and private services through referral to another agency, coordinating police responses with other agencies, correcting inadequacies in municipal services, and pressing for new services;

- Using mediation and negotiation skills to resolve disputes;

- Conveying information to the public to reduce anxiety and fear, to enable citizens to solve their own problems, elicit conformity with laws and regulations that are not known or understood, warn potential victims about their vulnerability and advise them of ways to protect themselves, demonstrate to individuals how they unwittingly contribute to problems, to develop support for addressing a problem, and acquaint the community with the limitations on the police and to define realistically what may be expected of the police;

- Mobilizing the community and making use of existing forms of social control in addition to the community;

- Altering the physical environment to reduce opportunities for problems to recur;

- Increased regulation, through statutes or ordinances, of conditions that contribute to problems;

- Developing new forms of limited authority to intervene and detain; and,

- Using civil law to control public nuisances, offensive behavior, and conditions contributing to crime.

Derek B. Cornish and Ronald V. Clarke (2003), working from the idea of situational crime prevention, develop a related but somewhat different list of techniques and specific programs including (Table 2-3):

- Increasing the *effort* that offenders must make by hardening targets, controlling access to facilities, screening exits, deflecting offenders, and controlling tools/weapons of criminal offending;

- Increasing the *risks* that offenders would face by increasing formal surveillance, reducing anonymity, utilizing place managers, extending guardianship, and facilitating natural surveillance;

- Reducing the *rewards* of criminal offending by removing targets, concealing targets, identifying property, disrupting markets, and denying benefits;

- Reducing the *provocations* of criminal offending by reducing frustrations and stress, avoiding disputes, reducing emotional arousal, neutralizing peer pressure, and discouraging imitation; and,

- Removing the *excuses* used by offenders to commit crime by setting rules, stimulating conscience, controlling disinhibitors, and facilitating compliance.

Obviously, these lists are partially overlapping and the prevention measures are presented in somewhat abstract language. Moreover, despite the obvious effort to be systematic and comprehensive, there is a somewhat ad hoc quality to the way the lists are developed and presented. It is important to recognize that these lists present methods and ideas that are still developing as the relatively young fields of problem-oriented policing and situational crime prevention move forward. The purpose of these lists is to

Table 2-3. Twenty-Five Techniques of Situational Prevention

Increase the Effort	Increase the Risks	Reduce the Rewards	Reduce Provocations	Remove Excuses
1. Target harden:	*6. Extend guardianship:*	*11. Conceal targets:*	*16. Reduce frustrations and stress:*	*21. Set rules:*
• Steering column locks and immobilisers	• Take routine precautions: go out in group at night, leave signs of occupancy, carry phone	• Off-street parking	• Efficient queues and polite service	• Rental agreements
• Anti-robbery screens		• Gender-neutral phone directories	• Expanded seating	• Harassment codes
• Tamper-proof packaging	• "Cocoon" neighborhood watch	• Unmarked bullion trucks	• Soothing music/muted lights	• Hotel registration
2. Control access to facilities:	*7. Assist natural surveillance:*	*12. Remove targets:*	*17. Avoid disputes:*	*22. Post instructions:*
• Entry phones	• Improved street lighting	• Removable car radio	• Separate enclosures for rival soccer fans	• "No Parking"
• Electronic card access	• Defensible space design	• Women's refuges	• Reduce crowding in pubs	• "Private Property"
• Baggage screening	• Support whistleblowers	• Pre-paid cards for pay phones	• Fixed cab fares	• "Extinguish camp fires"

3. Screen exits:
- Ticket needed for exit
- Export documents
- Electronic merchandise tags

4. Deflect offenders:
- Street closures
- Separate bathrooms for women
- Disperse pubs

5. Control tools/weapons:
- "Smart" guns
- Disabling stolen cell phones
- Restrict spray paint sales to juveniles

8. Reduce anonymity:
- Taxi driver IDs
- "How's my driving?" decals
- School uniforms

9. Utilize place managers:
- CCTV for double-deck buses
- Two clerks for convenience stores
- Reward vigilance

10. Strengthen formal surveillance:
- Red light cameras
- Burglar alarms
- Security guards

13. Identify property:
- Property marking
- Vehicle licensing and parts marking
- Cattle branding

14. Disrupt markets:
- Monitor pawn shops
- Controls on classified ads
- License street vendors

15. Deny benefits:
- Ink merchandise tags
- Graffiti cleaning
- Speed humps

18. Reduce emotional arousal:
- Controls on violent pornography
- Enforce good behavior on soccer field
- Prohibit racial slurs

19. Neutralize peer pressure:
- "Idiots drink and drive"
- "It's OK to say No"
- Disperse troublemakers at school

20. Discourage imitation:
- Rapid repair of vandalism
- V-chips in TVs
- Censor details of modus operandi

23. Alert conscience:
- Roadside speed display boards
- Signatures for customs declarations
- "Shoplifting is stealing"

24. Assist compliance:
- Easy library checkout
- Public lavatories
- Litter bins

25. Control drugs and alcohol:
- Breathalyzers in pubs
- Server intervention
- Alcohol-free events

Source: Cornish and Clarke (2003: 90).

provide practitioners with useful abstract ideas and supporting concrete examples of alternative responses to crime problems that will help further their creativity in developing appropriate interventions.

The crime triangle described earlier in Chapter 1 was developed from routine activity theory (see Chapter 3), and it has been reformulated to help problem solvers think about the response as well as the analysis (Figure 2-2). The latest formulation of the crime triangle adds an outer level of "controller" for each of the original three elements; problems are created when offenders and targets come together and controllers fail to act (Eck, 2003):

• For the target/victim, the *guardian* is usually someone who protects their own belongings or those of family members, friends, neighbors, and co-workers.

Figure 2-2. Revised Crime Triangle.

Source: Clarke and Eck (2005: section 9).

- For the offender, this is the *handler*, someone who knows the offender well and who is in a position to exert some control over his or her actions. Handlers include parents, siblings, teachers, friends, and spouses.

- For the place, the controller is the *place manager*, a person who has some responsibility for controlling behavior in the specific location such as a bus conductor or teacher in school (adapted from Clarke and Eck, 2003: 9).

When searching for appropriate responses, the revised crime triangle can help problem-oriented police think about what might be done to prevent offenders from reoffending by making better use of handlers, what victims can do to reduce the probability of being targets, and what changes could be made to the places where crimes occur (Clarke and Eck, 2003).

Finally, once an appropriate response has been identified, it has to be implemented. While this may seem obvious, implementing alternative crime prevention strategies can be very difficult in practice. Therefore, it is critically important to outline a response plan and identify responsible parties, state the specific objectives for the response, and carry out the planned activities (for more information on implementing responses, see www.popcenter.org).

Assessment

The crucial last step in the practice of problem-oriented policing is to assess the impact the intervention has had on the problem it was supposed to solve. Assessment is important for at least two different reasons. The first is to ensure that police remain *accountable* for their performance and for their use of resources. Citizens and their representatives want to know how the money and freedom they surrendered to the police are being used, and whether important results in the form of less crime, enhanced security, or increased citizen satisfaction with the police have been achieved. A second reason that assessment is important is to allow the police to *learn* about what methods are effective in dealing with particular problems. Unless the police check to see whether their efforts produced a result, it will be hard for them to improve their practices.

John Eck (2002) observed that it is important to distinguish between assessment and evaluation. Evaluation is a scientific process for determining whether the implemented responses caused any observable decline in the targeted problem. It begins as soon as the problem-solving process starts and continues throughout the stages of the SARA model. An *impact evaluation* focuses on questions of crime prevention effectiveness (e.g., did the problem decline? if so, did the implemented response cause the decline?), while a *process evaluation* focuses on questions of accountability and integrity in response implementation (e.g., did the response occur as planned? did all the response components work?). Since impact and process evaluations are complementary, Eck (2002) strongly recommends that problem solvers conduct both. Figure 2-3 presents a list of critical evaluation questions that should be asked at each stage of the problem-solving process (Eck, 2002). Assessment is the culmination of the evaluation process and represents the final stage where it is determined whether the targeted problem changed as a result of the implemented responses and decisions are made about continuing the response, trying alternative responses, and applying an "effective" response to other places, people, and situations.

The assessment of responses is a key element in facilitating an active exchange of "what works" in crime prevention among police departments. As Clarke (1998: 319) suggested: " . . . if law enforcement agencies do not have a mechanism to learn from others' mistakes and assist others to learn from their experiences, they will always be reinventing the wheel." The degree of rigor applied to the assessment of problem-oriented initiatives will necessarily vary across the size and overall importance of the problems addressed. Serious, large and recurrent problems, such as controlling gang violence or handling domestic disputes, deserve highly rigorous examinations. Other problems that are less serious, or common, such as a lonely elderly person making repeat calls to the police for companionship, are obviously not worth such close examinations. To meet the demands of measuring accountability and performance, problem-oriented police should, at a minimum, describe the scanning, response, and assessment phases by measuring inputs (i.e., monetary and organizational investments made in the project), activities and outputs (i.e., police efforts to produce results), and, to the extent possible, the outcomes of their initiatives (such as reduced crime and enhanced security). In general, problem-oriented police should strive to conduct more rigorous assessments of their responses with due consideration to time and resource constraints. Depending on the availability of funds, police departments should consider partnering with independent researchers to conduct systematic evaluations of their efforts. In the absence of such partnerships, Clarke (1998) suggested that

Figure 2-3. The Problem Solving Process and Evaluation.

Source: Eck (2002: 6).

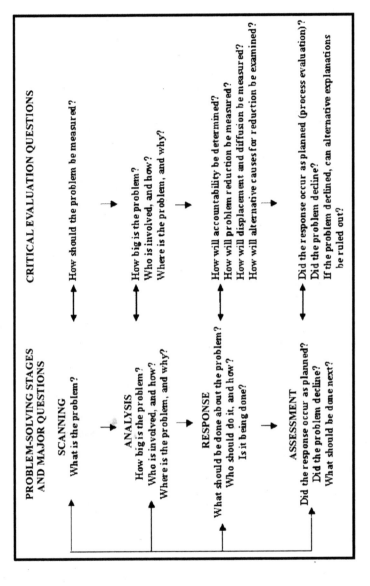

PROBLEM-SOLVING STAGES AND MAJOR QUESTIONS

SCANNING
What is the problem?

ANALYSIS
How big is the problem?
Who is involved, and how?
Where is the problem, and why?

RESPONSE
What should be done about the problem?
Who should do it, and how?
Is it being done?

ASSESSMENT
Did the response occur as planned?
Did the problem decline?
What should be done next?

CRITICAL EVALUATION QUESTIONS

How should the problem be measured?

How big is the problem?
Who is involved, and how?
Where is the problem, and why?

How will accountability be determined?
How will problem reduction be measured?
How will displacement and diffusion be measured?
How will alternative causes for reduction be examined?

Did the response occur as planned (process evaluation)?
Did the problem decline?
If the problem declined, can alternative explanations be ruled out?

police should carefully attempt to relate any observed results to specific actions taken, develop evaluation plans while the project is still being developed, present data on control groups when available, and, as will be discussed below, measure crime displacement. While the degree of rigor applied to the assessment of responses may vary, what must *not* be sacrificed is the goal of measuring results. This will keep the police focused on results rather than means, and that is one of the most important contributions of the idea of problem-oriented policing.

The value of focused crime prevention measures, such as specific applications of problem-oriented policing and situational crime prevention, has been called into question by the threat of crime displacement. This is the notion that efforts to prevent specific crimes will simply cause criminal activity to move elsewhere, to be committed in another way, or even to be manifested as another type of crime; thus negating any crime control gains (Repetto, 1976). This perspective on crime prevention developed from dispositional theories of criminal motivations, and the views of these skeptics were supported by early studies of crime prevention measures that found evidence of displacement (see, e.g., Chaiken et al., 1974; Mayhew et al., 1980). Later studies, however, have indicated that the purported inevitability of displacement was very much overestimated. Several reviews of situational crime prevention measures have concluded that crime displacement was absent or never complete (Hesseling, 1994; Eck, 1993a). In fact, some researchers have suggested that focused crime prevention efforts may result in the complete opposite of displacement – that anticipated crime control benefits are often greater than expected and "spill over" into places and situations beyond the targeted opportunity. Generally referred to as "diffusion of benefits," these unexpected gains have been reported by a number of studies on problem-oriented policing and situational crime prevention measures (see, e.g., Clarke and Weisburd, 1994; Weisburd and Green, 1995a). Although measurement of displacement and diffusion effects can be complex (Barr and Pease, 1990), both rigorous evaluations and simple assessments of problem-oriented policing intervention should attempt to assess the possibility of displacement and diffusion. This is an important step in learning the true impact of crime prevention efforts and determining whether the targeted problem should be reanalyzed and alternative responses implemented. Displacement and diffusion effects are discussed more fully in Chapter 7.

Current Issues in the Substance and Implementation of Problem-Oriented Policing

Researchers have found problem-oriented policing to be effective in controlling a wide range of specific crime and disorder problems, such as convenience store robberies (Hunter and Jeffrey, 1992), prostitution (Matthews, 1990), and alcohol-related violence in pubs and clubs (Homel et al., 1997), among many others. Sherman's (1997) review of problem-oriented policing evaluation findings and methods suggested that this strategy is "promising" in preventing crime. The National Research Council's Committee to Review Research on Police Policy and Practices also concluded that problem-oriented policing has promise in preventing crime because it uses a diverse range of approaches tailored to very specific crime problems (Skogan and Frydl, 2004; Weisburd and Eck, 2004). Figure 2-4 presents a summary of the committee's findings that effective police crime prevention strategies generally have a high level of focus and involve a wide array of tactics. Much of this research is reviewed in Chapters 3, 4 and 5.

Several recently published volumes of case studies provide a good sense of the work being done as well as the strengths and weaknesses of some of the better problem-oriented policing efforts (see, e.g., O'Connor Shelly and Grant, 1998; Sole Brito and Allan, 1999; Sole Brito and Gratto, 2000; Sampson and Scott, 2000). The concept seems to have survived what Gary Cordner (1998: 305) has identified as "first generation" issues, including:

- the view that problem-oriented policing was not "real" police work;

- the view that problem-oriented policing was a fine idea but not practical because of limited resources (e.g., time and personnel);

- the question of whether ordinary police officers had the analytic ability to conduct sophisticated problem-solving projects;

- the question of whether other government agencies had the capacity to meet police halfway in solving chronic community problems; and,

- the danger of raising the community's expectations above what can actually be achieved.

While these issues have not been completely resolved, the implementation of the concept has gone forward as more police managers grew more and more intrigued by the approach (Cordner, 1998).

Figure 2-4. Effectiveness of Police Strategies.

Source: Clarke and Eck (2005: Step 3).

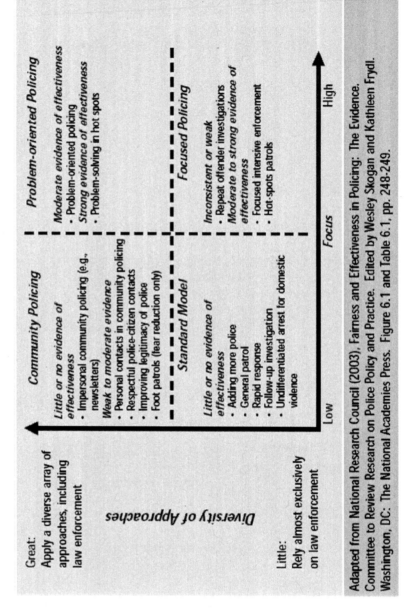

Adapted from National Research Council (2003), Fairness and Effectiveness in Policing: The Evidence. Committee to Review Research on Police Policy and Practice. Edited by Wesley Skogan and Kathleen Frydl. Washington, DC: The National Academies Press. Figure 6.1 and Table 6.1, pp. 248-249.

Although the problem-oriented approach has demonstrated much potential value in preventing crime and improving police practices, research has also documented that it is very difficult for police officers to implement problem-oriented policing strategies (Eck and Spelman, 1987; Clarke, 1998; Braga and Weisburd, 2006). Cordner and Biebel (2005) found that, despite 15 years of national promotion and a concerted effort at implementation within the San Diego Police Department, problem-oriented policing, as practiced by ordinary police officers fell far short of the ideal model. Cordner and Biebel suggested that it may be unreasonable to expect every police officer to continuously engage in full-fledged problem-oriented policing.

Cordner (1998) identified a number of challenging "second generation" issues in the substance and implementation of many problem-oriented policing projects. These issues include: the tendency for officers to conduct only a superficial analysis of problems and then rush to implement a response; the tendency for officers to rely on traditional or faddish responses rather than conducting a wider search for creative responses; and the tendency to completely ignore the assessment of implemented responses (Cordner, 1998). Indeed, the research literature is filled with a long history of cases where problem-oriented policing programs tended to lean toward traditional methods and where the problem-solving process was shallow.[1] Similarly, in his review of several hundred submissions for the Police Executive Research Forum's Herman Goldstein Award for Excellence in Problem-Oriented Policing, Clarke (1998) lamented that many recent examples of problem-oriented policing projects bear little resemblance to Goldstein's original definition. Clarke suggested that this misrepresentation puts the concept at risk of being pronounced a failure before it has been properly tested.

Deficiencies in current problem-oriented policing practices exist in all phases of the process. During the scanning phase, police officers risk undertaking a project that is too small (e.g., the lonely old man who repeatedly calls for companionship) or too broad (e.g., gang delinquency), either of which destroys the discrete problem focus of the project and leads to a lack of direction at the beginning of analysis (Clarke, 1998). In San Diego, most problem-oriented policing projects arose out of specific observations or complaints rather than from analysis of data or any other elaborate scanning methodology (Cordner and Biebel, 2005). Some officers skip the analysis phase or conduct an overly simple analysis that does not adequately dissect the problem or does not use relevant information from other agencies, such as hospitals, schools, and private businesses (Clarke, 1998). Based on his extensive experience with police departments implementing problem-oriented policing, Eck (2000) suggested that much problem analysis consists of a simple examination of police data coupled with the officer's working experience with the problem. Similarly, in their analysis of problem-oriented initiatives in 43 police departments in England and Wales, Read and Tilley (2000) found that problem analysis was generally weak, with many initiatives accepting the definition of a problem at face value, using only short-term data to unravel the nature of the problem, and failing to adequately examine the genesis of the crime problems. Cordner and Biebel (2005) also found that problem analyses conducted by San Diego police officers tended to be informal and limited. Officers rarely engaged in a discrete analysis phase during their projects; they gathered some information as they proceeded, integrating their analysis with the development of responses.

In the response phase, many problem-oriented policing projects rely too much on traditional police tactics (such as arrests, surveillance, and crackdowns) and neglect the wider range of available alternative responses. Read and Tilley (2000) found that officers selected certain responses prior to, or in spite of, analysis; failed to think through the need for a sustained crime reduction; failed to think through the mechanisms by which the response could have a measurable impact; failed to fully involve partners; and narrowly focused their responses, usually on offenders, among a number of other weakness in the response development process. Cordner and Biebel (2005) found that the most common method used by San Diego police officers to develop responses was "personal experience" (62%), followed by "brainstorming" (26%) and "informal discussions with other officers" (slightly more than 10%). Responses generally centered on enforcement – usually targeted enforcement by uniform patrol, directed or saturation patrol – and targeted investigations, plus one or two more collaborative or nontraditional strategies.

Finally, in the assessment or evaluation phase, Scott and Clarke (2000) observed that assessment of responses is rare and, when undertaken, it is usually cursory and limited to anecdotal or impressionistic data. In San Diego, Cordner and Biebel (2005) reported that the most common assessment measure, by far, was "personal observation" (51% of projects), followed distantly by analysis of radio calls (14%) and speaking to residents and businesses (13%).

Reflecting on these practical issues, Eck (2000) commented that the problem-oriented policing that is practiced today is but a shadow of the original concept. However, in their critical review, Braga and Weisburd (2006: 134) found value even in the imperfect implementation of problem-oriented policing:

> Our main conclusion is that there is a disconnect between the rhetoric and reality of problem-oriented policing, and that this is not likely to change irrespective of the efforts of scholars and policy makers. Indeed, we take a very different approach to this problem than others that have examined the deficiencies of problem-oriented approaches. We argue that there is much evidence that what might be called "shallow" problem solving and responses can be effective in combating crime problems. This being the case, we question whether the pursuit of problem-oriented policing as it has been modeled by Goldstein and others, should be abandoned in favor of the achievement of a more realistic type of problem solving. While less satisfying for scholars, it is what the police have tended to do, and it has been found to lead to real crime prevention benefits.

Scott (2006a) observed that policing, at its core, is an action-oriented occupation that tends toward impatience with deliberate analysis in favor of immediate and dramatic action. The determining factor in whether problem-oriented policing projects, however true to the ideal process, are successfully or unsuccessfully implemented is police desire. As Scott (2006a: 31) suggested:

> And, as with most human endeavors, desire is driven by individual or organizational self-interest, however determined. Problem-oriented policing is a promising means of enlightening that self-interest through rigorous analysis and careful weighing of alternatives, but the underlying desire to get problems solved through a new course of action would appear to be extrinsic to the concept itself. Accordingly, researchers and practitioners alike who are interested in advancing problem-oriented policing would do well to better understand why the best laid plans go oft awry.

Few police agencies have well established systems for ensuring that problem-oriented policing action plans are actually executed. Consequently, to the extent that action plans are implemented, it is usually due to the diligence, persistence, and perseverance of one or a few individuals (Scott, 2006a). This book is dedicated to these individuals and, hopefully, will inspire others to follow their lead.

NOTES

1. See Goldstein and Susmilch, 1982; Buerger, 1994a; Capowich et al., 1995; Eck and Spelman, 1984; Read and Tilley, 2000.

3. PREVENTING CRIME AT PROBLEM PLACES

Oakland, California – The Specialized Multi-Agency Response Team (SMART) program was developed by the Oakland Police Department to improve habitation conditions and reduce drug activity at addresses such as businesses, homes, and rental properties. The tactics of the SMART approach included: coordinating a team of city agencies to inspect properties identified as drug nuisances, coercing landowners to clean up blighted properties, posting "no trespassing" signs, enforcing civil law codes and regulatory rules, and initiating court proceedings against property owners who failed to comply with civil law citations. These alternative tactics were supplemented by traditional police enforcement efforts, such as focused patrols at nuisance places and increased arrests of drug dealers. The SMART program activities significantly reduced citizen calls to the police for narcotics offenses and improved the indoor and outdoor physical appearance at the targeted locations. Further analysis revealed that the crime prevention gains at the targeted areas "spilled over" and reduced narcotics activities in the areas surrounding the SMART locations (see Green, 1996).

* * *

Birmingham, England – The city center of Birmingham suffered from a large number of thefts of pocketbooks and wallets from the top of open shopping bags or from side pockets. These thefts were almost exclusively concentrated in the center of one of the largest retail markets in England, known as the Birmingham Bull Ring. Analyses of the problem revealed that existing conditions in the market facilitated thefts. In covered areas of the market, the lighting around the sales stalls was very poor. The poor lighting helped conceal the activities of thieves from customers, employees, and the police. The close arrangement of the stalls made the passageways very tight and congested for the customers. Constant bumping and close contact of market patrons also helped conceal offenders who were stealing wallets and pocketbooks from unsuspecting customers focused on shopping. To remedy this situation, improved lighting was installed to enhance surveillance of the market and the spaces between stalls were widened to prevent close contact between customers and potential offenders. These changes substantially reduced thefts in the markets. There seemed to have been a diffusion of crime prevention benefits, as thefts in nearby markets also declined (Poyner and Webb, 1997).

* * *

Geelong, Victoria, Australia – Geelong is the second largest city in the state of Victoria and the central business district of this city provides entertainment for the entire region. Groups of youth would "pub hop" among the numerous bars and taverns and this activity led to fights, intimidation, and a variety of crimes and incivilities. In response, the police, in partnership with the liquor commission and hotel licensees, led a cooperative effort to stop pub hopping. This initiative required liquor-serving establishments to require cover charges after 11:00 pm, prohibited unlimited reentry when a cover was paid (thus discouraging movements among bars), removed exemptions from cover charges for young women, who were used to lure crowds of young men, and banned special promotional prices for alcoholic drinks (including "happy hours"). The police also patrolled the establishments and enforced provisions against underaged drinking and public drinking. This cooperative effort led to a large decline in pub hopping and a notable reduction in serious assault rates (see Felson et al., 1997).

Why were these initiatives effective in preventing crime and disorder problems? These programs produced crime prevention gains because the interventions focused narrowly on the places where crime was concentrated and successfully modified the underlying conditions that caused crime to cluster at a few places. The appeal of focusing limited resources on a small number of high-activity crime places is straightforward. If we can prevent crime at these high crime places, or crime "hot spots," then we might be able to reduce total crime (Eck, 1997).

In this chapter, the definition of place suggested by John Eck (1997: 7-1) is used: "a place is a very small area reserved for a narrow range of functions, often controlled by a single owner, and separated from the surrounding area . . . examples of places include stores, homes, apartment buildings, street corners, subway stations, and airports." This chapter reviews the criminological research on problem places and synthesizes the prospects of place-oriented crime prevention strategies.

RESEARCH ON CRIME AND PLACE

Police officers have long recognized the importance of place in crime problems. Police officers know the locations within their beats that tend to be trouble spots and also are often very sensitive to signs of potential crimes across the places that comprise their beats. As Bittner (1970: 90) suggested in his classic study of police work, some officers know "the shops, stores, warehouses, restaurants, hotels, schools, playgrounds, and other public places in such a way that they can recognize at a glance whether what is going on within them is within the range of normalcy." The traditional response to such trouble spots typically included heightened levels of patrol and increased opportunistic arrests and investigations. Until recently, police crime prevention strategies did not focus systematically on crime hot spots and did not seek to address the underlying conditions that give rise to high-activity crime places.

Academic interest in the criminology of a place developed from research suggesting that micro-level variation in crime existed within communities. The observation that the distribution of crime varied within neighborhoods has existed for some time (see Hawley, 1944; Hawley, 1950; Shaw and McKay, 1942). However, due to limited analytical capacities, little empirical research examined this variance beyond the community level of analysis. With the advent of powerful computer systems and software packages in the late 1980s, two well known studies found that over 60 percent of crimes were committed at a few small places within communities in Boston (Pierce et al., 1988) and Minneapolis (Sherman et al., 1989). Even within the worst neighborhoods, research found that crime clustered at a few discrete locations, leaving blocks or areas relatively crime-free (Sherman et al., 1989). Further, research by Taylor and Gottfredson (1986) revealed conclusive evidence that linked this spatial variation to the physical and social characteristics of particular blocks and multiple dwellings within a neighborhood. Crime clustering at specific locations within specific neighborhoods has been reported in studies of a variety of crimes, including: burglary (Forrester et al., 1988, 1990; Farrell, 1995); convenience store robberies (Crow and Bull, 1975; Hunter and Jeffrey, 1992); gun crimes (Sherman and Rogan, 1995a); and drug selling (Weisburd and Green, 1994; Sherman and Rogan, 1995b).

The study of the variation of crime within communities has developed from an interest in improving crime control policies (Weisburd et al., 1992). The attributes of a place are viewed as key factors in explaining clusters of criminal events. For example, a poorly lit street corner with an abandoned building, located near a major thoroughfare, provides an ideal location for a drug market. The lack of proper lighting, an abundance of "stash" locations around the derelict property, a steady flow of potential customers on the thoroughfare, and a lack of defensive ownership (informal social control) at the place all generate an attractive opportunity for drug sellers. In many such cases, the police spend considerable time and effort arresting sellers without noticeably affecting the drug trade. The compelling criminal opportunities at the place attract sellers and buyers, and thus sustain the market. If the police want to disrupt the market, they should focus on the features of the place that causes the drug dealing to cluster at that particular location. This approach to focusing on the characteristics of high-crime locations is considered to be a radical departure from traditional criminological theories, which centered prevention efforts on the individual and ignored the importance of place (Sherman et al., 1989).

An important issue in the potential benefit of policing places is whether high-rate locations tend to remain "high rate" for a long time. The "criminal careers" of high-activity places have been found to be relatively stable, suggesting that place-oriented interventions do have potential crime prevention value. Spelman (1995) analyzed calls-for-service at high schools, housing projects, subway stations, and parks in Boston, and found that the risks at these public places remained fairly constant over time. Changes in risks over time at these locations were attributable to random processes or seasonal changes. In Spelman's analyses, 50 percent of calls at hot spots were generated by the unique characteristics of those locations that created criminal opportunities, such as the presence of bars, abandoned buildings or valuable goods, and a lack of proper management. Spelman (1995) suggested that, by focusing on the attributes of a place, police can control about 50 percent of crime at a particular place through problem-oriented interventions. On the other hand, 50 percent of calls were not attributed to the features of the place, and this suggested a substantial degree of instability in crime places over time. According to Spelman (1995: 135-137), "Operational personnel need specific objectives that can be reasonably achieved, and at least a rough idea of when to quit. For example, if problem solving can realistically reduce crime by, say, 40 percent in some locations, the line officers and neighborhood organizations err if they quit after a 10 percent reduction – there are many gains left on the table. They also err if they persist after a 38 percent reduction – there is little left to accomplish, and they could probably achieve more if they took on a different problem." Although long-run risks at the place were the most important source of variation, Spelman (1995) cautioned against identifying crime "hot spots" based on short time periods (such as one month). This is because random errors (i.e., a chance cluster of crime that suddenly appears and never recurs) and short-run changes in risk (i.e., a place may look especially hot at a particular time, such as during the summer months, but all locations were hot) were most important in explaining the clustering of crime at the place.

In Seattle, an analysis of crime trends at specific street segments over a 14-year period suggested that places have stable concentrations of crime events over time (Weisburd, Bushway, Lum, and Yang, 2004). The study also found that a relatively small proportion of places could be grouped as having steeply rising or declining crime trends, and that this subgroup of places was primarily responsible for overall city crime trends. Weisburd and his colleagues (2004) observed that city crime trends could be better understood as strong changes generated by a relatively small group of micro places over time rather than a general process evenly spread across the city landscape. This suggests that police departments dealing with sudden overall increases in particular types of crime should strategically focus on the small number of hot spot areas that drive these crime trends.

Beyond this observed clustering of criminal events, Eck and Weisburd (1995) identified four other types of research evidence that illuminate the role of place in crime. Facilities – such as bars, churches, and apartment buildings – have been found to affect crime rates in their immediate environment. But their impacts depend on the type of people attracted, the way the space is managed, and the possible crime controllers present (such as owners, security, or police). For example, Spelman (1993) found that the presence of unsecured, abandoned buildings on city blocks was positively associated with criminal activity. Felson (2006) identified eleven ways that abandoned sites – such as shells of factories, closed businesses, abandoned residences, and empty lots – can feed crime problems (Figure 3-1). Much

Figure 3-1. Abandoned Sites Can Feed Crime in 11 Ways.

Source: Felson (2006: 86). Reprinted with permission.

(Examples in italics)	
A. Crimes occur at abandoned sites, including lots or buildings.	
1. Brief offenses are committed there	*Prostitutes take customers to abandoned sites*
2. Ongoing offenses committed there	*Abandoned sites used as drug houses*
3. Site itself a crime target	*Copper pipes stripped from abandoned sites*
4. Personal crimes occur there	*Squatters are easy targets for attack*
B. Crimes occur near abandoned site.	
1. Place to stash contraband	*Local burglars hide the loot there*
2. Refuge for offenders	*People sell drugs outside, then take refuge*
3. Less supervision in vicinity	*Attacks occur on nearby streets*
C. An abandoned site nurtures crime beyond.	
1. Escape from parental controls	*Excellent hangout for young offenders*
2. Criminal continuity	*Offenders find past accomplices for another round of offenses*
3. Gang continuity	*Gangs' persistence more likely when they have a hangout*
4. New accomplices recruited	*New youths go to hangout, join in a car theft*

research points to the relationship between bars and crime in proximate areas (Block and Block, 1995; Roncek and Meier, 1991). However, most bars experience little crime while a few may be hot spots of crime (Homel and Clark, 1994; Sherman et al., 1992). As Eck (1997: 7-10) observed, "the behavior of bartenders and bouncers may contribute to violence in these places and changes in bar management practices (from server training and changes in legal liability of bartenders) may reduce assaults, drunk driving, and traffic accidents." As Clarke and Eck (2007) noted, only a small proportion of any type of facility will account for the majority of crime and disorder problems experienced or produced by the group of facilities as a whole.

A variety of physical and social characteristics known as site features can enhance or diminish the attractiveness of a place to offenders (Taylor 1997a, 1997b). Eck (1994) found evidence to suggest that "crack" and powder cocaine dealers prefer buildings with physical features that control access and prevent burglary. However, Eck (1994) also found that crack and powder cocaine dealers seem to prefer small apartment buildings with weak management. Apartment buildings with chronic drug dealing are often encumbered with debt, have lost value, and are often losing money or just breaking even for the owner. Landlords at such locations tend not to know how to control the behavior of their drug-selling residents or cannot afford to do much about drug selling. In contrast, the presence of attendants (Laycock and Austin, 1992) and of closed-circuit television (Poyner, 1991) have been found to reduce the number of auto thefts in parking lots. In short, features such as easy access, lack of guardians, inept or improper management, and the presence of valuable items influence the decisions that offenders make about the places where they choose to commit their crimes (Eck and Weisburd, 1995).

In a similar vein, studies of offender mobility have been interpreted as evidence of "rational and deliberate target searching behavior and the influence of personal characteristics and the distribution of crime targets on this behavior" (Eck and Weisburd, 1995:16). Weisburd and Green (1994) argued that drug markets within close proximity to each other have clear and defined boundaries, and they reported a high degree of territoriality for local drug sellers. Repeat arrestees were more likely to be arrested in a different district in the city than in a drug market a block or two away. In San Diego, Eck (1994) found a high proportion of drug dealers arrested at their home addresses. Offender mobility also seems to vary across gender, age, race, and crime types. For instance, robbers who victimize individuals do not seem to travel as far from home as robbers who attack commercial facilities (Capone and Nichols, 1976). Brantingham and Brantingham (1991b) show that target selection is a direct outgrowth of offender mobility patterns. Thus, offenders are attracted to areas with many potential targets and move from places with few targets to places with many targets (Rhodes and Conley, 1991). Studies of offender interviews have concluded that their target selection decision-making processes exhibit bounded rationality (Eck and Weisburd, 1995). Rengert and Wasilchick's (1990) research on residential burglars revealed that these offenders seek places with cues that indicate acceptable risks and gains, such as homes that are located on the outskirts of affluent neighborhoods. Such places are found during both intentional target searches and during offenders' daily legitimate routines.

Theoretical Perspectives Supporting the Importance of Crime Places

The study of crime events at places is influenced and supported by three complementary theoretical perspectives: rational choice, routine activities, and environmental criminology. The importance of focusing police resources on crime places is also informed by the "broken windows" thesis on the relationship between disorder and more serious crimes.

Rational Choice Perspective

The rational choice perspective assumes that "crime is purposive behavior designed to meet the offender's commonplace needs for such things as money, status, sex, and excitement, and that meeting these needs involves the making of (sometimes quite rudimentary) decisions and choices, constrained as these are by limits of time and ability and the availability of relevant information" (Clarke, 1995: 98; see also Cornish and Clarke, 1986). Rational choice theory makes distinctions among the decisions to initially become involved in crime, to continue criminal involvement, and to desist from criminal offending, as well as the decisions made to complete a particular criminal act. This separation of the decision-making processes in the criminal event from the stages of criminal involvement allows the modeling of the commission of crime events in a way that yields potentially valuable insights for crime prevention. A finding of particular importance to situational crime prevention is that the decision processes and information utilized in committing criminal acts can vary greatly across offenses; ignoring these differences and the situational contingencies associated with making choices may reduce the ability to effectively intervene (Clarke, 1995). In the case of places, modeling an offender's choice of committing crimes at one place over another may provide avenues for intervention. For example, a robber may choose a "favorite" spot because of certain desirable attributes that facilitate an ambush, such as poor lighting and untrimmed bushes. One obvious response to this situation would be to improve the lighting and trim the bushes.

The emphasis of the rational choice perspective on concepts of risk, reward, and effort in criminal decision making has been used to inform the development of situational crime prevention strategies that seek to change offender appraisals of criminal opportunities (Clarke, 1997). As suggested above, improving formal and natural surveillance in public spaces can be helpful in changing offender perceptions of risk. Welsh and Farrington (2004) found that a) closed-circuit television (CCTV) and improved street lighting were equally effective in reducing crime. More detailed analyses found that improved street lighting was more effective than CCTV in reducing crime in city centers and b) both were more effective in reducing property crimes than violent crimes (Welsh and Farrington, 2004). Table 2-3 in Chapter 2 details a variety of situational approaches to increasing the perceived risk of crime.

The rational choice perspective has also provided a theoretical grounding for the development of a "crime scripts" approach through its emphasis on the person-situation interaction in explanations of criminal events (Cornish, 1994). Interviews with offenders can be very informative in unraveling the nature of crime problems and the identification of responses. Many environmental criminologists argue that "opportunity makes the thief" and, as such, it is important to "always think thief" (Clarke and Eck, 2003: 11). The underlying idea is that any particular category of crime requires a set of standard actions to be performed in a particular order like a script in a play (Clarke and Eck, 2003). The use of such crime scripts can assist crime prevention designers in focusing their prevention efforts at different points in the series of actions that make up a crime. For example, a script analysis of the motivations of young vandals in the Greater London area found that the presence of graffiti, as well as the width of the fence surface and the materials out of which the fence was made, structured the offenders' choices in rating the attractiveness of fences to vandalize (Smith, 2003). The resulting implications for prevention included: the rapid removal of graffiti from fences to avoid sending cues that encourage additional graffiti writing (i.e., prompt graffiti removal reduces the rewards offenders receive from having their work displayed); the use of fences with narrow bars to decrease the surface area for graffiti writing; and the construction of fences from "hard" materials that were difficult for vandals to damage (Smith, 2003). Similarly, when New York City subway system personnel understood the motivation of "taggers" to "get up" (to see their handiwork displayed as the trains repeatedly traveled around the city), they succeeded in eliminating graffiti by implementing an immediate cleaning program (Sloan-Howitt and Kelling, 1990).

Routine Activity Theory

Rational choice is often combined with routine activity theory to explain criminal behavior during the crime event (Clarke and Felson, 1993). Rational offenders come across criminal opportunities as they go about their daily routine activities and make decisions whether to take action. The source of the offender's motivation to commit a crime is not addressed (it is assumed that offenders commit crimes for any number of reasons); rather, the basic ingredients for a criminal act to be completed are closely examined. Routine activity posits that a criminal act occurs when a likely offender converges in space and time with a suitable target (e.g., victim or property) in the absence of a capable guardian (e.g., property owner or security guard; see Cohen and Felson, 1979). The routine activity approach was used to demonstrate that increases in residential burglary in the United States between 1960 and 1970 could be largely explained by changes in the routine activities of households. During this time period, the number of empty homes during the day increased as the number of single-person households and female participation in the workforce grew. At the same time, households increasingly contained attractive items to steal, such as more portable televisions and other electronic goods. Burglary increased, as fewer capable guardians were present in the home to protect the new suitable targets from burglars.

As described in Chapter 1, the well-known crime triangle was developed from the key elements of routine activity theory. Most crime problems involve a mixture of repeat offenders, repeat victims, and repeat locations. Routine activity theory can assist in figuring out which of these three dimensions of a "repeat" crime problem is the most dominant (Clarke and Eck, 2003; Eck, 2003). A poorly managed tavern with repeated fights involving different participants is an example of a crime problem that may be most powerfully addressed through a place-based response. In this case, the setting continues to facilitate the problem events, even if handlers are available to suppress offending, and guardians are present to suppress victimization (Clarke and Eck, 2003). These insights would suggest that problem-oriented police should pay close attention to the characteristics and features of the place when devising appropriate prevention strategies.

Police often work with or create "place managers" to increase crime control guardianship at high-activity crime places (Felson, 1994). "Third-party policing," as this approach is often called, is defined as "police efforts to persuade or coerce organizations or non-offending persons, such as public housing agencies, property owners, parents, health and building inspectors, and business owners to take some responsibility for preventing crime or reducing crime problems" (Buerger and Mazerolle, 1998: 301). The police use a range of civil, criminal, and regulatory rules and laws to engage or force third parties into taking some crime control responsibility. The ultimate targets of third-party policing efforts are the people engaged in deviant and criminal behavior at the place, typically drug dealers, gang members, vandals, and petty criminals (Green, 1996). The engagement of place managers and the use of civil remedies[1] can be important situational strategies used by problem-oriented police officers seeking to control crime hot spots. Research has revealed that third-party policing is an effective mechanism to control drug problems and is a promising method of controlling violent crime, disorderly youth, and property crime problems (Mazerolle and Ransley, 2006).

Environmental Criminology

Environmental criminology, also known as crime pattern theory, explores the distribution and interaction of targets, offenders, and opportunities across time and space (Brantingham and Brantingham, 1991a). According to Eck and Weisburd (1995: 6):

> This occurs because offenders engage in routine activities. Environmental criminology is important in understanding the nature of crime at places because it combines rational choice and routine activity theory to explain the distribution of crime across places.

Understanding the characteristics of places, such as facilities, is important because these attributes give rise to the opportunities that rational offenders will encounter during their routine activities. Environmental criminologists unravel crime problems through studying offender decision-making processes and small (e.g., shopping mall or housing project) and intermediate-level (e.g., neighborhood or city) analyses of very specific types of crimes occurring at very particular locations in these areas (Brantingham and Brantingham, 1991a). Studies of environmental facilitators of crime have shown, for example, that commercial properties located near main roads have an increased risk of robbery, and affluent homes located adjacent to poorer areas are more likely to be burglarized. In both cases, the offenders' "journey to work" was greatly reduced by the proximity of the targeted places to the offenders' homes or to a major thoroughfare. A key insight from these studies was that the offender's target search time – the amount of effort expended by the offender to locate a suitable target – was related to the risk of victimization at that place (as described by Clarke, 1995). According to Marcus Felson (2006), offenders may find suitable targets through *personal knowledge* of the victim (e.g., your neighbor's son might know when you are away from your house), *work* (e.g., a burglar working as a telephone engineer might overhear that you will be taking vacation next week), or overlapping *activity spaces* (e.g., frequenting places where victims live, work, shop, or seek entertainment).

Felson (2006) also extended the insights provided by environmental criminology in his discussion of "crime habitats." A *specific* crime habitat encourages one type of crime in a certain area. For example, Felson (2006: 115) identified the University of Illinois at Urbana-Champaign as an "excellent habitat for bicycle theft" as its campus is dotted with bicycle racks that are often hidden by hedges and linked by a system of bicycle lanes that facilitate an easy escape. *Generic* crime habitats foster many types of crimes at a high rate in a defined geographic area. Felson (2006) identified three forms of generic crime habitats: discrete edges, connected edges, and a thick crime habitat (Figure 3-2). As originally identified by the Brantinghams (1991), discrete generic crime habitats foster many types of crimes at a high rate in a defined geographic area and develop along the edges between two neighborhoods. Victims are attracted to food stores, parks, and other amenities located between neighborhoods; offenders from each side blend with the diverse legitimate users, commit crime there, and leave with relative impunity (Felson, 2006). Connected edges allow offenders to roam more freely. Connectivity, assisted by mass transit and automobiles, allow victims and offenders to range farther, allows illegal markets to serve a wider area, and for crime to spread in new ways (Felson, 2006).

The interconnection of a multitude of abandoned sites with nearby edges creates thick crime habitats (Felson, 2006). Numerous abandoned

Figure 3-2. Three Types of Generic Crime Habitats.

Source: Felson (2006: 117). Reprinted with permission.

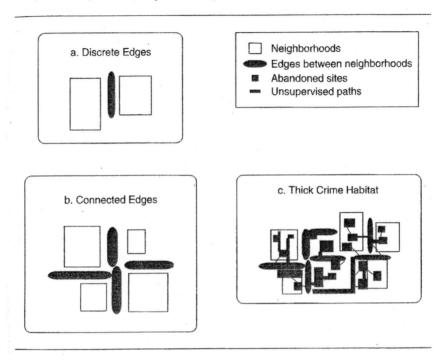

sites create an expanse of unsupervised space, where offenders can move freely, even on foot, and return to "home ground with the loot" (Felson, 2006: 118). In thick crime habitats, crime is dominant and legitimate business and community life has noticeably declined. Thick crime habitats also make it possible for crime to become "virulent." In its virulent form, criminal activity "attaches, invades, colonizes, and poisons conventional activities and the physical structures upon which they rely" (Felson, 2006: 121). To contain the growth of crime, problem-oriented policing and situational crime prevention strategies should be implemented to make sure that a narrow crime habitat does not thicken, two narrow crime habitats do not grow together, and existing thick crime habitats are fragmented (Felson, 2006).

The "Broken Windows" Thesis

[handwritten annotation: Disorder Linked to violent crime]

In their seminal "broken windows" article, Wilson and Kelling (1982) argued that social incivilities (e.g., loitering, public drinking, and prostitution) and physical incivilities (e.g., vacant lots, trash, and abandoned buildings) cause residents and workers in a neighborhood to be fearful. Fear of such incivilities causes many stable families to move out of the neighborhood and the remaining residents to isolate themselves and avoid others. As a result, anonymity increases and the level of informal social control (e.g., residents' willingness to intervene to protect their neighbor's property from crime) decreases. The lack of informal social control and escalating disorder also attract more potential offenders to the area, and this increases serious criminal behavior (see also Kelling and Coles, 1996). Wilson and Kelling (1982) argued that serious crime developed because the police and citizens did not work together to prevent urban decay and social disorder. In this section we examine the research on the relationship between disorder and more serious crime and the crime prevention value of policing disorder strategies. We do not examine, however, negative "externalities" that may be associated with aggressive policing initiatives, such as the potential for abuse, discrimination, and violations of civil liberties (see, e.g. Klockars, 1985; Golub et al., 2007).

The available research evidence on the connections between disorder and more serious crime is mixed. Skogan's (1990) survey research found disorder to be significantly correlated with perceived crime problems in a neighborhood, even after controlling for the population's poverty, stability, and racial composition. Further, Skogan's (1990) analysis of robbery victimization data from thirty neighborhoods found that economic and social factors' links to crime were indirect and mediated through disorder. However, Skogan's data were reanalyzed by Harcourt (1998, 2001), who questioned the strength of the relationship between disorder and perceived crime problems. In turn, Eck and Maguire (2000) then challenged the validity of Harcourt's conclusion. In his longitudinal analysis of Baltimore neighborhoods, Taylor (2001) found some support for the "broken windows" view that disorderly conditions lead to more serious crime. However, these results varied according to types of disorder and types of crime. Taylor (2001) suggested that other indicators, such as the initial levels of poverty and racial composition of the neighborhood, are more consistent predictors of later serious crimes than the disorders featured in the broken windows hypothesis.

Using systematic social observation data to capture social and physical incivilities on the streets of Chicago, Sampson and Raudenbush (1999) found that, with the exception of robbery, public disorder was not significantly related to most forms of serious crime when neighborhood characteristics (such as poverty, stability, race, and collective efficacy) were considered. Sampson and Raudenbush's findings have been criticized on methodological grounds by Jang and Johnson (2001).

The scientific research evidence on the crime control effectiveness of broad-based broken windows policing strategies, such as quality-of-life programs and order-maintenance enforcement practices, is also mixed. However, there seems to be more research evidence supporting the crime prevention value of broken windows policing strategies than refuting it. The New York City Police Department (NYPD) provides the best known example of a broad-based (or "macro") policy of order-maintenance policing, as it is well documented that officers became more aggressive in making arrests for minor offenses during the 1990s (Sousa and Kelling, 2006). Using misdemeanor arrests as a proxy for order-maintenance activities, Kelling and Sousa (2001) found that the NYPD strategy was associated with a significant reduction in violent crime in the 1990s, after controlling for economic, demographic, and drug use variables. A similar analysis by Corman and Mocan (2002) found that increased misdemeanor arrests in New York City during the 1990s had a significant impact on robbery and motor vehicle theft, after controlling for economic and criminal justice factors.

Other macro-level analyses have also generated results supportive of broad-based policing disorder strategies. In California, controlling for demographic, economic, and deterrence variables, a county-level analysis revealed that increases in misdemeanor arrests were associated with significant decreases in felony property offenses (Worrall, 2002). Finally, an analysis of robbery rates in 156 American cities showed that aggressive policing of disorderly conduct and driving-under-the-influence reduced robberies (Sampson and Cohen, 1988).

Many observers, however, have argued that it is very difficult to credit a generalized order-maintenance strategy with the crime drop in New York in the 1990s. The NYPD implemented the broken windows strategy within a larger set of organizational changes framed by the Compstat management accountability structure for allocating police resources (Silverman, 1999). As such, it is difficult to establish the independent effects of broken windows policing relative to other strategies implemented as part of the Compstat process (Weisburd et al., 2003). Other scholars have suggested that a number of rival causal factors, such as the decline in New York's crack epidemic, played a more important role in the crime drop than the policing strategy (Blumstein, 1995; Bowling, 1999). Some academics have noted that the crime rate was already declining in New York before the implementation of any of the post-1993 police reforms, and that New York's decline in homicide rates was not significantly different from declines experienced in surrounding states and in other large cities that did not implement aggressive enforcement policies during that time period (Karmen, 2000; Eck and Maguire, 2000).

Other evaluations have not found significant crime prevention gains associated with broad-based policing strategies that target disorder. A recent reanalysis of the Kelling and Sousa (2001) data did not find that a generalized broken windows strategy, as measured by increased misdemeanor arrests, yielded significant reductions in serious crimes in New York City between 1989 and 1998 (Harcourt and Ludwig, 2006, 2007). An evaluation of a quality-of-life policing initiative focused on social and physical disorder in four target zones in Chandler, Arizona also did not find any significant reductions in serious crime associated with the strategy (Katz et al., 2001). Finally, an evaluation of a one-month police enforcement effort to reduce alcohol and traffic-related offenses in a community in a Midwestern city did not find any significant reductions in robbery or burglary in the targeted area (Novak et al., 1999).

In contrast, two recent studies of the impact of order-maintenance policing in New York City supported the idea that policing disorder prevents more serious crime. Rosenfeld, Fornango, and Renfigo (2007) analyzed the effects of order-maintenance arrests on precinct-level robbery and homicide trends in New York City between 1988 and 2001, and concluded that the approach generated small but significant crime reduction gains. Using a different analytic approach, Messner and his colleagues (2007) analyzed homicide trends in 74 New York City police precincts between 1990 and 1999. They found that misdemeanor arrests generated significant reductions in total homicide rates, with the largest impacts on gun homicide rates. This is consistent with Fagan, Zimring, and Kim's (1998) observation that the kinds of changes in policing associated with the broken-windows approach might be effective, in part, because it results in taking more guns off the streets through increased police-citizen contacts.

Research on high activity crime places reveals that disorder clusters in space and time with more serious crimes. In their closer look at crime in Minneapolis hot spots, Weisburd and his colleagues (1992) found that assault calls-for-service and robbery of person calls-for-service were significantly correlated with "drunken person" calls-for-service. In Jersey City, New Jersey, Braga and his colleagues (1999) found that high-activity violent crime places also suffered from serious disorder problems.

The concentration of disorder at a place provides compelling opportunities for criminals. Abandoned buildings and vacant lots, for example, provide unguarded places for drug dealers selling their product and concealment for robbers looking to ambush an unsuspecting passerby. In contrast to the literature on broad-based policing disorder strategies applied to large geographic areas, the research evidence on dealing with disorderly conditions in specific hot spot locations reveals consistent crime prevention gains associated with a more focused approach.

As will be further discussed in the next chapter, problem-oriented policing strategies that modify the crime opportunity structure at specific places by addressing disorder have important impacts on criminal behavior.

STRATEGIES TO PREVENT CRIME
AT PROBLEM PLACES

Figure 3-3 presents a continuum of strategies, ranging from traditional to innovative, that police can use to control crime at high-activity crime places (see Braga and Weisburd, 2006). At one extreme, police departments use traditional, incident-driven strategies to control crime in the community. Although these activities coincidentally cluster in space and time, these opportunistic enforcement strategies are not specifically targeted at problem places and the limitations of this approach are, as discussed earlier, well known.

Based on Eck's (1993b) examination of alternative futures for problem-oriented policing, problem-solving efforts can be divided into "enforcement" and "situational" problem-oriented policing (POP) programs. *Enforcement*-oriented POP interventions concentrate mostly traditional tactics at high-risk times and locations. Although these programs are "problem-oriented" in a global way, their tactics do not employ the individualized treatments for crime problems advocated by Herman Goldstein (1990). These enforcement-oriented POP interventions concentrate mainly on the time and location of crime events, rather than focusing on the characteristics and dynamics of a place that make it a hot spot for criminal activity.

Figure 3-3. Continuum of Police Strategies to Control High Activity Crime Places.

Source: Braga and Weisburd (2006: 146).

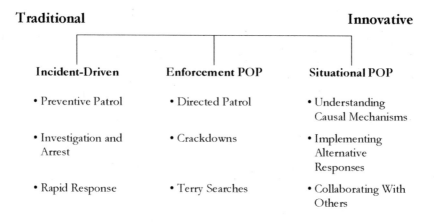

At the more innovative end of the continuum is Goldstein's (1990) vision of *"situational"* problem-oriented policing, in which police agencies undertake thorough analysis of crime problems at places, collaborate with community members and other city agencies, and conduct a broad search for situational responses to problems. The next two sections examine these two problem-solving approaches to controlling crime at problem places.

Problem-Oriented *Enforcement* Interventions

Efforts to concentrate police enforcement efforts in high-risk places, commonly known as "hot spots" policing, have been found to be effective in controlling crime (Braga, 2001, 2005a). These focused police enforcement efforts include traditional tactics, such as directed patrol and heightened levels of traffic enforcement. They also include alternative strategies, such as the aggressive enforcement of laws and ordinances regulating disorderly behavior in public places, and problem-oriented policing interventions with superficial problem analysis, limited situational responses, and limited engagement of the public. In essence, these approaches seek to modify the criminogenic routine activities of places by increasing actual and perceived risks of detection and apprehension in a very small area. Offenders seeking to commit crimes at particular places may be deterred by increased police presence and activity. Increasing patrol car presence in high-crime locations may be the simplest way to generate crime prevention gains. Increasing police contact with serious offenders through disorder enforcement, conducting *Terry* stops,[2] and implementing crackdowns – a massive short-term swamping of law enforcement resources in a specific area – may extend these crime prevention gains.

The first evaluation of "hot spots" policing was in Minneapolis, Minnesota. Researchers designed the Minneapolis Hot Spots Patrol Experiment to address the theoretical and methodological shortcomings of the Kansas City Preventive Patrol Experiment. Sherman and Weisburd (1995) suggested that most of the crime in the Kansas City treatment districts occurred in only a few places and, as a result, that the Kansas City study's uniform application of preventive patrol across all places in the treatment districts weakened the intervention and did not truly assess the effects of varying levels of preventive patrol on crime. In the initial mapping of crime in Minneapolis, 3 percent of all addresses generated over 50 percent of citizen calls-for-service; 110 distinct crime hot spot intersections were identified and randomly allocated to control and treatment groups (Sherman et al., 1989; Sherman and Weisburd, 1995). Fifty-five hot spots received the normal level of patrol, while the experimental 55 locations received 250 percent more police presence.

The results of the Minneapolis study were impressive: they challenged the Kansas City experiment's assertion that varying levels of patrol do not affect crime. Overall reported crime in the treatment areas was reduced by 13 percent and robbery was reduced by 20 percent (both statistically significant results; Sherman and Weisburd, 1995). Further, researcher observations of disorder noted a 50 percent reduction in experimental hot spots when compared to control places (Sherman and Weisburd, 1995). A follow-up study by Koper (1995) of the optimal amount of time that patrol cars should spend in hot spots found that patrol stops should last between 11 and 15 minutes; after that, continued police presence during a single patrol stop brings diminishing returns.

In Jersey City, the effects of problem-oriented enforcement policing on street-level drug markets were examined. Fifty-six hot spots of drug activity were identified and randomized in statistical blocks to treatment and control groups for inclusion in the Drug Markets Analysis experiment (Weisburd and Green, 1995a). The control strategy consisted of arrest-oriented opportunistic enforcement, while the experimental treatment followed a step-wise approach that involved building intelligence on drug activity in the market, working with citizens in the area, police crackdowns, and maintaining crime prevention gains by conducting routine surveillance of the treated places and increasing police patrols of the area as needed (Weisburd and Green, 1995a). The results of the experiment revealed a significant reduction in disorder-related calls-for-service in treatment places relative to control places.

In Kansas City, Missouri, the effects of court-authorized raids on crack houses were examined (Sherman and Rogan, 1995a). The Kansas City Crack House Raid experiment reported modest decreases in citizen calls-for-service and crime offenses at targeted blocks relative to control blocks. These effects that decayed within two weeks of the raids (Sherman and Rogan, 1995a).

A police patrol project to reduce gun violence in Kansas City centered on patrol beats where gun violence, drive-by shootings, and homicides were 20 times higher than the national average (Sherman et al., 1995). The Kansas City Gun Project found that a strategy of aggressive order maintenance in the target areas (i.e., directed patrols aimed at stopping cars breaking minor road rules and subsequent *Terry* searches of the automobile for illegal guns) increased the number of guns seized by 65 percent and reduced gun crimes by nearly 50 percent (Sherman et al., 1995; Sherman and Rogan, 1995b). A separate study found that the community strongly supported the intensive patrols and perceived an improvement in the quality of life in the treatment neighborhood (Shaw, 1995). The study did not, however, attempt to measure how the individuals who were stopped and searched by the police felt about the program.

Jersey City was also the research site for a problem-oriented policing project to control violent crime places (Braga et al., 1999). The program and experimental design followed the steps of the SARA model. During the scanning phase, 56 violent crime hot spots were identified and matched into 28 pairs for evaluation purposes. Twelve pairs were randomly allocated to treatment and control conditions. Treatment places received focused problem-solving attention from the Jersey City Police Department's Violent Crimes Unit (VCU), while the control places were not assigned to a special unit and received the routine amount of traditional police strategies that such places would experience (i.e., arbitrary patrol interventions and routine follow-up investigations by detectives). Similar to the findings of other examinations of police problem solving described earlier, the Jersey City study found that translating problem-solving theory into practice was difficult for the officers. The complex and varied problems at the high-activity violent crime places presented a substantive challenge to the problem-solving officers charged with preventing crime at the places (Braga and Weisburd, 2006).

Figure 3-4 presents the diverse problems encountered by the Jersey City VCU officers at one hot spot location. Problems at the place could be viewed as either problems in their own right or as an underlying condition or correlate of other problems. For example, an abandoned building could be viewed as a problem by virtue of its hazardous, dilapidated conditions and unsightly appearance, but it might also serve as a magnet or clustering point for a host of other problems such as drug selling, public drinking, or illegal dumping. A street corner drug market was definitely viewed as a problem, but it could also be categorized as a contributing factor to other issues such as trash, loitering, and public drinking that, in turn, caused the area to be even more attractive to drug sellers. Often these social and physical problems were deeply intertwined, and direct "causes" of problems

Figure 3-4. Characteristics of Jersey City Hot Spot Locations.

Source: Author's original research.

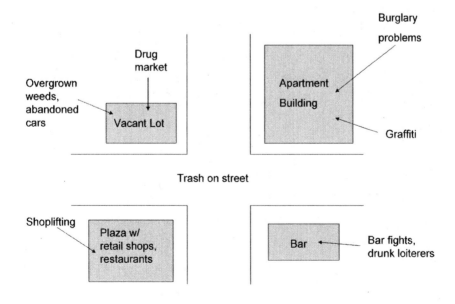

were difficult to pinpoint. In their closer look at the Jersey City problem-oriented policing experiment, Braga and Weisburd (2006) made three general observations about the complexities of problems at places: problems could be common among several places; a problem could arise from multiple underlying conditions or factors; and several problems could arise from a single cause or be related to one problem.

The complexities of crime and disorder problems at places and the difficulties encountered by police officers in implementing the problem-oriented approach have generally led to limited problem analysis, the use of mostly traditional law enforcement responses, reliance on situational responses that are often not directly linked to the violent crime problems at a place, and a lack of community involvement (Braga and Weisburd, 2006). Consistent with the literature that links disorder and violent crime (Skogan, 1990; Wilson and Kelling, 1982; Kelling and Coles, 1996), the Jersey City VCU officers believed that the violence – which distinguished these places from other areas of the city – was closely related to the disorder of the place. Therefore, many plans to control the violence at a place were actually targeted at these social and physical disorder problems. Although specific tactics and priorities varied from place to place, the officers certainly did not limit themselves to addressing violent crime; the officers generally attempted to control their places by cleaning up the environment via aggressive order maintenance and making physical improvements such as securing vacant lots or removing trash from the street. Therefore, in practice the "treatment" comprised a collection of specific problem-oriented tactics that could be broadly categorized as a "policing disorder" strategy. The Jersey City Police Department's program to control violent places went beyond the tactics of most problem-oriented enforcement interventions, but still fell short of situational problem-oriented policing. On the continuum of police strategies to control high-activity crime places, the program as implemented would fit between enforcement and situational POP interventions.

Despite falling short of problem-oriented situational policing, the Jersey City strategy resulted in statistically significant reductions in total calls-for-service and total crime incidents, as well as varying reductions in all subcategories of crime types, in the treatment places relative to control places (Braga et al., 1999). Analyses of systematic observation data collected during the pre-test and post-test periods revealed that social disorder and physical disorder were significantly reduced at the treatment places relative to controls (Braga et al., 1999). Pre-test and post-test interviews with key community members suggested that community perceptions of places improved at 7 of 12 treatment places (Braga, 1997).

A similar study evaluated the effects of problem-oriented policing interventions on crime and disorder hot spots in Lowell, Massachusetts (Braga and Bond, 2007). Thirty-four hot spots were matched into 17 pairs, and one member of each pair was allocated to treatment conditions in a randomized block field experiment. Responsibility for implementing the problem-oriented policing intervention at the treatment places was assigned to the captains who managed Lowell's three police sectors. Within each sector, lieutenants and sergeants spent time analyzing official data sources and discussing problems with community members. As in other studies, the problem analysis and community engagement in the Lowell Policing Crime and Disorder Hot Spots project was generally weak and the implemented strategy more closely resembled a general policing disorder strategy rather than nuanced situational POP responses. Nevertheless, the impact evaluation revealed that the strategy generated significant reductions in crime and disorder calls-for-service at the treatment places relative to the control places.

The Lowell evaluation also found that the strongest crime prevention benefits were driven by situational changes in the physical environment at the crime and disorder hot spots (Braga and Bond, 2007). Misdemeanor arrests for disorderly behavior generated much smaller crime prevention gains in the experimental places. The Lowell police officers' strategies to ameliorate physical incivilities and improve surveillance at places (thereby changing site features and facilities) may have diminished the number of easy criminal opportunities and, thus, discouraged offenders from frequenting the experimental places. These findings suggest that, when adopting a broad-based "policing disorder" approach to crime prevention, police departments should use an approach that seeks to change the physical conditions that give rise to crime problems rather than a zero-tolerance policing model that focuses on a subset of social incivilities (such as drunken people, rowdy teens, and street vagrants) and that seeks to remove them from the street via arrest. Misdemeanor arrests obviously play a noteworthy role in dealing with disorder; however, arrest strategies do not directly deal with physical conditions. An exclusive commitment to increasing misdemeanor arrests isn't the most powerful approach to community crime prevention, and it may undermine police relationships in disadvantaged, urban communities where partnership is most needed and where distrust between the police and citizens is most profound.

Despite the gap between the desired application of the approach and its actual implementation, the problem-oriented policing approach was found to be effective in reducing crime and disorder in both Jersey City and Lowell. This suggests that problem-oriented policing interventions may not need to be implemented in the ways envisioned by Herman Goldstein in order to produce a crime prevention effect. Perhaps simply focusing police resources on identifiable risks that come to the attention of problem-oriented policing projects, such as crime hot spots, may be enough to produce crime control gains. This is a striking result considering the large body of research that shows the ineffectiveness of many police crime prevention efforts (Visher and Weisburd, 1998). Of course, this does not mean that had the police more fully implemented the problem-oriented approach they might have achieved even greater crime prevention benefits. However, if the problem-oriented policing model is unlikely to be fully implemented in many police environments, police scholars and practitioners should at least encourage a middling level of problem solving, rather than leaving police officers with a sense that they have usually missed the mark in their practices (Braga and Weisburd, 2006). As discussed in Chapter 1, such mid-level problem solving may be the most that can be expected, and may lead in any case to significant crime prevention benefits.

Beyond thinking about the relative crime prevention value of enforcement-oriented POP programs, practitioners and policy makers need to know more about community reaction to increased levels of police enforcement action. Police effectiveness studies have traditionally overlooked the effects of policing practices upon citizen perceptions of police legitimacy (Tyler, 2000; Tyler, 2001). Does the concentration of police enforcement in specific hot spots lead citizens to question the fairness of police practices? The results of the Kansas City Gun project suggest that residents of communities suffering from high rates of gun violence welcome intensive police efforts against guns (Shaw, 1995). However, some observers question the fairness and intrusiveness of such approaches and caution that street searches, especially of young men and minorities, look like police harassment (Moore, 1980; Kleck, 1991). Focused and aggressive police enforcement strategies have been criticized as resulting in increased citizen complaints about police misconduct and abuse of force in New York City (Greene, 1999). As in the case of understanding the effectiveness of police strategies, the potential impacts of enforcement actions on police legitimacy may depend in good part on the types of strategies used and the context of the hot spots affected. But whatever the impact, we need to know more about the effects of enforcement problem-oriented interventions on the communities that the police serve.

Problem-Oriented *Situational* Interventions

Although enforcement-oriented POP interventions have produced crime control gains and have added to law enforcement's array of crime prevention tools, it is commonly assumed that police could be more effective if they focused their efforts on the criminogenic attributes that cause a place to be "hot." In other words, adding an increased level of guardianship at a place by optimizing patrol is a step in controlling crime, but reducing criminal opportunities by changing site features, facilities, and the management at a place (e.g., adding streetlights, razing abandoned buildings, and mobilizing residents) may have a more profound, and longer lasting, effect on crime. However, as described above, research has found that it is difficult for police officers to develop situational POP interventions to control the complex problems that cause a place to be hot (Braga and Weisburd, 2006; Braga et al., 1999).

In successful place-oriented problem-solving ventures, the situational interventions designed to control places have been as varied and multi-dimensional as the problems they sought to address at the place. These successful situational POP efforts have also been characterized by effective partnerships with outside agencies. Three noteworthy projects are described below that illuminate the varied nature of the responses applied to problem places as well as the crime prevention benefits of developing situational responses that are directly linked to the nature of crime problems at places.

The Jersey City Public Housing Project

Jersey City was the site for a problem-oriented policing project designed to address serious crime problems in six public housing projects (Mazerolle et al., 2000; Mazerolle and Terrill, 1997). At each of the participating housing projects, a problem-oriented site team was created comprising community members, police officers, tenant representatives, a civilian site manager, and a social service liaison. These teams held monthly meetings to identify the places that were associated with serious crime and drug market problems, unravel the circumstances contributing to these problems, coordinate the implementation of place-specific interventions, and report the progress made on the problem-oriented initiatives. During the scanning phase, two distinct types of problem places were identified: outdoor common areas (such as parking lots, playgrounds, and walkways), and individual apartments (Mazerolle and Terrill, 1997). The targeted common areas received situational responses to alter criminal opportunities, such as changing the public phones to allow only outgoing calls and installing floodlights in poorly lit areas (Mazerolle et al., 2000). The police supplemented these alternative responses with heightened levels of traditional policing tactics such as surveillance and serving warrants. At problem-prone individual apartments, counseling and treatment were provided to leaseholders with drug and alcohol problems and to families with histories of lease violations (Ready et al., 1998). If the tenants of these "nuisance" apartments did not take advantage of the services, they were advised that noncompliance would lead to eviction. If social services were deemed to be inadequate to deal with these problems, the problem-solving teams used more aggressive tactics such as eviction or having tenants arrested.

An evaluation of this program revealed that the problem-oriented strategies, as compared to traditional strategies used prior to the program, led to fewer serious crime calls-for-service over time and, at two sites, to reductions in violent, property, and vehicle-related crimes (Mazerolle et al., 2000).

The Surfer's Paradise Safety Action Project

Surfers Paradise, a large tourist resort area in Queensland, Australia, suffered from violence, public drunkenness, and disorder problems around its pubs and clubs (Homel et al., 1997). Research revealed a variety of risk factors for violence, such as inappropriate drink promotions, large groups of young males "bar hopping" from place to place, crowding, lack of comfort, aggressive behavior by bar staff and security personnel, and inept practices in dealing with drunken patrons (Homel et al., 1997). A Safety Action Project team composed of important stakeholders – such as the city council, the health department, police officers, liquor-licensing commission, and university researchers – set forth to deal with this difficult set of problems.

Four task groups were charged with tackling the different aspects of the disorder and violence problems. The "Safety of Public Spaces" task group audited factors in the physical environment that prevented Surfers Paradise from being a safe recreational area. Auditors drawn from the community recorded pertinent information about the physical characteristics of specific places (e.g., lighting levels, problems with informal and natural surveillance, and the availability of emergency phones). The results of the audits included recommendations for changes that were forwarded to the project team. The "Security and Policing" task group focused on training licensees and security personnel in ethics and good practices, management skills, staff recruitment, conflict resolution, venue security, civil and criminal law, incident reporting, handling emergency, and improving communications and relations with police officers. The "Security and Policing" task force also implemented a pilot program of shuttle bus services to ensure safe transport of patrons out of the area and to reduce the incidence of drunk driving. The "Community Monitoring" task group focused on disseminating information on the Safety Action Project and promoting a positive image of Surfers Paradise. The "Venue Management" task group attempted to improve relationships between the liquor license commission, the police, and licensees as well as promote the responsible delivery of alcoholic beverages to patrons. Most importantly, this fourth task group set about changing risky business practices such as drink discounting, serving underaged persons, jumbo serving sizes of glasses and jugs, potent drink strength, unlimited entries for patrons, overcrowding premises, not serving food to offset effects of liquor, and continuing to serve alcohol to dangerously intoxicated persons.

The business practices of each pub and club were assessed using a standard risk assessment instrument filled out by the manager, one security officer, one bar staff member, and a member of the Project team. The key to this approach was to get the pubs and clubs to accept responsibility for the control of their establishment and self-regulate their behavior, regardless of any external enforcement. In a group setting, resolutions of identified problems were agreed upon, implemented, and codified in an individualized house policy. Compliance with the house policies was monitored and enforced by a Monitoring Committee overseen by the health department, nightclub licensees, hotel business representatives, the city council, and the chamber of commerce, among others.

Noteworthy reductions in violence and disorder followed the implementation of the problem-solving initiatives. Analyses of observational data revealed that verbal abuse declined by 82 percent, arguments by 68 percent, and assaults by 52 percent (Homel et al., 1997). The Surfers Paradise Safety

Action Project has been replicated in three cities in Australia. An evaluation of these efforts revealed a 75 percent decrease in assaults and 49 percent decrease in verbal aggression within the venues in the three cities (as described in Homel et al., 1997). While these results are certainly encouraging, Homel and his colleagues (1997) also noted that some of the problem patrols have been displaced to other sites and that follow-up observation indicated a rise in violence and a cessation of compliance with the code.

The New York Port Authority Bus Terminal Project

The New York Port Authority Bus Terminal had fallen into such an advanced state of disrepair that Felson and his colleagues (1996) entitled their study of a comprehensive plan to clean up the facility, "Redesigning Hell." Noteworthy problems included phone hustlers placing illegal international phone calls for free from inside the terminal, a bustling community of homeless persons taking over whole sections of the terminal (with accompanying public urination and defecation, drug use, blocking access routes, and aggressive panhandling), solicitation by male prostitutes, prostitution in the parking structure, and criminal interdependence with the surrounding Times Square area.

Sixty-two interventions were instituted at the terminal including: closing off spaces, improved shopping, cleaning, increased enforcement, and other measures to remove situations that facilitated offending or increased the number of patrons and their ability to watch each other (Table 3-1). Beyond addressing physical conditions that facilitated the development of a large homeless population in the terminal, the Port Authority addressed the homeless problem through a "refer or arrest" process. In partnership with social service agencies, this process allowed the police to offer loitering homeless persons alternative places and programs. If that offer was refused, the officer could ask the person to leave the terminal. If that request was ignored, the officer could make an arrest. The phone hustling problem was addressed by various measures, including reducing the number of pay phones, removing phones' international dialing capacity, and disabling the keypads to prevent the routing of fraudulent calls through the exchange systems of private businesses (Bichler and Clarke, 1996).

Analyses of official crime data revealed that robberies and assaults were significantly reduced in the station (Felson et al., 1996). Noting that robberies and assaults also declined in the surrounding area, Felson and his colleagues (1996) suggested that either outside crime prevention efforts

Table 3-1. List of 62 Specific Tactics Employed to Reduce Crime and Disorder in the Port Authority Bus Terminal, New York City

A.   *Increasing Visibility*

1.   Install new lighting
2.   replace bulbs in old lighting
3.   clean light reflectors and fixtures
4.   brighten signs
5.   put in white ceilings
6.   use light color paint and brighter tile on walls
7.   use glass for internal walls
8.   avoid walls that obstruct line of sight
9.   make columns no wider than necessary
10. make stores easy to see into and out from
11. use special stripping and sealing chemicals on floors
12. locate information boots, kiosks, advertising, and newsstands to reduce obstruction.

B.   *Close nooks and improve natural supervision*

13. install pushcarts and place them strategically
14. renovate the food court
15. avoid interior doors
16. avoid direct access to extra stairwells
17. keep stairs away from street entries
18. close off areas under stairwells
19. close in areas between columns
20. bring walls out to columns
21. close emergency stairs off-hours
22. block off much of bus station off-hours
23. use only sawtooth gates off-hours
24. centralize ticketing
25. improve street entrances to the building
26. put merchants in key places, and to fill in empty spots
27. replace police cars with golf carts in parking structure
28. use clear glass panels on waiting room walls
29. wall up unneeded areas
30. block walls around bus gates against transient takeovers
31. block elevators from public use
32. block off construction areas with plywood

Table 3-1. *(continued)*

C. *Improve flows*

    33. arrange better stairway and escalator flow pattern.
    34. streamline vertical and horizontal circulation.
    35. use Agents to solve problems and to keep traffic moving

D. *Discourage loitering and hustling in other ways.*

    36. get rid of low brick walls to discourage transients
    37. put pyramid-shaped brick and plastic spikes on window ledges
    38. put attractive paper in windows of unoccupied shops.
    39. construct control center to block balcony and "meat market"
    40. get rid of benches
    41. put in flip seats
    42. use technology and design to get rid of phone hustlers
    43. locate information kiosks at doors
    44. keep sex magazines out of sight
    45. set up house phones for emergency, information, red caps
    46. set up new public address system
    47. use legal powers to evict transients
    48. use programs to offer alternative services to transients
    49. hire coordinator for transient services
    50. bring police and social workers together on transient problem
    51. train police in dealing with transients
    52. increase supervision of police officers dealing with transients
    53. strengthen communication between police and business tenants

E. *Improve retailing*

    54. bring in chain retailers
    55. bring in better retail management
    56. provide fax machine to retail tenants
    57. redesign space specifically for retailers
    58. replace restaurant which house hustlers with a benign tenant
    59. get rid of management which let people sleep in bowling alley
    60. close the betting shop
    61. do not welcome hard-drinkers in bowling alley bar
    62. remove violent video games

Source: Felson et al. (1996: 70-71).

or a diffusion of crime prevention benefits may have accounted for the decreases in crime outside the terminal. An annual survey of terminal patrons that commenced with the 1991 cleanup revealed noteworthy declines in incivilities and disorder in the terminal.

Preventing Thefts from Parked Cars in Charlotte, North Carolina

In Charlotte, North Carolina, a problem-oriented policing project was implemented to reduce thefts from cars parked in the center-city (Clarke and Goldstein, 2003). A detailed analysis of the theft problem revealed that the risk of theft was much greater in parking lots than in parking decks; these higher risks were associated with inadequate fencing, poor lighting, and the absence of lot attendants. Based on these analyses, the recommended responses included (adapted from Clarke and Goldstein, 2003: 276-277):

1. The Charlotte-Mecklenburg Police Department and the district attorney's office would continue to develop aggressive policies of arresting offenders, seeking convictions, and seeking severe sentences for repeat offenders.

2. Parking lot operators would be asked to post the addresses of their lot at the entrance(s) of each lot. This would assist victims in reporting thefts, help police in responding to calls for assistance, and assist future analysis of larcenies from automobiles by allowing these to be assigned to the specific lot in which the larceny occurred.

3. Changes would be sought in the city's zoning ordinance that required, for aesthetic purposes, that all new lots be surrounded by screening (which in practice is usually a fence) that is no less than four feet in height and can have no more than 25 percent of its surface left open. These fences, most often solid, have reduced surveillance of lots by passing motorists, pedestrians, and police officers on patrol. Furthermore, lots established before the ordinance came into effect in 1993 (and its amendment in 1995), which constitute a majority of all lots, were not required to have screening. The proposed new ordinance would require "see through" fences to be erected for all new lots and, within a period of two or three years, for all existing lots.

4. With the cooperation and agreement of lot operators, the police would seek to implement a rating scheme that would result in every lot being graded for its security on a number of variables. Grades would be

determined by either the police or the building inspector and would be posted at the lot entrances, in the same way that health inspection results are posted for Charlotte's restaurants. This proposal was intended to provide a strong incentive for parking facility operators to improve security.

5. Funds would be sought for a security bike patrol for the lots. The patrol would be trained in what to look for, how to focus patrols for greatest effect, how to deal with suspicious persons, and when and how to call the police (their radios would be compatible with police radios). The patrols would give the customers and employees of area businesses the same type of security that private patrols give to customers and employees at large shopping malls.

A new closed-circuit television (CCTV) surveillance system was also installed by private security companies charged with monitoring particular lots. Before the plan was fully implemented and the CCTVs were operational, the targeted lots experienced an unexpected 38 percent decrease in larcenies from motor vehicles (Clarke and Goldstein, 2003). The evaluators credited increased police and security patrol attention given to the high-risk lots after the problem-oriented policing process commenced. The decline in larcenies continued as the newly devised situational strategies were implemented, and the authors anticipated that these strategies would contribute to a long-term, permanent reduction in larcenies from automobiles.

Concluding Thoughts on the Crime Prevention Mechanisms at Work in Place-Oriented Strategies

The important lesson for police practitioners and academics is that problem-oriented situational and enforcement policing interventions change the criminal dynamics of problem places in important ways. The rational choice perspective and routine activities theory provide useful frameworks to speculate on the theoretical mechanisms underlying these effects at problem places.

According to the rational choice perspective, offenders consider risks, effort, and rewards when contemplating criminal acts (Cornish and Clarke, 1986). Increased police presence and order-maintenance activities at places serve as powerful deterrents to criminal and disorderly conduct. For example, in the Minneapolis hot spots patrol experiment, Sherman and Weisburd (1995: 646) claimed evidence of place-specific "micro-deterrence" associated with increased police presence in hot spot areas. These tactics also increase the certainty of detection and apprehension at places, communicate that disorderly behavior will no longer be tolerated at places, and raise potential offenders' perceptions of risk at places (Cook, 1980; Zimring and Hawkins, 1973; also Koper, 1995). These perceptions of increased risks also influence the behavior of an array of would-be offenders.

Changes in the physical environment may also discourage potential offenders from frequenting an area by altering criminal opportunities at a place. The presence of abandoned buildings, for instance, attracts offenders to places (Spelman, 1993). The abandoned building may serve as a location for muggers to conceal themselves while waiting for a victim to pass, a drinking spot for disorderly youth, or a space to stash or sell drugs. If the derelict building were secured, fewer potential offenders would enter the area because the necessary effort to commit crimes at the places would increase. Strategies to ameliorate physical incivilities (thereby changing site features and facilities) may have diminished the number of easy opportunities at the place and, thus, discouraged offenders from frequenting the experimental places.

Complementing the rational choice perspective, routine activities theory focuses on the criminal event and posits that criminal events occur when potential offenders and suitable targets converge in space and time in the absence of a capable guardian (Cohen and Felson, 1979). The increased presence of police augments the level of guardianship in targeted places. Heightened levels of patrol prevent crimes by introducing the watchful eye of the police as a guardian to protect potential victims from potential offenders. According to the "broken windows" hypothesis, reductions in physical and social incivilities at places send clear signals to potential criminals that lawbreaking will no longer be tolerated. Offenders make choices about the places they frequent based on cues at the site, and are likely to select places that emit cues where risks are low for committing crimes (Eck and Weisburd, 1995). Changing the perceptions of potential offenders by controlling disorder and changing easy criminal opportunities may reduce their numbers at the place. Therefore, since victims and offenders often share the same social milieus (Lauritsen et al., 1991; Garofalo, 1987), these changes will also reduce the number of potential victims at the place.

Kleiman suggested that this phenomenon occurred in the reductions in violent crime and property crime from a crackdown on street-level heroin sales in Lynn, Massachusetts (1988: 23):

> A plausible explanation would be that street drug markets involve concentrations of both likely aggressors and attractive victims: attractive both because they have money and drugs worth stealing and because they are less likely than average to complain to the police. In addition, business disputes among drug dealers and between drug dealers and drug customers may result in violence rather than litigation. Breaking up the drug market disperses potential victims and offenders making it less likely they will come in contact with one another.

In the examples described in this chapter, problem-oriented interventions focused on problem places changed the relationships between offenders, targets, and guardians. Reduced crime rates followed these changes in the dynamics of problem places.

NOTES

1. "Civil remedies are procedures and sanctions provided in civil statutes and regulations that are used in programs to prevent crime. These remedies include efforts to persuade or coerce non-offending their parties, such as landlords and property owners, to take action in their buildings, as well as the use of restraining orders and injunctions against loitering or congregating in gangs, enhanced enforcement of housing and nuisance codes, and other measures" (Green Mazerolle and Roehl, 1998: 1).
2. In the case of *Terry v. Ohio* (1968), the U.S. Supreme Court upheld the right of the police officers to conduct brief threshold inquiries of suspicious persons when they have reason to believe that such persons may be armed and dangerous to the police or others. In practice, this threshold inquiry typically involves a safety frisk of the suspicious person.

4. CONTROLLING HIGH-ACTIVITY OFFENDERS

August 29, 1996, Boston, Massachusetts – More than 20 members of the Intervale Posse, a street gang in Boston's Roxbury neighborhood, are arrested in an early-morning sweep after a nearly 9-month investigation. Fifteen of the arrestees face Federal drug charges and 10-year minimum mandatory sentences; many face even stiffer sanctions. In the weeks after the arrests, Boston's Ceasefire Working Group – composed of frontline members of the Boston Police Department's gang unit, the departments of probation and parole, the U.S. Attorney's and county prosecutor's offices, the Office of the State Attorney General, school police, youth corrections, social services, and others – meets with gangs around the city, goes to youth detention facilities to talk with inmates, and speaks to assemblies in Roxbury public schools. The message Ceasefire members deliver is simple and direct: "The city is not going to put up with violence any longer. We know who's behind the gang violence. We're warning gangs to stop; if they don't, there are going to be consequences. There are people here who want to help you – we can offer services, job training, protection from your enemies, whatever you need – but the violence is going to stop. The Intervale Posse was warned, they didn't listen, and they're gone. This doesn't have to happen to you. Just put your guns down" (Kennedy, 1998: 2).

* * *

May 1997, Lowell, Massachusetts – One by one, 20 of Lowell's worst young troublemakers are brought into a meeting with 14 representatives of seven city and state agencies. In two additional meetings, the authorities meet with a group of 35 less chronic offenders and 16 members of a city street gang. The message basically is the same as Boston's. "We just wanted to tell you that we know who you are," says assistant district attorney Michael Ortiz. "If you continue to get into trouble, you're going to end up in jail, or hurt, or even dead. But if you want to get out of a gang or back into school, or you want a job or counseling, we're here to help" (Kennedy, 1998: 2).

* * *

June 1997, Minneapolis, Minnesota – A dozen members of the Bogus Boyz, a street gang composed of members ejected from other gangs and notorious for street violence, are arrested on federal weapons charges after a short, intensive investigation spearheaded by the Minneapolis Police Department's gang unit, in cooperation with federal authorities. At the same time, teams of police and probation officers hit the streets to visit some 250 individuals identified by the gang unit as the city's most chronic gang offenders. The teams tell the gang members: "The Bogus Boyz's arrests were no accident. The Bogus Boyz were violent, and their violence won them this treatment. This is how the city is doing things from now on. We've got a dozen agencies, from probation to the Feds, meeting regularly and focusing on gang violence. Where we find it, we're going to act. Gang officers visit injured gang members – victims of assaults by other gangs – in the hospital and say to them: 'This is a terrible thing that's happened to you. But understand, we're going to deal with it. Retaliation will not be tolerated. Remember the Bogus Boyz' " (Kennedy, 1998: 2).

A number of jurisdictions have been experimenting with new problem-oriented frameworks to understand and respond to gun violence among gang-involved offenders. These interventions are based on the "pulling levers" focused deterrence strategy (discussed below), which focuses criminal justice and social service attention on a small number of chronically offending gang members responsible for the bulk of urban gun violence problems (Braga, Kennedy, and Tita, 2002). While the research evidence on the crime prevention value associated with the approach is still developing, the pulling levers strategy has been embraced by the U.S. Department of Justice as an effective approach to crime prevention. In his address to the American Society of Criminology, former U.S. National Institute of Justice Director Jeremy Travis (1998) announced that, "[the] pulling levers hypothesis has made enormous theoretical and practical contributions to our thinking about deterrence and the role of the criminal justice system in producing safety."

Pioneered in Boston to halt youth violence, the pulling levers framework has been applied in many American cities through federally sponsored violence prevention programs such as the Strategic Alternatives to Community Safety Initiative and Project Safe Neighborhoods (Coleman et al., 1999; Dalton, 2002). In its simplest form, the approach consists of: selecting a particular crime problem, such as youth homicide; convening an interagency working group of law enforcement practitioners; conducting research to identify key offenders, groups, and behavior patterns; framing a response to offenders and groups of offenders that uses a varied menu of sanctions ("pulling levers") to stop them from continuing their violent behavior; focusing social services and community resources on targeted offenders and groups to match law enforcement prevention efforts; and directly and repeatedly communicating with offenders to make them understand why they are receiving this special attention (Kennedy, 1997; Kennedy, 2006).

Although focusing police resources on dangerous offenders has long been an attractive idea, most police departments have not formally adopted these programs. The selective focusing on a small number of active offenders raises important questions of fairness, and of whether such approaches threaten individuals' rights to equal protection and due process. In this chapter, the criminological evidence on the concentration of offending amongst a few highly active criminals and the relevance of "co-offending" are reviewed; early police programs that focus on repeat offenders are discussed; new approaches to the strategic prevention of gang- and group-involved violence are presented; and the potential for preventing crime by repeat offenders through other frameworks is described.

Most approaches to controlling repeat offenders described in this section focus on the strategic management of criminal justice actions. However, as suggested in the section below on controlling crime facilitators, such as guns, it is important to remember that alternative responses to controlling highly active criminals are available. Situational strategies such as those described in Chapter 3 on places and in Chapter 5 on victims may be used to good effect in controlling the behavior of chronic offenders without launching high-intensity enforcement programs. For example, with regard to drunk driving problems, preventive measures such as controls over bars and bartenders may reduce the number of intoxicated drivers on the road. Increased use of safety belts and strategic engineering of roads may effectively reduce injuries and deaths arising from alcohol-involved automobile accidents. The point is that problem-oriented police should be encouraged to follow the recommendations of Herman Goldstein (1990) and conduct an "uninhibited" search for possible responses and not to limit themselves to only thinking about improving enforcement actions when dealing with repeat offender problems. As suggested in the introduction to this book, crime prevention strategies targeting places, offenders, and victims obviously converge and often seem to be just mirror reflections.

Research on the Distribution of Criminal Offending and "Co-Offending"

Police officers have long known from experience that a small number of criminals account for a large share of the crime problem, and some detectives have attempted to prevent crimes by "working" particular criminals rather than particular crimes (see, e.g., Lane, 1971). Research has confirmed that a small number of chronic offenders generate a disproportionate share of crime.

In their classic study of nearly 10,000 boys in Philadelphia, Wolfgang et al. (1972) revealed that the most active 6 percent of delinquent boys were responsible for more than 50 percent of all delinquent acts committed. Laub and Sampson's (2003) close examination of a small set of persistent violent offenders reported that these men had been arrested an average of 40 times over the course of their criminal careers (the most active offender had been arrested 106 times) and had spent an inordinate amount of times in prison and jails. Over their lifetimes, these men had been incarcerated an average of 75 days each year. Similarly, the Rand Corporation's survey of jail and prison inmates in California, Michigan, and Texas revealed that, in all three states, the most recidivist 10 percent of active offenders had committed some 50 percent of all crimes, and that 80 percent of crimes had been committed by only 20 percent of the criminals (Chaiken and Chaiken, 1982). Moreover, the worst 1 percent of offenders had committed crimes at an extremely high rate – more than 50 serious offenses per year (Rolph et al., 1981).

In his review of the literature on repeat offenders, Spelman (1990) observed that frequent offenders do not specialize, are usually drug addicts, and are more persistent. In the Rand survey in three states, about two-thirds of all offenders had specialized in either violent or property crimes; however crime "generalists" had committed about twice as much property crime as the property crime specialists and about twice as much violent crime as the violent crime specialists (Chaiken and Chaiken, 1982). Although most *criminals* are specialists, most *crimes* are committed by highly active "violent predators" (Spelman, 1990). In his review of data from the Arrestee Drug Abuse Monitoring (ADAM) system, Kleiman (1997) concluded that the population of heavy drug users consists mainly of frequent offenders. Kleiman (1997) further noted that, among offenders, the use of expensive drugs predicts both high-rate offending and persistence in crime. Chaiken and Chaiken (1982) found that most frequent offenders also deal drugs in high volume. Frequent offenders also have longer "criminal careers" than the typical offender. While the average criminal career for an adult offender lasts no more than six or seven years (Blumstein et al., 1986), frequent offenders persist for between nine and ten years (Spelman, 1986). Finally, as frequent offenders gain more experience they become more difficult to apprehend. Spelman's (1990) analysis of the probability of arrest per crime among offenders who commit crimes at different rates revealed that high-rate offenders run substantially lower risks of arrests than others. This pattern was true for both property and personal crimes.

These studies suggest that focusing on the worst offenders is a particularly efficient use of limited police resources. As Spelman (1990: 7) suggested:

> The offense rates show the typical criminal to be a casual, low-rate offender, committing only a few crimes each year. For them, crime probably supplements a low-paying, legitimate job. But the 90th percentile offender is a full-time criminal, committing one or more crimes per day. Thus a few offenders commit crimes 40 or 50 times as often as the average active criminal; assuming all other factors equal, incarcerating one of them should be 40 to 50 times more effective in reducing crime.

Given that prisons have become increasingly overcrowded, if police officers can effectively focus their crime prevention efforts on a small number of highly active offenders, then crime can be reduced without further burdening the limited resources of the criminal justice system. Moore and his colleagues observed that opportunities exist to increase the selectivity of police crime prevention actions that are both just and effective; they suggest the following basic principles to guide experimentation in this area (1984: 168-169):

- Program procedures must be described in detail, not only to make the program effective, but also to allow for political and legal oversight.

- Procedures for designating dangerous offenders must be defined in detail and there must be some mechanism for allowing offenders to know about and challenge the designation. A procedure must be established for removing the designation if a person who has been on the street for a certain length of time without convictions or arrest for offenses.

- Reactive programs that are put into practice after a crime has been committed contain fewer risks to fairness and due process than those that operate before a criminal act has been committed (e.g., that use field intelligence on dangerous offenders).

- Programs should be evaluated in terms not only of arrests, indictments, convictions, and sentences, but also of the characteristics of those arrested and ultimate outcomes, including observed effects on serious crime. This is particularly important for the evaluation of selective arrest strategies because the purpose is to have a greater impact on crime rates through a smaller number of arrests focused on an unusually active group of offenders.

When considering the prospects for focusing on repeat offenders, an important dimension to consider is "co-offending": the commission of crimes by groups of offenders. Felson (2003: 151) described how access to accomplices is inherently criminogenic:

> Likely co-offenders not only reinforce one another's criminal impulses, but also provide each other with information and direct assistance in carrying out illegal acts. The information they can provide includes what crime targets are located where, as well as how to attack these targets, avoid apprehension, escape with loot, dispose of stolen goods, and/or win physical contests. These are simple lessons, but a little shared crime knowledge can go a long way.

Not only can co-offenders exchange knowledge, but they can also provide one another with several types of direct assistance in carrying out offenses. It is easier to carry out a property crime with someone to monitor, distract, or thwart particular guardians against the crime. Accomplices can bring different skills to the scene – one is more powerful, another runs faster, another has a keener eye. With criminal violence, two can intimidate or overpower more readily than one. Even individuals who are going to commit crime anyway can be more efficient when they act together. In short, easy access to each other under suitable circumstances causes offenders to commit more crimes.

Youth, in particular, commit crimes, as they live their lives, in groups (Zimring, 1981). This observation is particularly important because young offenders account for a disproportionate share of the most serious crimes. For example, conflicts between youth street gangs have long been noted to fuel much of the serious street violence in major cities (Klein and Maxson, 1989; Curry, Ball, and Fox, 1994; Miller, 1975). City-level studies have found gang-related motives in more than one-third of homicides in Chicago (Block and Block, 1993), 50 percent of the homicides in Los Angeles's Hollenbeck area (Tita, Riley, and Greenwood, 2003), and 75 percent of homicides in Lowell, Massachusetts (Braga, McDevitt, and Pierce, 2006). In his recent review of juvenile self-report surveys, Warr (2002) reported that most studies found between 50 and 75 percent of juvenile crimes had been committed in the company of others.

When considering youth crime, the strategy of focusing resources on a lone offender who participates in several groups may do little to prevent crimes because of the continuation of the co-offending groups (Sherman, 1992a). As such, offender-based policing strategies targeting youthful offenders should consider focusing on groups rather than particular individuals. The Boston Gun Project, discussed below, is one example of focusing criminal justice resources on groups of chronic youth offenders. Reiss (1988) observed that both adults and juveniles may be vulnerable to the suggestive influence of "Typhoid Marys": people who accumulate high numbers of co-offenders. These people serve as "carriers" of criminal ideas across social networks and their presence in particular groups could facilitate criminal action. Sherman (1992a) suggested that identifying and incarcerating these "idea men" may produce greater crime prevention benefits then apprehending lone offenders who do not spread criminal ideas around.

Police Repeat Offender Programs

Police repeat offender programs may employ varying combinations of reactive and proactive tactics. In their review of existing police "career criminal" programs, Martin and Sherman (1986) described the array of reactive and proactive tactics. Reactive tactics have included: prioritized service of warrants against identified career criminals, notification of the prosecutor when a career criminal is arrested, and augmentation of evidence through locating additional witnesses, or obtaining information about other cases against the offender. Proactive tactics have included the use of decoys, surveillance, "buy-bust" schemes, and phony fencing operations.

Moore and his colleagues (1984) reviewed six studies of selective police enforcement programs. They observed that a police focus on dangerous offenders does seem to increase the probability that such persons will be arrested and that crime will be reduced. Moore and his colleagues also stressed that case preparation matters a great deal in felony cases involving serious offenses among strangers. The precision and determination of the traditional investigative actions carried out by the police make important differences in rates of indictment, conviction, and felony-time sentences for important cases. Similarly, in New York City, an interim evaluation of an experimental effort to improve the quality of felony case preparation revealed that indictments for all robbery arrests had increased, conviction rates for all robbery arrests (including cases refused by the prosecutor) had increased, and sentences of more than a year in prison for convicted robbers had increased in one experimental precinct relative to a control precinct (McElroy et al., 1981). These results suggest that police can produce high-quality cases and, if they do, that the dispositions will be much stronger.

According to Moore and his colleagues (1984), some promising evidence that a police focus on dangerous offenders increases the probability that they will be arrested and that crime will be reduced was presented in an evaluation of the San Diego Police Department's Career Criminal Program (Boydstun et al., 1981). This program centered on: (1) improved investigation and case preparation, (2) special attention to crimes in which a dangerous offender was a suspect, and (3) identification and suppression of crime series through proactive investigations. The evaluation suggested that only the first and second strategies were in place during the "career criminal" period of the project, which primarily targeted robbery and burglary. The evaluation results for the early phases of the program, when the focus on repeat offenders was not fully operational, revealed that arrests for robbery had declined a little while the actual level of robbery in the community had declined as well. These results suggest that the robbery arrests were successfully focused on high-rate offenders. In later phases of the program, the results were less impressive as the program shifted away from a reactive investigative focus to a proactive patrol focus.

In Kansas City, proactive patrol focused on dangerous offenders led to increased arrests and convictions of dangerous offenders when compared to less focused strategies (Pate et al., 1976). However, the evaluation of these strategies also revealed that the arrests were for less serious offenses and had a weaker evidentiary basis. This implies that targeting patrol efforts on dangerous offenders has the potential of raising fairness and due process concerns if such an approach is not implemented with an emphasis on improving the quality of investigation and case preparation.

The Police Foundation's examination of the effectiveness of Washington, DC's Repeat Offender Project (ROP) concluded that the creation of selective apprehension units was a promising strategy for major urban police departments (Martin and Sherman, 1986). The ROP unit's objective was to identify and apprehend two types of active recidivists: those already wanted on one or more warrants who could be arrested on sight, and those believed to be criminally active but not currently wanted. ROP's criterion for selecting both types of targets was "the belief that the person is committing five or more Part I offenses per week" (Martin and Sherman, 1986: 157). ROP's target selection was aided by routine information on the department's major violators, the criminal histories of recent arrestees, daily crime reports from each district, and specially prepared weekly lists of all people wanted on three or more felony warrants. A controlled experiment revealed that ROP substantially increased the likelihood of arrest among targeted persons. Quasi-experimental data showed that ROP arrestees had longer and more serious criminal histories when compared to a sample of arrestees of officers in other units. The Police Foundation evaluation also found that ROP arrestees were more likely to be prosecuted and convicted on felony charges and more likely to be incarcerated. Although ROP officers were much less productive in overall arrest numbers than officers in other units, this cost was offset by the greater seriousness of the current and past offenses of the ROP arrestees (Martin and Sherman, 1986).

The Rand Corporation used a randomized field experiment to evaluate the impact of efforts at post-arrest case enhancement by a special repeat offender unit of the Phoenix Police Department (Abrahamse, Ebener, Greenwood, Fitzgerald, and Kosin, 1991). Repeat Offender Program (ROP) unit detectives and Maricopa County prosecutors agreed upon nine criteria to be used as a basis for identifying potential ROP candidates. These criteria included:

- *Current activity.* Current activity involves participation in criminal events, either as a perpetrator or as an accomplice.

- *Substance abuse.* A drug or alcohol problem may be suggested by failure in a treatment program, a prior record of illegal sales of drugs, or association with known drug users.

- *Lifestyle.* A candidate may appear to be living beyond his or her means of support, or may have associates who are heavily involved in crime.

- *Probation failure.* Although not in itself conclusive evidence of a high-rate offender, probation failure is often associated with high-rate offending.

- *Felony convictions.* The committee took note of prior felony convictions in the last 10 years.

- *Prior juvenile record.* At what age did the candidate come to the attention of the criminal justice system?

- *Past informant activity.* High-rate offenders often make excellent informants, but the Phoenix Police Department adopted a policy that prohibits use of an ROP target as an informant without prior approval of a captain or higher authority. Past informant activity, however, was used as one criterion for the program.

- *Family background.* Has the candidate committed property crimes against family members? Is the candidate married? Are any family members involved in crime?

- *Method of operation.* What types of arrest have been made in the past? Does the candidate attract attention because of the brazen nature of the crime committed? Is the candidate willing to confront victims directly? (Abrahamse et al., 1991: 147-148).

Over the course of the one-year study time period, the ROP unit's six detectives and cooperating prosecutors handled 257 cases assigned to the target group. ROP detectives did not directly investigate crimes committed by targeted offenders. Rather, they coordinated pre-arrest activities (such as notifying officers of open warrants for targeted offenders), and post-arrest activities (such as working with prosecutors on additional charges and walking warrants through the court system to ensure higher bail release bonds), and, with probation officers, prepared strong pre-sentence investigation reports that would make a case for harsher penalties for targeted offenders.

Analysis of case disposition patterns showed no significant increase in conviction rates for ROP cases relative to the control group, but there were significant increases in the likelihood of commitment to prison and in the length of term imposed (Abrahamse et al., 1991). The proportion of convicted offenders who were imprisoned increased by 9.2 percent (from 63.4 to 72.7 percent), or an additional 21 offenders. The average sentence length for imprisoned ROP offenders increased by 18 months (from 73 to 91 months). The Rand research team attributed these impacts on case outcomes to several aspects of the ROP program. Most important were "the unit's efforts to develop information on additional charges and on the defendant's prior record, the close and cooperative relationship that ROP detectives developed with the prosecutors handling their cases, and the prosecutors' willingness to hold out for tougher agreements in negotiating case settlements" (Abrahamse et al., 1991: 165). The evaluators concluded that there were no apparent reasons why similar units could not be implemented in other police departments and their ultimate success will depend on the quality and amount of information they possess for identifying target offenders, the degree of cooperation already existing between police and prosecutor, and the degree to which cooperation can be increased (Abrahamse et al., 1991).

The National Research Council's Committee to Review Research on Police Policy and Practices carefully noted that the evaluations of the Washington, DC and Phoenix, Arizona repeat offender programs only examined the apprehension effectiveness of these programs (Skogan and Frydl, 2004). These studies represented "only indirect examinations of their effect on reducing crime, and conclusions about their crime reduction effectiveness rely on ancillary assumptions about the effectiveness of selective incarceration and incapacitation" (Skogan and Frydl, 2004: 241).

While the research evidence suggests that repeat offender programs are successful in apprehending and increasing punishments for dangerous offenders, police departments considering the adoption of such approaches need to be aware that there is very limited evidence of their direct crime prevention value.

In his excellent review of the strengths and limits of targeting repeat offenders, William Spelman (1990: 60-61) identified three overriding problems faced by repeat offender programs that could affect their crime control effectiveness.

- *The information problem.* Criminal justice agencies are decentralized organizations; information is broadly distributed among line personnel. Because accurate, timely information is critical to target selection and operations, it is essential that each agency find a way to get everyone involved in the repeat offender effort. Because most repeat offender activities were undertaken by special units, few agencies sustained the involvement of other units in the department. *PREVENTING TIMELY INTEL*

- *The mobility problem.* The most frequent and experienced offenders are also the most mobile. Because municipal government is fractured in most metropolitan areas, this means that no single police agency (and, in many areas, no single prosecution or probation agency) will have full information about an individual offender's activities. To prevent mobile offenders from slipping through the cracks, the criminal justice agencies within the metropolitan area must work together to identify, arrest, and convict repeat offenders.

- *The chain problem.* Surveillance, case preparation, and prosecution are all links in a chain. If the chain is broken at any point, by any agency, the offender will not be incapacitated. Virtually all police, prosecution, and probation and parole programs were implemented by only one of the agencies along the chain, so it was frequently broken.

Dealing with these problems is vital to the success of repeat offender efforts. In his review, Spelman (1990) detailed the experiences of three jurisdictions that dealt with these problems as they planned and implemented their programs. Readers interested in learning more about the experiences of these jurisdictions should read his text closely.

The Boston Gun Project and the "Pulling Levers" Approach to Controlling Dangerous Offenders

The Boston Gun Project was a problem-oriented policing enterprise expressly aimed at taking on a serious, large-scale crime problem – homicide victimization among young people in Boston. Like many large cities in the United States, Boston experienced a large sudden increase in youth homicide between the late 1980s and early 1990s. Boston youth homicide (ages 24 and under) more than tripled – from 22 victims in 1987 to 73 victims in 1990. Youth homicide remained at a high level well after the 1990 peak; Boston averaged about 44 youth homicides per year between 1991 and 1995 (Braga et al., 2001; and see Figure 4-1).

The Boston Gun Project proceeded by: (1) assembling an interagency working group of largely line-level criminal justice and other practitioners; (2) applying quantitative and qualitative research techniques to assessing the nature of, and dynamics driving, youth violence in Boston; (3) developing an intervention designed to have a substantial, near-term impact on youth homicide; (4) implementing and adapting the intervention; and (5) evaluating the intervention's impact (Kennedy et al., 1996a). The project implemented what is now known as the "Operation Ceasefire" intervention, which began in the late spring of 1996.

The trajectory of the Boston Gun Project and of Operation Ceasefire is by now well known and extensively documented.[1] Briefly, the working group of law enforcement personnel, youth workers, and researchers diagnosed the youth violence problem in Boston as one of patterned, largely vendetta-like ("beef") hostility amongst a small population of chronic offenders, and particularly among those involved in some 61 loose, informal, mostly neighborhood-based groups. These groups were called "gangs" in Boston, but were not Chicago- or LA-style gangs (see Figures 4-2 and 4-3). These 61 gangs consisted of between 1,100 and 1,300 members, representing less than 1 percent of the city's youth between the ages of 14 and 24. Although small in number, these gangs were responsible for more than 60 percent of youth homicides in Boston.

The Operation Ceasefire "pulling levers" strategy was designed to deter violence by reaching out directly to gangs, telling them explicitly that violence would no longer be tolerated, and backing up that message by "pulling every lever" legally available when violence occurred (Kennedy, 1997, 1998). Simultaneously, youth workers, probation and parole officers, and later churches and other community groups offered gang members services and other kinds of help. The Ceasefire Working Group delivered this message in formal meetings with gang members, through individual police and probation contacts with gang members, through meetings with inmates at secure juvenile facilities in the city, and through gang outreach

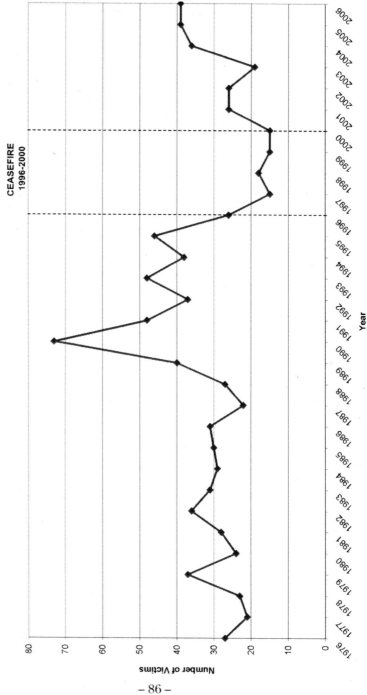

Figure 4-1. Youth Homicide in Boston, 1976–2006, Victims Ages 24 and Under.

Source: Author's original research.

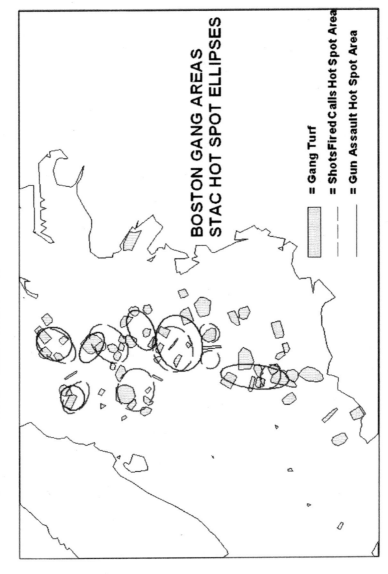

Figure 4-2. Gangs and Gang Violence in Boston.

Source: Author's research files.

Figure 4-3. Boston Gang Conflict Network.

Source: Kennedy et al. (2001: 23).

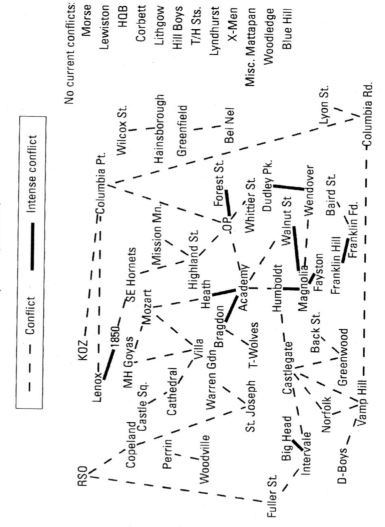

workers. The deterrence message was not a "deal" with gang members to stop violence. Rather, it was a promise to gang members that violent behavior would evoke an immediate and intense response. If gangs committed other crimes but refrained from violence, the normal workings of police, prosecutors, and the rest of the criminal justice system dealt with these matters. But if gang members hurt people, the Working Group concentrated its enforcement actions on them.

When gang violence occurred, the Ceasefire agencies addressed the violent group or groups involved, drawing from a menu of all possible legal "levers." The chronic involvement of gang members in a wide variety of offenses made them, and the gangs they formed, vulnerable to a coordinated criminal justice response. The authorities could disrupt street drug activity, focus police attention on low-level street crimes such as trespassing and public drinking, serve outstanding warrants, cultivate confidential informants for medium- and long-term investigations of gang activities, deliver strict probation and parole enforcement, seize drug proceeds and other assets, ensure stiffer plea bargains and sterner prosecutorial attention, request stronger bail terms (and enforce them), and bring potentially severe federal investigative and prosecutorial attention to gang-related drug activity. The multitude of agencies involved in the Working Group assessed each gang that behaved violently and subjected them to such "crackdowns." These operations were customized to the particular individuals and characteristics of the gang in question, and could range from probation curfew checks to U.S. Drug Enforcement Administration (DEA) investigations.

The Ceasefire crackdowns were not designed to eliminate gangs or stop every aspect of gang activity, but to control and deter serious violence. To do this, the Working Group explained its actions against targeted gangs to other gangs, as in: "This gang did violence, we responded with the following actions, and here is how to prevent anything similar from happening to you." The ongoing Working Group process regularly watched the city for outbreaks of gang violence and framed any necessary responses in accord with the Ceasefire strategy. As the strategy unfolded, the Working Group continued communication with gangs and gang members to convey its determination to stop violence, to explain its actions to the target population, and to maximize both voluntary compliance and the strategy's deterrent power.

A central hypothesis within the Working Group was the idea that a meaningful period of substantially reduced youth violence might serve as a "firebreak" and result in a relatively long-lasting reduction in future youth violence (Kennedy et al., 1996a). The idea was that youth violence in Boston had become a self-sustaining cycle among a relatively small number of youth, with objectively high levels of risk leading to nominally self-protective behavior such as gun acquisition and use, gang formation, tough "street" behavior, and the like: this behavior then became an additional input into the cycle of violence (Kennedy et al., 1996a). If this cycle could be interrupted, a new equilibrium at a lower level of risk and violence might be established, perhaps without the need for continued high levels of either deterrent or facilitative intervention. The larger hope was that a successful intervention to reduce gang violence in the short term would have a dispro-portionate, sustainable impact in the long term.

Impact of Operation Ceasefire

A large reduction in the yearly number of Boston youth homicides followed immediately after Operation Ceasefire was implemented in mid-1996. As discussed earlier, Boston averaged about 45 youth homicides per year be-tween 1991 and 1995. In 1996, with Ceasefire in place for roughly half the year, the number of Boston youth homicides decreased to 26 and then further decreased to 15 in 1997, a level below that characteristic of Boston in the pre-epidemic period. The low level of youth homicides continued through 1998 (18), 1999 (15), and 2000 (18). After the Ceasefire interven-tion was no longer in place (see Braga and Winship, 2006 for a discussion), Boston youth homicide steadily increased between 2001 and 2006 (Figure 4-1).

A U.S. Department of Justice (DOJ)-sponsored evaluation of Operation Ceasefire revealed that the intervention was associated with a 63 percent decrease in the monthly number of Boston youth homicides, a 32 percent decrease in the monthly number of shots-fired calls, a 25 percent decrease in the monthly number of gun assaults, and, in one high-risk police district given special attention in the evaluation, a 44 percent decrease in the monthly number of youth gun assault incidents (Braga et al., 2001). The evaluation also suggested that Boston's significant youth homicide reduc-tion associated with Operation Ceasefire was distinct when compared to youth homicide trends in most major U.S. and New England cities (Braga et al., 2001).

Other researchers, however, have observed that some of the decrease in homicide may have occurred without the Ceasefire intervention in place as violence was decreasing in most major U.S. cities. Fagan's (2002) cursory review of gun homicide in Boston and in other Massachusetts cities sug-gested a general downward trend in gun violence that existed before Opera-tion Ceasefire was implemented. Levitt (2004) analyzed homicide trends over the course of the 1990s and concluded that innovative policing strategies, such as Operation Ceasefire in Boston and "broken windows" policing and Compstat in New York, had only limited impacts on homicide. According to Levitt, other factors – such as increases in the number of police, the rising prison population, the waning crack-cocaine epidemic, and the legalization of abortion – can account for nearly the entire national decline in homicide, violent crime, and property crime in the 1990s. But in their analysis of homicide trend data for the 95 largest U.S. cities during the 1990s, Rosenfeld, Fornango, and Baumer (2005) found some evidence of a sharper youth homicide drop in Boston than elsewhere; they suggested that the small number of youth homicide incidents precluded strong conclusions about program effectiveness based on their statistical models. And in his examination of youth homicide trends in Boston, Ludwig (2005) suggested that Ceasefire was associated with a large drop in youth homicide. However, given the complexities of analyzing city-level homicide trends, Ludwig concluded that some uncertainty remained about the exact contribution of Ceasefire to the near two-thirds drop in Boston youth homicide.

The National Research Council's Panel on Improving Information and Data on Firearms (Wellford, Pepper, and Petrie, 2005) concluded that the DOJ-sponsored Ceasefire evaluation (Braga et al., 2001) offered compelling evidence associating the intervention with the subsequent decline in youth homicide. However, the panel also suggested that many complex factors affect youth homicide trends, and therefore it was difficult to specify the exact relationship between the Ceasefire intervention and subsequent changes in youth offending behaviors. While the DOJ-sponsored evaluation controlled for existing violence trends and certain rival causal factors – such as changes in the youth population, drug markets, and employment in Boston – there could have been complex interaction effects among these factors not measured by the evaluation that could have accounted for some meaningful portion of the decrease. The evaluation was not a randomized, controlled experiment. Therefore, because of the non-randomized control group research design, it was not possible to rule out the possibility that some factor other than Ceasefire was the key cause of the youth homicide decline.

Violence Prevention Mechanisms Associated with the Pulling Levers Strategy

As part of the U.S. Office of Juvenile Justice and Delinquency Prevention (OJJDP) National Youth Gang Suppression and Intervention Program,

Spergel and Curry (1990, 1993) surveyed 254 law enforcement, school, and community representatives in 45 cities and six institutional sites about their gang intervention programs. From these survey data, Spergel and Curry developed a typology of interventions these areas used to deal with gang problems, grouping them into four broad categories: (1) suppression, (2) social intervention, (3) opportunity provision, and (4) community organization. Although Operation Ceasefire was a problem-oriented policing project centered on law enforcement interventions, the multidimensional and complex activities of the program fell into all four categories. The elements of strategy that involved community organization, social intervention, and opportunity provision certainly supported and strengthened the ability of criminal justice agencies to reduce gang violence (Braga and Kennedy, 2002). Thus, the Boston experience suggests that a multidimensional mix of interventions is a desirable way to approach complex and sensitive problems like urban youth gang violence.

The typical law enforcement suppression approach assumes that most street gangs are criminal associations that must be attacked through an efficient gang tracking, identification, and targeted enforcement strategy (Spergel, 1995). The basic premise of this approach is that improved data collection systems and coordination of information across different criminal justice agencies will lead to more efficiency and to more gang members being removed from the streets, rapidly prosecuted, and sent to prison for longer sentences (Spergel, 1995). Typical suppression programs include: street sweeps in which police officers round up hundreds of suspected gang members; special gang probation and parole caseloads in which gang members are subjected to heightened levels of surveillance and more stringent revocation rules; prosecution programs that target gang leaders and serious gang offenders; civil procedures that use gang membership as the basis for arrests for conspiracy or unlawful associations; and school-based law enforcement programs that include surveillance and buy-bust operations (Klein, 1993).

Operation Ceasefire and Deterrence

These suppression approaches are loosely based on deterrence theory (Klein, 1993). Deterrence theory posits that crimes can be prevented when the costs of committing the crime are perceived by the offender to outweigh the benefits of committing the crime (Zimring and Hawkins, 1973; Gibbs, 1975). Most discussions of the deterrence mechanism distinguish between "general" and "specific" deterrence – also called "special" deterrence (Cook,

1980). General deterrence is the idea that the general population is dissuaded from committing crime when it sees that punishment necessarily follows the commission of a crime. Specific deterrence involves punishment administered to individual criminals with the intent of discouraging them from committing crimes in the future. Much of the literature evaluating deterrence focuses on the effect of changing certainty, swiftness, and severity of punishment associated with certain acts on the prevalence of those crimes.[2]

Law enforcement agencies attempt to influence the behavior of gang members or eliminate gangs entirely by dramatically increasing the certainty, severity, and swiftness of criminal justice sanctions. Unfortunately, gangs and gang problems usually continue in the wake of these intensive operations. Malcolm Klein (1993) suggested that law enforcement agencies do not generally have the capacity to "eliminate" all gangs in a gang-troubled jurisdiction, nor do they have the capacity to respond in a powerful way to all gang offending in such jurisdictions. Pledges to do so, though common, are simply not credible to gang members. Klein (1993) also observed that the emphasis on selective enforcement by deterrence-based gang suppression programs may increase the cohesiveness of gang members, who often perceive such actions as unwarranted harassment, rather than cause them to withdraw from gang activity. Therefore, suppression programs may have the perverse effect of strengthening gang solidarity.

The Operation Ceasefire intervention is, in its broadest sense, a deterrence strategy. However, the Ceasefire working group recognized that, in order for the strategy to be successful, it was crucial to deliver a credible deterrence message to Boston gangs. Therefore, the Ceasefire intervention targeted those gangs that were engaged in violent behavior rather than expending resources on those who were not. In addition to any increases in certainty, severity, and swiftness of sanctions associated with youth violence, the Operation Ceasefire strategy sought to obtain deterrence through *advertising* the law enforcement strategy, and through the personalized nature of its application. It was crucial that gang youth understood the new regime that the city was imposing. The "pulling levers" approach attempted to prevent gang violence by making gang members believe that consequences would follow on violence and gun use and choose to change their behavior.

The effective operation of general deterrence is dependent on the communication of punishment threats to the public. As Zimring and Hawkins (1973: 142) observed: " . . . the deterrence threat may best be viewed as a form of advertising." One noteworthy example of this principle was of the 1975 Massachusetts Bartley-Fox amendment, which introduced a mandatory minimum one-year prison sentence for the illegal carrying of firearms. The high degree of publicity attendant upon the amendment's passage, some of which was inaccurate, was found to increase citizen compliance with existing legal stipulations surrounding firearm acquisition and possession, some of which were not in fact addressed by the amendment (see Beha, 1977). Zimring and Hawkins (1973: 149) further observed that, " . . . if the first task of the threatening agency is the communication of information, its second task is persuasion." There is also evidence that crime prevention measures may reduce crime before they are implemented, an effect known as an "anticipatory" benefit (Smith et al., 2002). Offenders may be influenced by the perception that the risk of committing crime has changed. Pre-implementation publicity campaigns have been found to produce anticipatory reductions in criminal offending (Johnson and Bowers, 2003).

A key element of the Operation Ceasefire strategy was the delivery of a direct and explicit "retail deterrence" message to a relatively small target audience regarding what kind of behavior would provoke a special response and what that response would be. Law enforcement agencies in Boston strove to achieve deterrence by increasing the cost to offenders of gang-related violence. The deterrence principles applied in the Operation Ceasefire intervention could be regarded as a "meso-deterrence" strategy. Beyond the particular gangs subjected to the intervention, the deterrence message was applied to a relatively small audience (all gang-involved youth in Boston) rather than to a general audience (all youth in Boston), and it operated by making explicit cause-and-effect connections between the behavior of the target population and the behavior of the authorities. Knowledge of what happened to others in the target population was intended to prevent further acts of violence by gangs in Boston.

Operation Ceasefire and Social Intervention Programs

Beyond deterring violent behavior, Operation Ceasefire was also designed to facilitate desired behaviors among gang members through social service intervention, opportunity provision, and community organization. As Spergel (1995) observed, coordinated strategies that integrate these varied domains are most likely to be effective in dealing with chronic youth gang problems. Social intervention programs encompass both social service agency-based programs and detached "streetworker" programs; opportunity provision strategies attempt to offer gang members legitimate opportunities and means to success that are at least as appealing as available illegitimate options (Curry and Decker, 1998; Spergel, 1995; Klein, 1995). Boston streetworkers were key members of the Operation Ceasefire Working Group and, along with the Department of Youth Services (juvenile corrections) caseworkers, probation officers, and parole officers in the group, added a much needed social intervention and opportunity provision dimension to the Ceasefire strategy. With these resources, the Ceasefire Working Group was able to pair criminal justice sanctions, or the promise of sanctions, with help and with services. When the risk to drug dealing gang members increases, legitimate work becomes more attractive, and when legitimate work is more available, raising risks will be more effective in reducing violence. The availability of social services and opportunities were intended to increase the Ceasefire strategy's preventive power by offering gang members any assistance they may want: protection from their enemies, drug treatment, and access to education and job training programs, and the like.

Community organization strategies to cope with gang problems include attempts to create community solidarity, networking, education, and involvement (Spergel and Curry, 1993). The Ten Point Coalition of activist black clergy played an important role in organizing Boston communities suffering from gang violence (Winship and Berrien, 1999; Braga and Winship, 2006). As will be described in Chapter 6, Ten Point clergy were an invaluable resource to Operation Ceasefire as they helped to legitimate the strategy in the eyes of the community, conducted street work and home visits with high-risk gang youth, and provided a strong moral voice at the gang forums in the presentation of Ceasefire's anti-violence message.

Replications of the "Pulling Levers" Strategy in Other Jurisdictions

At first blush, the effectiveness of the Operation Ceasefire intervention in preventing violence may seem unique to Boston. Operation Ceasefire was constructed largely from the assets and capacities available in Boston at the time and deliberately tailored to the city's particular violence problem. Operational capacities of criminal justice agencies in other cities will be different and youth violence problems in other cities will have important distinguishing characteristics. However, the basic working group problem-solving process and the "pulling levers" approach to deterring chronic offenders are transferable to violence problems in other jurisdictions. A number of cities have begun to experiment with these analytic frameworks and have experienced some encouraging preliminary results. Consistent with the problem-oriented policing approach, these cities have tailored the approach to fit their violence problems and operating environments.

In East Los Angeles, a DOJ-sponsored replication of Operation Cease-fire experienced noteworthy difficulty keeping the social service and community-based partners involved in the interagency collaboration (Tita, Riley, Ridgeway, Grammich, Abrahamse, and Greenwood, 2004). However, the law enforcement components of the intervention were fully implemented: they focused on two gangs engaged in ongoing violent conflict. The quasi-experimental evaluation revealed that the focused enforcement resulted in significant short-term reductions in violent crime and gang crime in targeted areas relative to matched comparison areas (Tita et al., 2004). In Stockton, California, a rigorous evaluation of the Operation Peacekeeper gang violence reduction intervention also found a significant decrease in gun homicide associated with the pulling levers approach (Braga, 2008; see also Wakeling, 2003; Braga, 2005b).

A quasi-experimental evaluation of the Indianapolis Violence Reduction Partnership found that the pulling levers strategy was associated with a 42 percent reduction in homicide in Indianapolis (McGarrell, Chermak, Wilson, and Corsaro, 2006). When compared to homicide trends in the nearby cities of Cleveland, Cincinnati, Kansas City, Louisville, and Pittsburgh, Indianapolis was the only city experiencing a statistically significant decrease in homicide during the study time period.

In Chicago, a quasi-experimental evaluation of a Project Safe Neighborhoods gun violence reduction strategy found significant reductions in homicides in treatment neighborhoods relative to control neighborhoods (Papachristos, Meares, and Fagan, 2007). The largest effect was associated with preventive tactics based on the pulling levers strategy, such as offender notification meetings that stress individual deterrence, normative change in offender behavior, and the respectful treatment of offenders in presenting them with the choices they have to make to ensure that they do not commit gun violence in their neighborhoods.

The Lowell "Pulling Levers" Project

An interagency task force implemented a pulling levers strategy to prevent gun violence among Hispanic and Asian gangs in Lowell, Massachusetts (Braga, McDevitt, and Pierce, 2006). While the Lowell authorities felt very confident about their ability to prevent violence among Hispanic gangs by pursuing a general pulling levers strategy, they felt much less confident about their ability to prevent Asian gang violence by applying the same set of criminal justice levers. As Malcolm Klein (1995) suggested previously, Asian gangs display some key differences from typical black, Hispanic, and white street gangs. They are more organized, have identifiable leaders, and are far more secretive. They also tend to be far less territorial and less openly visible. Therefore, their street presence is low compared to other ethnic gangs. Relationships between law enforcement agencies and the Asian community are often characterized by mistrust and a lack of communication (Chin, 1996). As such, it is often difficult for the police to develop information on the participants in violent acts to hold offenders accountable for their actions.

During the intervention time period, the Lowell Police Department (LPD) had little reliable intelligence about Asian gangs in the city (Braga et al., 2006). The LPD had attempted to develop informants in the past, but most these efforts had been unsuccessful. With the increased focus on Asian gang violence, the LPD increased its efforts to develop intelligence about the structure of the city's Asian gangs and particularly the relationship between Asian gang violence and ongoing gambling that was being run by local Asian businesses. Asian street gangs are sometimes connected to adult criminal organizations and assist older criminals in extortion activities and protecting illegal gambling enterprises (Chin, 1996). In many East Asian cultures, rituals and protocols guiding social interactions are well defined and reinforced through a variety of highly developed feelings of obligation, many of which are hierarchical in nature (Zhang, 2002). This facilitates some control over the behavior of younger Asian gang members by elders in the gang.

In Lowell, the Cambodian and Laotian gangs were composed of youth whose street activities were influenced by "elders" of the gang (Braga et al., 2006). Elders were generally long-time gang members in their 30s and 40s who no longer engaged in illegal activities on the street or participated in street-level violence with rival youth. Rather, these older gang members were heavily involved in running illegal gambling dens and informal casinos that were operated out of cafes, video stores, and warehouses located in the poor Asian neighborhoods of Lowell. The elders used young street gang members to protect their business interests and to collect any unpaid gambling debts. Illegal gaming was a very lucrative business that was much more important to the elders than any ongoing beefs the youth in their gang had with other youth (Braga et al., 2006). In contrast to acquiring information on individuals responsible for gun crimes in Asian communities, it was much easier to detect the presence of gambling operations through surveillance or a simple visit to the suspected business establishment.

The importance of illegal gaming to influential members of Asian street gangs provided a potentially potent lever to law enforcement in preventing violence. The authorities in Lowell believed that they could systematically prevent street violence among gangs by targeting the gambling interests of older members. When a street gang was violent, the LPD targeted the gambling businesses run by the older members of the gang. The enforcement activities ranged from serving a search warrant on the business that housed the illegal enterprise and making arrests to simply placing a patrol car in front of the suspected gambling location to deter gamblers from entering. The LPD coupled these tactics with the delivery of a clear message: "When the gang kids associated with you act violently, we will shut down your gambling business. When violence erupts, no one makes money" (Braga et al., 2006: 40). Between October 2002 and June 2003, the height of the focused attention on Asian gangs, the LPD conducted some 30 searches of illegal gambling dens, which resulted in more than 100 gambling-related arrests (Braga et al., 2006).

An impact evaluation found that the Lowell pulling levers strategy was associated with a 43 percent decrease in the monthly number of gun homicide and gun aggravated assault incidents (Braga, Pierce, McDevitt, Bond, and Cronin, 2008). A comparative analysis of gun homicide and gun aggravated assault trends in Lowell relative to other major Massachusetts cities also supported a unique program effect associated with the pulling levers intervention.

While this approach to preventing violence among Asian street gangs represents an innovation in policing, it is not an entirely new idea. The social control exerted by older Asian criminals over their younger counterparts is well documented in the literature on Asian crime. For example, in his study of Chinese gangs in New York City, Ko-Lin Chin (1996) suggests that gang leaders often exert influence over subordinate gang members to end violent confrontations so they can focus their energies on illegal enterprises that make money. The prospect of controlling street violence by cracking down on the interests of organized crime is also familiar to law enforcement. In his classic study of an Italian street gang in Boston's North End, Whyte (1943) described the activities of beat officers in dealing with outbreaks of violence by cracking down on the gambling rackets run by organized crime in the neighborhood. Nevertheless, the systematic application of this approach, coupled with a communications campaign, represents an innovative way to deal with Asian street gang violence.

There is less experience in applying the pulling levers approach to other problems. In High Point, North Carolina, a pulling levers strategy has been aimed at eliminating public forms of drug dealing such as street markets and crack houses by warning dealers, buyers, and their families that enforcement is imminent (Kennedy, 2006). The project employed a joint police-community partnership to identify individual offenders, notify them of the consequences of continued illegal activity, and provide supportive services through a community-based resource coordinator. A preliminary assessment of the pulling levers drug market intervention found noteworthy reductions in drug and violent crime in High Point's West End neighborhood (Frabutt, Gathings, Hunt, and Loggins, 2004).

Controlling Repeat Offenders Who Abuse Drugs and Alcohol

As discussed earlier, frequent offenders often abuse drugs. Kleiman (1997: 200) observed, " . . . if heavy users account for 80 percent of the cocaine, and if three-quarters of them are in the criminal justice population, then 60 percent of the total cocaine is sold to persons under (nominal) criminal justice supervision." To make a visible dent in the drug consumption of addict-offenders, Kleiman (1997) therefore proposed a system that extends the supervisory capacity of drug courts and diversion programs to a larger proportion of offenders for longer periods. The system would substitute, to the maximum extent possible, testing and automatic sanctions for treatment services and personal attention from a judge. Kleiman calls this approach *coerced abstinence,* and describes the system as follows (1997: 205-206):

- Probationers and parolees are screened for cocaine, heroin, or methamphetamine use, through drug tests and reviews of records.

- Those identified as users, either at the beginning of their terms or by random testing thereafter, are subject to twice weekly drug tests. They may choose any two days of the week and any times of day for the tests as long as the two chosen times are separated by at least 72 hours. In effect, there is no window for undetected use.

- Every positive test earns the offender a brief (perhaps two-day) period of incarceration. (The length of the sanction and whether and how sharply sanctions should increase with repeated violations, are questions best determined by trial and error, and the best answer may very from place to place.) Missed drug tests count as positive tests (perhaps the sanction for missing a drug test should be greater than the sanction for a positive drug test in order to discourage failing to show up for a drug test).

- The sanction is applied immediately, and no official has authority to waive or modify it. (But perhaps employed users with no recent failures should be allowed to defer their confinement until the weekend to avoid the risk of losing their jobs.) The offender is entitled to a hearing only on the question of whether the test result is accurate; the penalty itself is fixed.

- After some long period (perhaps six months) without missed or positive drug tests, or, alternatively, the achievement of some score on a point system that measures good behavior, offenders are eligible to less frequent testing. Continued good conduct leads to removal to inactive status with only random testing.

While this approach to controlling offenders is primarily based in the courts and carried out by probation and parole officers, police would play an important role in the enforcement of the conditions of this program. The interesting proposition for improved crime prevention, which is relevant to police efforts to control serious offenders, is the attempt to get deterrence "right" for highly active drug offenders. Kleiman (1997) observed that, for the reckless and impulsive offender, deferred and low-probability threats of severe punishment are less effective than immediate and high-probability threats of mild punishment. Current practices for dealing with offenders rely too much on severity of sanctions at the expense of certainty and immediacy. Kleiman suggested that abstinence from drug use ought to be made a condition of liberty for addict-offenders and that this condition ought to be enforced with frequent tests and predictable sanctions.

Although this approach has not yet rigorously evaluated, Kleiman (1997) presented encouraging results from four pilot programs. For example, Santa Cruz County, California, instituted aggressive testing of known heroin users on probation in the late 1980s, coupled with a focused crackdown on street-level dealing. Although no formal examination of the relationship between testing and burglary rates was conducted, the county reported a 22 percent reduction in burglaries in the following year, while the number of burglaries slightly increased in surrounding counties.

In Oahu, Hawaii, the principles of coerced abstinence are being applied in a new pilot program, called H.O.P.E. (Hawaii's Opportunity Probation with Enforcement). By closely monitoring probationer behavior and rapidly punishing violations with relatively mild sanctions – typically a few days in jail – the program provides much-needed structure to offenders whose lives are often in disarray (Hawken and Kleiman, 2007). The formula H.O.P.E. follows for controlling hard-drug use in the criminally active population is fairly simple (Hawken and Kleiman, 2007):

- Weekly randomized testing (or twice-weekly scheduled testing), to eliminate any "safe window" for undetected drug use.

- Fixed sanctions on a set schedule: As little as two days in jail is adequate, so long as enforcement is reliable, with sentence length increasing gradually for successive violations.

- A formal warning to the probationer in open court, putting him on notice that violations have consequences.

- As short a time as possible between violations and sanctions. (For offenders with paycheck jobs, the first sanction could be deferred to the following weekend.)

- Quick service of bench warrants on those who abscond.

- Treatment services for those who prove unable to comply on their own.

A preliminary assessment suggests the approach has considerable value in controlling the behavior of high-risk probationers. A group of methamphetamine-using probationers with records of poor compliance were put on the H.O.P.E. drug-testing-and-sanctions program and given a formal warning by a judge (Hawken and Kleiman, 2007). Immediately after the initial warning was issued, half of the probationers conformed and never needed to be sanctioned. Hawken and Kleiman (2007) reported that the overall rate of missed and "dirty" drug tests went down by more than 80 percent. In response to these promising results, Hawaii's legislature has appropriated funds to expand that pilot program to 1,000 of the 7,200 felony probationers on Oahu.

Police Efforts to Prevent Drunk Driving

Another way to control offenders is by increasing the number of contacts between them and the police. Police efforts to prevent drunk driving are one example; increased contacts between police and serious offenders who commit minor crimes via a policing disorder strategy is another well-known application described in the previous chapter. Drunk drivers range from chronic alcoholics who routinely drink and drive to minor and infrequent alcohol users who occasionally take the risk of driving a car while intoxicated (Jacobs, 1988). Although repeat drunk drivers comprise a relatively small proportion of the total population of drivers, they are disproportionately responsible for alcohol-related crashes and other problems associated with drunk driving.

According to a recent review by Michael Scott (2006b: 4), between one-third and three-fourths of drivers arrested for drunk driving have been previously charged with the offense, those who drink and drive at least twice per month account for about 90 percent of all drunk driving trips, and between one-third and one-half of those charged with drunk driving will be charged again in the future.

Studies examining the effectiveness of severe punishments for drunk driving have suggested that tough laws do not deter drunk drivers (Ross et al., 1990; Ross, 1992). The support for increasing the penalties associated with drunk driving comes from the belief that the threat of swift, certain, and severe punishment can reduce undesirable behavior. However, under routine police enforcement patterns, the probability of being arrested for drunk driving is, in reality, quite low (Jacobs, 1988). For every drunk driving arrest, an estimated 500 to 2,000 violations go undetected by the police (U.S. National Highway Traffic Safety Administration, 1995). Moreover, the stiff penalties associated with drunk driving have caused an increased number of defendants to pursue full jury trials that take an extended period of time to resolve (Ross, 1992). Therefore, punishment for those arrested for drunk driving is generally slow and uncertain. The typical criminal justice system response to drunk driving, unfortunately, does not seem to prevent intoxicated persons from getting behind the wheel of a car.

In contrast to the literature on the effects of severe punishment on drunk driving, the ability of the police to control drunk driving through focused enforcement efforts is quite promising. As part of a large scale review of the criminology literature for the U.S. Congress, Lawrence Sherman (1997: 24) wrote that: " . . . the evidence on drunk driving . . . is one of the great success stories of world policing."

A series of quasi-experimental evaluations of proactive drunk driving arrest strategies suggested a clear cause and effect; when drunk driving arrests increase, car crashes from drunk driving decrease (see Ross, 1992 for a review). Homel (1990) suggested that the ability of the police to control drunk driving appears to be a direct and linear function of the amount of effort they put into it. Benson and his colleagues (2000) also found that the availability of police resources can affect the probability of arrest for drunk driving, which suggests that systematic and sustained police efforts could be effective in controlling drunk driving. Thus, by increasing the certainty of detection, police crackdowns on drunk driving produce a deterrent effect among potential drunk drivers.

Scott (2006b) suggested two methods through which the police can raise the perception among drinking drivers that they will be stopped and investigated for drunk driving: first, by increasing the total number of drivers stopped by the police; and second, by improved detection of alcohol impairment once a stop is made. Clearly, police need to significantly increase the number of stops of suspected drunk drivers during times when the risk of a drunk driving crash is high. This can be achieved through increasing the amount of patrol time of officers looking for drunk drivers, streamlining the arrest process, encouraging citizens to report drunk driving, and increasing the emphasis placed on drunk driving interdiction and enforcement (Scott, 2006b).

Highly visible sobriety checkpoints can also be used to increase drinking drivers' perceived risk of being stopped and arrested. Sobriety checkpoints have been shown to reduce the incidence of drunk driving and alcohol related crashes by 15 to 25 percent (Scott, 2006b). Officers should also be trained in detecting physical and verbal cures that indicate drunkenness (such as the Standardized Field Sobriety Test, which assists officers in recognizing alcohol impairment), and make use of preliminary breath-testing devices (to detect the presence of elevated levels of alcohol in the driver's blood system; Scott, 2006b).

In Madison, Wisconsin, researchers reasoned that, since the percentage of drinking drivers arrested was very low and the criminal justice system could handle only a small number of cases, problem-oriented policing could have a significant deterrent effect by increasing the number of contacts with drinking drivers without expending the enormous resources it would take to process them through the criminal justice system (Goldstein and Susmilch, 1982). They believed that an increased expectation of being caught would be enough to deter many drunk drivers. Recognizing a limited capacity to arrest all drunk drivers, the research team developed a set of alternatives to making an arrest. These alternatives included (Goldstein and Susmilch, 1982: 118):

- Make the driver walk home.

- Have one of the other individuals in the stopped vehicle take over, provided that he or she is not also impaired.

- Call a cab for the driver and secure the vehicle.

- Insist that the driver take time out to eat.

- Remove the ignition key and either hide it in the vehicle where it is not easily accessible (e.g., in the trunk), or deposit it at some point (e.g., the police station) with information left with the driver as to where it can be picked up.

Criteria were recommended for guiding police in determining who should be arrested and who should only be warned. Beyond increasing contacts to deter drunk drivers, these alternatives were also developed to reduce the likelihood of accidents. Unfortunately, this plan was not implemented because it generated little support from within the police department (Goldstein and Susmilch, 1982).

Controlling Crime Facilitators: Keeping Guns Away from Dangerous Offenders

Crime facilitators are things such as automobiles, credit cards, and weapons that are essential tools in committing certain kinds of crimes (Clarke, 1997). Approaches used to controlling crime facilitators have included: personalizing credit cards with photos of the proper owner to prevent misuse; serving beer in plastic mugs to prevent the use of glass mugs as weapons; removing or altering pay phones in drug market areas to block their use in dealing; introducing Caller-ID (a screening device that allows the person answering the phone to read the number calling) to reduce obscene and annoying phone calls; and creating identification procedures to reduce check fraud (for a review, see Clarke, 1997).

Guns in the hands of criminals and juveniles are crime facilitators that are of great concern to police departments. Criminal misuse of guns kills or injures tens of thousands of Americans every year. The threat of such violence imposes a heavy burden on our standard of living, not only on groups that have the highest victimization rates, but also on the entire community. By one estimate, this burden amounts to $80 billion per year (Cook and Ludwig, 2000). In the United States, there are some 258 million privately owned firearms, including 93 million handguns (Wellford, Pepper, and Petrie, 2005). This immense stockpile serves as a source of guns to juveniles and other prohibited persons, who may obtain them through a variety of means. Although there is much debate about proper gun control measures to reduce legal access to guns, insufficient emphasis is placed on the fact that only about one of every six firearms used in crime was legally obtained (Reiss and Roth, 1993). Unlike narcotics or other contraband, the illegal supply of guns does not begin with illegal smuggling or in clandestine factories. Virtually every crime gun in the United States starts out, at least initially, in the legal market. Clearly, there is a problem with illegal gun acquisition from regulated and unregulated legal sources and there is a corresponding need to intervene in these markets to make it more expensive, inconvenient, or legally risky to obtain firearms for criminal use.

In their review of the various sources of data on the illegal supply of firearms, Braga, Cook, Kennedy, Moore (2002) suggested that, in the parlance of environmental regulation, illegal gun markets consist of both a) "point sources," such as ongoing diversions through scofflaw dealers and trafficking rings; and b) "diffuse sources," such as acquisitions through theft and informal voluntary sales. A reasonable conclusion is that, as in the case of pollution, both point sources and diffuse sources are important (see also Cook and Braga, 2001). Braga and his colleagues (2002) also speculated that the mix of point and diffuse sources differs across jurisdictions depending on the density of gun ownership and the strictness of gun controls. For example, systematic gun trafficking from retail point sources may be more difficult in jurisdictions with stricter controls on the purchase and sale of firearms, such as Boston and New York, than in looser-control jurisdictions such as Atlanta and Dallas. Given that there is a mix of concentrated and diffuse sources, the potential effectiveness of supply-side enforcement may also vary across jurisdictions.

Figure 4-4 presents a conceptual scheme of the flow of firearms to criminals and juveniles. Other than theft, there are three broad mechanisms through which criminal consumers acquire firearms from licensees: straw purchases, "lying and buying," and buying from a dealer who is willing to ignore regulations. A straw purchase occurs when the actual buyer, typically someone who is too young or otherwise proscribed, uses another person to execute the paperwork. Prohibited persons can purchase firearms directly by showing false identification and lying about their status. In some cases the seller is knowingly involved, and may disguise the illegal transaction by falsifying the paper record of sale or reporting the guns as stolen. After firearms are diverted from legal commerce, it is quite likely that they

Figure 4-4. Illegal Supply of Firearms.

Source: Braga et al. (2002a: 337).

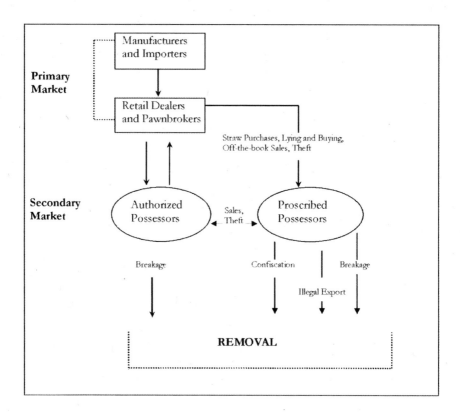

will be put to use in criminal activity. It appears that most guns used by criminals, especially by young offenders, have been acquired relatively recently, reflecting the fact that street criminals tend to have brief careers (Blumstein et al., 1986). Guns have value in exchange as well as in use. Based on interviews with youthful offenders, Cook and his colleagues (1995) reported that guns were valuable commodities for youth to trade for services, money, drugs, or other items. Youthful offenders may be active both as sellers and buyers of guns through informal networks of family, friends, and street sources (Wright, Sheley, and Smith, 1992). Incarcerated felons who reported selling or trading stolen guns identified a varied list of customers including friends, fences, drug dealers, strangers on the street, pawn-shops, retail gun stores, and family members (Wright and Rossi, 1994).

Effective supply-side efforts to reduce the supply of available guns would help increase the price of guns sold to prohibited persons and increase the "effective price" of acquiring guns – the time and hassle required to make a "connection" to buy guns (see Moore, 1973, 1976). The benefit of this approach would be an increased incentive for criminals and youths to economize on gun possession and use. As guns become scarcer and more valuable, they will be slower to buy and quicker to sell, thus reducing the percentage of their criminal careers in which they are in possession of a gun (Kennedy, 1994).

Local police departments can quite possibly be effective at disrupting local gun markets, but only if they concern themselves with gathering the necessary intelligence and acting on it. Most police departments have focused on getting guns off the street instead of focusing on where the guns are coming from (Moore, 1980; Moore, 1983b). In recent years, however, police practices have changed in many major cities due in part to efforts by the Bureau of Alcohol, Tobacco, Firearms, and Explosives (ATF) and the U.S. Department of Justice to form partnerships to reduce the availability of guns to youth and criminals (see, e.g., ATF 2000a; ATF 2000b). Heightened enforcement of federal laws against illegal gun trafficking is also a major component of the current U.S. Department of Justice-sponsored Project Safe Neighborhoods initiative to reduce gun violence in each of the 94 U.S. Attorney judicial districts in the United States (www.psn.gov). A key to these partnerships is the comprehensive tracing of all firearms recovered in a jurisdiction to their first sale at retail source and the strategic analysis of trace information to identify suspicious purchase and sales patterns indicative of illegal gun trafficking (Cook and Braga, 2001; Pierce, Braga, Hyatt, and Koper, 2004). Analyses of firearms trace data have documented that a disproportionate number of firearms recovered in crimes were first purchased recently at retail; this suggests that illegal diversions of firearms from retail commerce are a significant problem worth addressing.

Local problem-oriented policing projects hold great promise for creating a strong response to illicit firearms markets. The problem-oriented approach provides an appropriate framework to uncovering the complex mechanisms at play in illicit firearms markets and to developing tailor-made interventions to disrupt the gun trade. The complexity and diversity of illegal gun markets suggests that there is no single best policy or approach to disrupting the illegal supply of guns across the numerous jurisdictions in the United States. Jurisdictions interested in reducing the availability of guns should develop a portfolio of interventions based on problem-solving partnerships among federal, state, and local authorities. By analyzing the nature of particular gun trafficking problems, law enforcement can develop a systematic plan to shut down supply lines rather than simply pursuing ad hoc enforcement actions against specific individuals.

The Boston Gun Project

The most famous illustration of a problem-oriented approach was the afore-mentioned Boston Gun Project. Based on an analysis of the local illegal gun market, the resulting strategy was appropriately focused on the illegal diversion of new handguns from retail outlets in Massachusetts, southern states along Interstate 95, and elsewhere (Kennedy et al., 1996). For investigative and tactical purposes, guns with quick "time-to-crime" (the time between the first retail purchase and its ultimate recovery by the police) offered law enforcement an opportunity to identify illegal gun traffickers. New guns have passed through fewer hands and this makes it much easier for law enforcement to investigate its diversion and its diverters, and to mount prosecutions. Records are likely to be more complete and more available; individuals listed on paperwork are easier to find; guns are less likely to have been resold, given away, or stolen; and the chain of transfers to illicit consumers is likely to be shorter (Kennedy et al., 1996). The key elements of the Ceasefire gun market disruption strategy were (summarized from Kennedy, Braga, and Piehl, 2001):

- Expanded focus of local, state, and federal authorities to include *intrastate* firearms trafficking in Massachusetts in addition to interstate trafficking.

- Focused enforcement attention on traffickers of the makes and calibers of handguns most used by gang members.

- Focused enforcement attention on traffickers of handguns that had short time-to-crime intervals and, thus, were most likely to have been trafficked. The ATF Boston Field Division implemented an in-house tracking system that flagged handguns whose traces revealed a short time-to-crime interval.

- Focused enforcement attention on traffickers of handguns used by the city's most violent gangs.

- Attempts to restore obliterated serial numbers of confiscated handguns and subsequently investigate trafficking based on these restorations.

- Support for these enforcement priorities through strategic analyses of data generated by the Boston Police Department and ATF's comprehensive tracing of crime guns and by developing leads from the systematic debriefing of gang-affiliated arrestees and those involved in violent crime.

- Deliberate communication of successful investigations and prosecutions of gun traffickers to deter others from diverting firearms from retail sources to criminals and youth in Boston.

The results of a DOJ-funded evaluation found that Operation Ceasefire's focus on close-to-retail diversions of handguns was associated with significant decreases in the percentage of handguns recovered by the Boston Police that were new (Braga and Pierce, 2005). While data on street prices of new handguns paid by criminals were not available, the evaluation findings suggest that the supply-side enforcement strategy increased the "effective price" of new handguns by making it riskier to acquire these firearms for illegal possession and criminal use. As described earlier, the Boston supply-side approach was implemented in conjunction with a powerful deterrence-based demand-side strategy to reduce youth violence. Unfortunately, the gun-trafficking investigations and prosecutions followed the implementation of a very successful deterrence strategy and their effects on gun violence could not be independently established (Braga et al., 2001). Nevertheless, the results provide some much needed research evidence that supply-side strategies can be used to good effect in shutting down direct pipelines of illegal guns to criminals.

The South Los Angeles Gun Project

In 2001, with the support of a grant from DOJ, researchers at Rand initiated a research and program development effort to understand the nature of illegal gun markets operating in Los Angeles (Riley, Pierce, Braga, and Wintemute, 2001). The primary goal of this project was to determine whether a data-driven, problem-solving approach could yield new interventions aimed at disrupting the workings of local illegal gun markets serving criminals, gang members, and juveniles in the Los Angeles Police Department's 77th Street Policing District area (South Los Angeles). The analyses of illegal gun markets serving criminals in the target area revealed that many crime guns were first purchased at "local" licensed dealers (Ridgeway, Pierce, Braga, Tita, Wintemute, and Roberts, 2007). That is, contrary to the conventional wisdom that crime guns were being trafficked across state borders from places with less stringent regulations such as Arizona and Nevada, a majority of the guns used in crimes had been purchased in Los Angeles County.

Based on their investigative experience, an interagency law enforcement working group suggested that the local nature of the market was driven by prohibited possessors who were having local friends or family members conduct straw purchases for them (Ridgeway et al., 2007). The working group felt strongly that, since the person conducting the straw purchase did not have a criminal history forbidding them from making legal purchases, this population could potentially be deterred from initiating this illegal activity. The working group organized a "letter campaign" intervention that attempted to dissuade legal firearm purchasers from selling or transferring their firearms to others without filing the necessary paperwork with the state (Figure 4-5). New gun buyers received a notification letter during their 10-day waiting period, before they picked up their newly-purchased firearms, informing them of their responsibilities as a gun owner and warning that their firearm can be traced back to them if used in a crime. The key idea of this new gun market disruption strategy was to deter small-scale straw purchasers from picking their firearms and from making other illegal purchases in the future. While a rigorous evaluation of this initiative was not possible (see Ridgeway et al., 2007), there was some evidence that purchasers in the targeted area were less likely to pick up their guns from the dealer after receiving the letter.

The St. Louis Firearm Suppression Program

The St. Louis Firearm Suppression Program (FSP) was an innovative effort that sought parental consent to search for and seize the guns of juveniles (Decker and Rosenfeld, 2004; Rosenfeld and Decker, 1996). While this program was not explicitly focused on "dangerous" offenders or on disrupting illegal gun markets, it represented a problem-solving program to prevent gun violence by disarming a very risky population of potential gun offenders – juveniles.

The FSP was operated by the St. Louis Metropolitan Police Department's Mobile Reserve Unit, which is a police squad dedicated to responding to pockets of crime and violence throughout St. Louis (Rosenfeld

Figure 4-5. Letter Used in Los Angeles Gun Market Disruption Strategy.

Source: Ridgeway et al., 2007.

Office of the Attorney General for the State of California
Office of the Los Angeles City Attorney
Los Angeles Police Department

July 29, 2005

Name
Address
Los Angeles, CA 90001

Dear Mr./Ms. Name,

As you know, gun violence is a serious problem in Los Angeles. We understand that you have recently purchased a gun. It is important that we all do our part to store guns safely and keep guns out of the hands of kids and criminals. We are working in collaboration with the federal program called Project Safe Neighborhood (PSN).

As partners in keeping the streets safe in your neighborhood we want to remind you of your obligations as a gun owner.

If you ever decide to sell or give your gun to someone, you must complete a "Dealer Record of Sale" (DROS) form. These forms can be obtained and completed at any gun store. Remember, it is a crime to transfer a gun to anyone without first filling out this form.

If the police recover a gun that was involved in a crime, the Los Angeles City Attorney will prosecute the gun's previous owner if that owner did not complete the "Dealer Record of Sale" form. Please make sure you go to a firearms dealer and fill out that form if you want to sell or give away your firearm.

You can help us make Los Angeles a safer community by preventing your gun from ending up in the wrong hands.

Thank you,

Rockard J. Delgadillo
Los Angeles City Attorney

Bill Lockyer, Attorney General
State of California

William J. Bratton, Chief
Los Angeles Police Department

Figure 4-6. Consent Form Used in St. Louis FSP Strategy.

Source: Decker and Rosenfeld (2004: 10).

ST. LOUIS METROPOLITAN POLICE DEPARTMENT
MOBILE RESERVE SECTION
FIREARM SUPPRESSION PROGRAM

CONSENT TO SEARCH AND SEIZE

Police Officers of the Mobile Reserve Section are currently engaged in a Firearm Suppression Program. The purpose of this Firearm Suppression Program is to locate and recover illegal and/or unregistered firearms. As part of this program said officers agree that should any illegal or unregistered firearms be located in the residence the person authorizing the search of the premises will not be charged with illegal possession of a firearm.

Having authority to authorize a search of the premises, do hereby grant officers of the St. Louis Metropolitan Police Department permission to search and remove any illegal and/or unregistered firearms.

POLICE OFFICER _____   SIGNATURE _____

DATE _____   OF _____
                                              (Address)

FIREARMS SEIZED:

_____

_____

_____

MPD FORM MobReserve-1 (2/95)

and Decker, 1996). Home searches were initiated based on citizen requests for police service, reports from other police units, and information gained from other investigations. As Rosenfeld and Decker (1996: 204) described, " . . . an innovative feature of the program is its use of a 'Consent to Search and Seize' form to secure legal access to the residence. Officers inform the adult resident that the purpose of the program is to confiscate illegal firearms, particularly those belonging to juveniles, without seeking criminal prosecution. The resident is informed that she will not be charged with the illegal possession of a firearm if she signs the consent form" (Figure 4-6). While it was operating, the FSP generated few complaints from the persons who were subjected to the search, but received criticism from local representatives of the American Civil Liberties Union, which questioned the possibility of receiving real consent to search when a person is standing face-to-face with two police officers (Rosenfeld and Decker, 1996).

A key component of the program was to respond to problems identified by citizens, so the success of the program was reliant on effective police-community relationships. By seeking and acquiring community input into the process of identifying and confiscating guns from juveniles, the St. Louis Metropolitan Police Department developed a model of policing gun violence that put a premium on effective communication and trust with the community: something not found in most problem-oriented policing projects. As Rosenfeld and Decker (1996) observed, the FSP also was designed to send a clear message that juvenile firearm possession will not be tolerated by the police or the community because it places individuals at risk and threatens public safety. Unfortunately, while this program gained national attention for its innovative approach and seemed to be a very promising route to disarming juveniles, the Mobile Reserve Unit underwent a series of changes that caused the program to be stopped and restarted several times; the subsequent incarnations of the FSP did not adopt the same approach as the original program (Decker and Rosenfeld, 2004). As such, a rigorous impact evaluation of gun violence prevention effects associated with the original FSP was not completed. However, a process evaluation of the original FSP documented that consent to search was given by adults at 98 percent of the addresses visited, that 50 percent of the searches netted at least one gun, and that 510 guns were seized over an 18-month period (Decker and Rosenfeld, 2004).

Concluding Thoughts on Keeping Guns Out of "High Risk" Hands

There is little evaluation evidence to confirm the value of a supply-side approach to reducing gun violence. Given the high stakes in this area, systematic "experimentation" with different market disruption tactics appears warranted. A variety of promising supply-side measures are available, some of which have been tried. While many conclusions are necessarily speculative, some lessons have been learned. For instance, gun buy-back and exchange programs have been popular in a number of jurisdictions, but they appear to have only symbolic value (Kennedy, Piehl, and Braga, 1996b). Evaluations indicate that gun buy-backs have had no observable effect on either gun crime or firearm-related injury rates (see, e.g. Callahan, Rivara, and Koepsell, 1994; Wellford et al., 2005).

It is possible that the important pathways of gun trafficking for particular types of offenders at any given moment may not be important after a year's time. For instance, Braga and Pierce (2005) reported some evidence that Boston criminals substituted older handguns for new handguns as a result of the focused efforts to shut down illegal diversions of recently purchased guns. This suggested that Boston law enforcement agencies needed to focus their attention on alternative sources of firearms such as theft, illegal diversions of secondhand guns from retail outlets, and unregulated transfers from secondary market sources such as unlicensed dealers selling guns at gun shows and flea markets. The potential for substitution is precisely the reason that developing new crime intelligence methodologies to analyze local gun markets is essential to improving the capacity of local jurisdictions to respond to illegal gun trafficking (Pierce et al., 2004). If proven methodologies exist to identify pathways of gun trafficking, law enforcement agencies can reassess the situation, diagnose the alternate supply channel, and implement a response to reduce the flow of guns to the street. This fits well with the problem-oriented policing philosophy and advances a key component of the process – the analysis of problems. Police officers need better-developed technologies for analyzing complex crime problems, and this research provides a vehicle for law enforcement agencies to think strategically about a very difficult problem – the illegal gun trade.

Pricing Offenders Out of Stolen Goods Markets

Another method used to identify and apprehend repeat offenders involves "anti-fencing" or property sting operations in which undercover police officers typically pose as receivers of stolen goods. While studies suggest that these approaches may apprehend larger numbers of criminally active offenders than traditional law enforcement practices, the research evidence supporting the crime prevention value of these approaches is very weak (Skogan and Frydl, 2004).

The ERASOR Problem-Solving Process

Researchers from the Policing and Reducing Crime Unit of the Home Office in London suggested tackling stolen good markets through an inter-agency market-reduction approach that develops tailor-made responses to local problems (Sutton et al., 2001). The general premise of the market-reduction approach is that reducing the traffic in stolen goods will reduce the motivation to steal. This is accomplished by convincing thieves that transporting, storing, and selling stolen goods has become at least as risky as it is to steal goods in the first place (Sutton et al., 2001). As in efforts to disrupt the illegal gun trade, an effective market-reduction approach would help increase the price of stolen goods sold to illicit consumers and increase the time and hassle required by offenders to make a connection to sell and buy stolen goods.

Although it is commonplace for police officers to ask arrested thieves about their *modus operandi,* they do not usually ask detailed questions about how they sell their stolen goods. Sutton and his colleagues (2001) suggested the ERASOR (Extra Routine And Systematic Opportunistic Research) problem-solving process, which involves: interviewing offenders and crime analysis to identify "hot products" and associated theft problems; unraveling the nature of illegal goods markets (how, where, and when); prioritizing markets to target, developing market disruption tactics and publicizing these efforts; developing effective partnerships with the community; adjusting responses as markets and theft patterns change; assessing the effectiveness of the implemented strategies; and consolidating the lessons learned from the experience for use in a variety of settings.

A key component of the market-disruption approach is to inform offenders and the wider public that there will be an increased risk involved in selling and buying stolen goods. Sutton and his colleagues (1998) suggested several approaches to enhancing the deterrent effect of the market-reduction approach, such as arranging "arrest days" for dealers of stolen goods, taking the press along for media coverage, and implementing a long-term campaign to "name and shame" local dealers and consumers of stolen goods.

Sutton and his colleagues (2001) identified several approaches to reducing trade in five main types of stolen goods markets (Sutton 1998: 2001):

- *Commercial Fence Supplies and Commercial Sales Markets.* Investigative resources should focus on thieves and fences; particular attention should be paid to business people who buy stolen goods so that the thieves who supply them will need to invest greater effort and face greater risks if they want to convert stolen property into cash. Tactics to achieve this may include: using intelligence and ERASOR information to identify the shops and businesses that thieves visit to sell stolen goods; introducing legislation that requires traders to elicit proof of identify and keep records of transactions for second-hand goods transactions; using "test-selling" to see if businesses are complying with the new code of practice; and enlisting interagency support to crack down on any irregularities committed by businesses known to deal in stolen goods.

- *Residential Fence Supplies Markets.* Identifying and arresting residential fences may control these illicit markets; these individuals may also deal drugs since theft is a common way to finance drug abuse. Therefore, it may be worth combining efforts with local drug-market disruption schemes. This approach may attack the market by using existing and ERASOR information to figure out who the local drug dealers and fences are, who they deal with, and how they operate; setting up mobile CCTV cameras and surveillance teams to gather evidence by observing the homes of known or suspected residential fences; and joining with interagency partners, such as housing associations and local housing authority departments, to evict those trading out of residential addresses.

- *Network Sales Markets.* These markets may be reduced by: arresting any fences known to be involved in wider dealing networks; using media campaigns to implement local "rule setting" schemes and thereby removing any ambiguity in what is and is not acceptable behavior at the local level; and running publicity campaigns to discourage people from buying stolen goods and encouraging the reporting of persons who do so to the police or to special telephone hotlines.

- *Hawking Markets.* Consumers may be "innocent" when they buy in commercial supplies markets, but are not so innocent when they buy goods cheaply in pubs or at their doorstep. In these markets, surveillance measures might work alongside tactics aimed at increasing awareness of the consequences of buying stolen goods. Some suggested tactics would include: analyzing ERASOR information and existing criminal intelligence information to identify housing estates and pubs where hawkers frequently sell stolen goods; setting up special telephone hotlines to invite the public to inform on pubs and clubs where hawking is taking place; and arresting hawkers and their customers.

The "North Town" and "South Town" Experiments

Between 1999 and 2002, the Home Office funded two police forces (called "North Town" and "South Town") to experiment with the market-reduction approach. The goal was to reduce rates of burglary and theft by directing multi-agency activity less at the thieves themselves than at the disruption of stolen goods markets (Hale, Harris, Uglow, Gilling, and Netten, 2004). In both areas, great emphasis was placed on the collection and collation of intelligence on local stolen goods markets through activities such as inspecting the records of second-hand shop dealers, examining second-hand sales in the advertising press, conducting local business and resident surveys, carrying out interviews with offenders, and undertaking traditional investigative techniques.

In North Town, intelligence analysis generated early arrest targets at a low level of the local criminal hierarchy. But as work progressed, additional links were established enabling more sophisticated targeting to be developed against individuals on a higher level of existing criminal networks (Hale et al., 2004). In an effort to prevent economically motivated thefts, North Town police officers and treatment service providers connected low-level drug offenders serving short sentences to social services and treatment options. North Town also engaged in a publicity campaign to encourage the public to share information on stolen goods markets and emphasize both the moral unacceptability of handling stolen goods as well as the legal risks.

Police officers in South Town adopted a more systematic approach in addressing stolen goods markets by adopting Sutton's marketplace typology (1998) described above. Commercial outlets, hawkers selling directly to strangers at the door or in pubs, and residential fences were identified as targets for intervention (Hale et al., 2004). Several initiatives were developed from this problem-oriented framework, one of which centered on intelligence analysis suggesting that significant numbers of second-hand commercial shops in South Town were used as outlets for stolen goods. Second-hand shopkeepers were recruited and agreed to keep records of all transactions, including the date, time and details of the purchased article, and of the seller, sometimes including a photograph of the seller with the goods (Hale et al., 2004). Officers monitored these records for suspicious purchase and sales patterns; these activities resulted in 35 people being charged with theft offenses. In addition to focusing on disrupting identifiable stolen goods markets, South Town also initiated a property marking and recording program, and launched a marketing campaign to communicate the message about the consequences of buying stolen goods to the general public.

The evaluators reported that the process of engaging the market reduction approach was very promising (Hale et al., 2004). The North Town and South Town police forces learned much about intelligence gathering and analysis, the nature of the stolen goods markets, and multi-agency cooperation in launching new interventions. Unfortunately, the evaluators also reported that it was impossible to demonstrate the impact of these projects on crime rates (Hale et al., 2004: 9):

> In South Town there was a significant reduction in average monthly-recorded burglary in a dwelling in the period after the tactics were adopted. However, the force as a whole saw similar reductions making it questionable whether the successes in South Town were attributable simply to the MRA. For other forms of burglary the picture was clearer with a significantly larger fall in average monthly rates in South Town as compared to the force as a whole.
>
> For burglary in a dwelling, North Town shows a similar picture with no evidence of substantially reduced levels compared to the rest of the force. Similarly, there is no evidence of any impact on the "burglary other" figures. There is, however, one point worth noting. If June 2001, the date the Police Operations Manager arrived, is taken as the point at which the project began to function effectively, the following months showed a 9.4 per cent reduction in average recorded figures for burglary in a dwelling compared to 7.1 per cent force-wide. Although weak, this suggests the co-ordination of intelligence gathering may be beginning to have an impact.

The market reduction approach seems to have considerable value in generating knowledge on the activities of offenders participating in ongoing illegal stolen goods transactions and devising new interventions to disrupt these illicit markets. Additional research, however, is necessary to determine whether the approach has value in preventing theft problems.

Concluding Thoughts on the Prospects of Offender-Oriented Strategies

The observation that a small number of highly active offenders generate a large share of the crime problem is an important insight for law enforcement agencies with limited resources to prevent crime. Many serious urban crime problems, for example gang violence, are driven by groups of these criminally active individuals. In some respect, it is fundamentally good news for the police that repeat offending and regular contact with the criminal justice system make these offenders particularly vulnerable to focused police efforts. These individuals identify themselves through their chronic offending, and this provides a readily available mechanism through which to detect and incapacitate them. Removing these high-activity offenders from the street, deterring them from continuing their offending, and keeping crime facilitators such as guns away from them will have an important impact on crime. However, it is also important to recognize that police efforts to control active offenders must be carried out in a way that is fair and does not violate individual rights. Inappropriate applications of selective apprehension approaches will undoubtedly cause the community to question the legitimacy of the police. Beyond crime prevention, communities demand policing strategies to be fair and just. Sacrificing positive relationships with the community is too high a price for the benefits of pursuing potentially unacceptable practices.

Beyond incapacitating serious offenders, many of the approaches described in this chapter are exercises in deterrence and in getting deterrence right. Although sanctions for many crimes are quite severe, criminal justice is usually not administered in a way that is certain or swift. The criminal justice system is also not very good at sending clear messages to offenders about the risks they face when committing crimes. Police departments interested in dealing with crime through a focus on highly active offenders will want to develop programs that effectively increase the likelihood of detection and apprehension, make punishment more certain (even if it is through mechanisms such as arrests for other offenses or constant scrutiny), and underscore these increased risks to offenders by mounting an effective communications strategy.

NOTES

1. See: Kennedy et al., 1996a; Kennedy et al., 1997; Kennedy, 1997; Kennedy, 1998; Braga et al., 2001.
2. See: Cook, 1977; Cook, 1980; Blumstein et al., 1978; Sherman and Berk, 1984; Paternoster, 1987; Cameron, 1988; Weisburd et al., 1995; Sherman, 1990.

5. PROTECTING REPEAT VICTIMS

Kirkholt public housing estate in Rochdale, England – The Kirkholt public housing estate suffered from a burglary rate that was
double the rate of similar high-crime housing. Further analyses
revealed that nearly half of the households burglarized in December 1986 had been burglarized earlier in the year, and that once
a home had been burgled, its chance of a repeat burglary was
four times the rate at homes that had not been burgled at all.
The burglary prevention strategy concentrated on previously victimized homes and consisted of two key elements. First, residents
of the five or six homes around a previously victimized dwelling
were enlisted to watch the home. Second, coin-fed fuel meters,
that were found to be attractive to burglars, were replaced with
conventional fuel billing. The strategy resulted in a 75 percent
reduction in burglary for the entire Kirkholt estate, not just the
protected houses (Pease, 1991).

*   *   *

Edmonton, Alberta, Canada – In 1989 and 1990, the city of Edmonton began to take a closer look at its domestic violence problem.
The Edmonton Police Department analyzed citizen calls-for-service and found that 21 percent of domestic violence calls were
repeat calls from the same households. The police department
also found that in about 70 percent of domestic violence calls
constables were not filing any charges at all. The Edmonton police
implemented several responses to the problem. First, all officers
were trained on the complexity and dynamics of family violence
and what is needed to facilitate victim protection. Analysts found

that most officers were not charging offenders because they thought the victim had to be willing to pursue the charges. Second, analysts recommended training of supervisors on report approval, family violence investigations, and problem-solving approaches to domestic violence incidents. Third, a program was initiated to alert constables to repeat domestic violence locations and offenders. In 1991, a therapeutic response was included in the response. Social workers were teamed with detectives to develop case-tailored plans of action to stop the violence, ensure victims' safety, and connect both victim and perpetrator with the resources they needed. An evaluation of this program found that 97 percent of victims who worked with the collaborative team made positive changes in their lives compared to 63 percent in the comparison group. Forty-seven percent left their abusive relationship, compared to 26 percent in the comparison group. Finally, the police charge rate increased from less than 30 percent to 70 percent (Sampson and Scott, 2000: 35-36).

* * *

New York State – During the 1980s, Suringer Singh Panshi, a New York physician, earned the media nickname "Dracula, Inc.: Bloodsucker of the Decade." In 1986, Panshi lost his license to practice medicine after he had been prosecuted for false billings. He subsequently went into the laboratory business and purchased two labs in Queens and one on Long Island. His scam involved purchasing blood from addicts and Medicaid mills and then falsely charging New York State for thousands of blood tests that had never been ordered, referred, or authorized by physicians that were not medically necessary. In 1986, the Panshi Mills billed Medicaid a combined total of $1 million; in 1987, more than $12 million; and in 1988, over $31 million. By then, Panshi employed more than a dozen or more "blood collectors"; they set up blood-drawing centers in small apartments and prowled the streets in search of donors – most drug addicts – paying them $10 per vial. As of February 1988, the three Panshi labs accounted for more than 20 percent of all Medicaid billings by the state's laboratories, even though there were nearly 450 labs in the state. Emergency room physicians discovered the scam after a rash of anemic patients received extensive blood transfusions; these patients repeatedly returned to the hospital after selling as much as a quart of blood two or three times per week. On August 4, 1988, Panshi was convicted of stealing over $3.6 million from Medicaid. As a result of a small number of criminal prosecutions of similar scofflaw labs, New York's statewide clinical lab billings dropped from a high of nearly $170 million in 1988 to just over $20 million in 1992 – an 88 percent reduction (Sparrow, 2000).

These anecdotes suggest that protecting the repeat victims may be a promising avenue for police in reducing overall levels of crime. Criminological research has demonstrated that small proportions of the population, and of victims, suffer large proportions of all criminal victimizations. As such, preventing repeat victimization may prevent a large percentage of all crimes. Focusing on repeat victims also provides the police with an opportunity to detect more serious offenders, as well as addressing specific problems within crime hot spots. Police should be particularly attentive to repeat victims of crime because those victims may develop serious emotional scars (Shaw, 2001) and feel less positive about their neighbors and neighborhoods (Mawby, 2001), and they often have significantly lower levels of satisfaction with overall police performance (van Dijk, 2001). This chapter reviews the dimensions of repeat victimization; examines the link between policing hot spots and protecting repeat victims; describes a noteworthy repeat burglary prevention project; and discusses the prevention of repeat domestic violence and fraud.

THE DIMENSIONS OF REPEAT VICTIMIZATION

Repeat targets can include an individual, a group of persons, a property (residential, commercial, or other), a motor vehicle, or some other single target (Farrell, 1995). Repeat victimization can involve either the same or different types of crime against a single target.

In the United States, 10 percent of the victims are involved in 40 percent of the victimizations (Spelman and Eck, 1989). Using data from the 1992 British Crime Survey, Farrell and Pease (1993) reported that 4 percent of people experience 44 percent of all victimizations. In his review of the international research evidence on repeat victimization, Farrell

(1995) found that the 2 or 3 percent of victim survey respondents who are most commonly victimized report between a quarter and a third of all incidents.

Repeat victimization is not a random occurrence, and vulnerable individuals are prone to repeat victimization by the same type of crime (Reiss, 1980). Repeat victims can include individuals who are repeatedly victimized by the same offender (e.g., spouse assault cases) and individuals who are repeatedly victimized by a variety of offenders (e.g., a local merchant who is repeatedly visited by shoplifters, robbers, and vandals). The "lifestyle" theory of victimization suggests that differential risks of victimization are related to differential exposure to offenders (Hindelang et al., 1978). Exposure to potential offenders varies with the characteristics of the victim (age, race, place of residence, etc.) as well as the victim's lifestyle (Clarke, 1992). Work and leisure activities, such as drinking alcohol in public or using public transportation late at night, can increase an individual's risk of victimization.

For individuals with particularly risky lifestyles, the probability of victimization can be quite high. For example, during Boston's youth homicide epidemic in the early to mid-1990s, youth gang members stood a roughly one in seven chance of being killed at some point during an average nine-year-long duration of gang membership (Kennedy et al., 1996a). Youth gunshot wound victims treated in Boston emergency rooms often had scars from past gun and knife wounds (Rich and Stone, 1996). Routine activity theory – which describes crime events in terms of likely offenders and suitable targets converging in space and time in the absence of a capable guardian (Cohen and Felson, 1979) – also suggests that repeat victimization can be influenced by the activities and vulnerabilities of the victim. As Clarke (1992) observed, the implication is that modifying patterns of activity may reduce the risks of victimization.

Farrell et al. (2002) suggested that repeat crimes can be understood in terms of "risk heterogeneity" and "event dependency." Risk heterogeneity refers to the persisting attributes of repeat victims that make them more attractive to offenders relative to other potential victims. For example, a violent father may be more likely to repeatedly assault his 120-pound wife rather than his 250-pound college-age son who plays football. Event dependency involves one crime that leads to another for the same victim. In the case of burglary, for instance, the same dwelling could suffer repeat burglaries because the successful offender decided to make a return visit to exploit a suitable target, or informed his criminal associates of the easy opportunity, or because the initial break-in caused the dwelling to become somehow more attractive to other burglars (e.g., the broken lock on the door had not yet been replaced). Unfortunately, many burglary victims do not heed crime prevention advice from police (Scott, 2004a). Weak doors, door frames, window frames, and window locks contribute to forced-entry burglaries and many low-income victims lack the resources to improve these house features (Scott, 2004a).

Pease (1998) explained repeat victimization by distinguishing between "boost" accounts and "flag" accounts. Like event dependency, boost accounts explain repetitions in terms of offenders' positive experiences at the initial offense; the likelihood of subsequent victimization for the same target is increased (or "boosted"). Flag accounts explain repeated victimization in terms of the unusual attractiveness or vulnerability of specific targets to a variety of offenders (sending a signal or "flag" to them). Some professions, such as taxi drivers, have much higher victimization rates than others, and some "hot" products, such as sports cars attractive to joy riders, also increase the likelihood of repeat victimization (Clarke and Eck, 2003).

An important dimension of revictimization is the length of time between one victimization and the next. Research demonstrates that the risk of revictimization is greatest in the period immediately after the preceding victimization and that this risk declines over time (Farrell, 1995). Thus, a study of residential burglary in Saskatoon, Canada revealed that the likelihood of a repeat burglary at a residence within a month was over 12 times the expected rate of burglary. But that repeat rate declined to less than twice the expected rate when burglaries six months apart were considered. An analysis of the repeat burglaries within a single month revealed that half of the second burglaries occurred within seven days of the first (Polvi et al., 1990, 1991). Similarly, in a study of families suffering violent racial attacks on an estate in the East End of London, Sampson and Phillips (1992) found that 67 percent of the 30 families in the study had been repeatedly victimized and that subsequent attacks were most frequent within the first week of the first attack. The most heavily victimized family was harassed, on average, once every six days. Further, it is well established that domestic violence is frequently a repeated crime (Crowell and Burgess, 1996). An analysis of domestic dispute calls to the police revealed a "heightened risk period" for repeat domestic violence victimizations; when a woman calls the police, she is more likely to call them repeatedly within a short period of time (Farrell et al., 1993). This body of research suggests that crime prevention measures need to be implemented as soon as possible following victimization and that temporary measures to provide security during the high-risk period after victimization may be an efficient and effective way to prevent crime (Farrell, 1995).

Pease and Laycock (1998) argued that repeat victimization provides two types of opportunities for crime prevention: (1) crime deflection and (2) the detection of offenders. Crime deflection involves turning offenders away from crime targets. For example, to reduce fighting at soccer matches in Britain, rival groups of fans have been segregated in the stadium, and their arrivals and departures have been scheduled to avoid waiting periods that promote trouble (Clarke, 1983). Repeat victimization facilitates the detection of offenders because it gives law enforcement an opportunity to predict where and when crimes will occur. As many as 80 percent of repeat burglary victims are likely to have been revictimized by the same offender (Pease, 1998).

From interviews with offenders, Anderson and Pease (1997) learned the degree to which burglary and theft repeats are rational and market-driven. Repeats involved less risk, since the place was known, including its escape routes; offered the prospect of capturing new, insurance-replaced goods, which will attract a better price; and permitted offenders to learn the value of goods known to remain available during the period between offenses. Anderson and Pease (1997) also found that substantial change (or perceived substantial change) at places previously targeted decreased the likelihood that the same offenders would target these places again. Gill and Pease (1998) revealed that bank robbers who targeted the same branch more than once were more serious offenders than those who did not repeat offenses against the same target. The prospects of apprehending chronic offenders by protecting repeat victims underscore the potential crime prevention value of this approach.

"Virtual" Repeats and "Near Repeats"

Examining repeat victimization patterns can also assist in making predictions about those who are not yet victims. "Virtual repeat victimization" refers to instances where offenders select targets because they have already offended against similar or identical targets (Pease, 1998). As Farrell (2005: 147) described:

> For example, the same make and model of car offers similar prospects to offenders. If the car is parked in a similar location or situation, the virtual-repeat is all the more identical. Nearby households with

the same layout are prone to virtual repeats because, for the offender, there is a good chance that the same types of efforts and skills are needed, and the risks and rewards are similar to those of the previous target. These virtual repeats provide a useful angle for thinking about crime prevention: whether virtual-repeat victimization occurs due to a target's design (easy to break into), its location (in an unlit area) or its high resale value and low traceability (for example, a laptop, a portable MP3 player), can influence the choice of tactics for a preventive response.

The victimization of a target located next to one that was victimized previously is referred to as "near-repeat victimization." A series of studies have shown that the risk of burglary is communicable – properties next to a newly burgled home are for a time victimized at a rate that is much higher than would be expected on the basis of chance alone (Townsley et al., 2003; Johnson and Bowers, 2004). The increased burglary risk is communicated to neighboring households and, for any given distance, there is a greater risk for homes on the same side of the street as the burgled home (Johnson and Bowers, 2004). The elevation in risk is tempo-rary, however, and diminishes as the distance from the burgled property increases. According to Johnson and Bowers (2007), more detailed analyses revealed that the increased risk was communicated to houses up to 400 meters away and for a period of one month after the original burglary event. Figure 5-1 presents how burglary risks were communicated at the street level following the original incident in the county of Merseyside, United Kingdom (Johnson and Bowers, 2007). These insights suggest that problem-oriented police officers should give priority to protecting homes close to the initial burgled home over the next several weeks.

As the key ideas in this section suggest, addressing repeat victimization is an important consideration in developing effective crime prevention strategies. Based on their extensive review of the existing literature, Gloria Laycock and Graham Farrell (2003) developed seventeen reasons why the prevention of repeat victimization is an attractive strategy for policing (Fig-ure 5-2).

The Convergence of High-Crime Areas, Crime Hot Spots, and Repeat Victimization

While focusing on repeat victims may be a particularly valuable way to detect and apprehend highly active offenders, it also provides a way to better focus police efforts at crime hot spots. Indeed, since both hot spots

Figure 5-1. The Communicability of Burglary Risk.

Source: Johnson and Bowers (2007: 207).

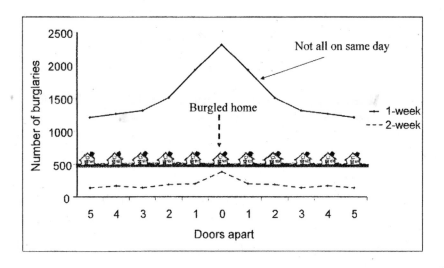

policing and protecting repeat victims involve the prevention of repeated crimes, it is conceptually difficult to draw a distinct line between the two approaches. Common themes include the use of empirical data to identify crime patterns, a policy interest in predicting the next crime or victimization, and an interest in identifying the causal mechanisms of crime (Farrell, 1995).

Pease and Laycock (1996) suggested that repeat targets could be thought of as "hot dots" of crime on a crime map. This conception of repeat targets facilitates the description of different types of problems within a troubled neighborhood, ranging from hot dots to hot spots to high-crime areas. In the search for appropriate responses to crime problems, it could be very important to distinguish between high-crime areas, crime hot spots, and repeat victimization. In this discussion, a high-crime area is simply a larger hot spot area, such as a high-crime public housing site, rather than a specific location, such as a common playground area within the public housing site. Figure 5-3 provides a conceptual framework for how high-crime areas, hot spots, and repeat victimizations can overlap; this

Figure 5-2. Seventeen Reasons for Policing to Prevent Repeat Victimization.

Source: Laycock and Farrell (2003: 216-217).

---

(1) Preventing repeat victimization is a crime prevention activity and hence pursuant to the most fundamental of police mandates (as defined since Robert Peel's original list of principles).

(2) Targeting repeat victimization is an efficient means of allocating, in time and space, scarce police resources to crime problems.

(3) Preventing repeat victimization is an approach that is relevant to all crimes with a target. It has been shown to be a feature of crimes including hate crimes, domestic and commercial burglary, school crime (burglary and vandalism), bullying, sexual assault, car crime, neighbor disputes, credit card fraud and other retail sector crime, domestic violence and child abuse. Even murder can be the repeat of attempted murder.

(4) Police managers can use repeat victimization as a performance indicator (Tilley, 1995). These can range from the national to the local level.

(5) Preventing repeat victimization naturally allocates resources to high crime areas, crime hot spots, and the most victimized targets (Bennett, 1995, Townsley et al., 2000).

(6) Preventing repeat victimization may inform the allocation of crime prevention to nearby targets (near-repeats) and targets with similar characteristics (virtual repeats; Pease, 1998).

(7) Preventing repeat victimization is a form of "drip feeding" of prevention resources (Pease, 1992). Since all crime does not occur at once, police resources need only be allocated as victimizations occur from day to day.

(8) Preventing repeat victimization is even less likely to result in displacement than unfocused crime prevention efforts (Bouloukos and Farrell, 1997).

(9) Preventing repeat victimization may be even more likely to result in a diffusion of crime control benefits (Clarke and Weisburd, 1994) than more general crime prevention. Offenders will be made uncertain and more generally deterred by changed circumstances at the most attractive and vulnerable targets.

(10) Preventing repeat victimization can generate common goals and positive work between police and other agencies (such as housing, social services, and victim organizations), which may in turn facilitate broader co-operation.

(11) Focusing on repeat victimization empowers police officers to do something tangible and constructive to help crime victims and for policing to become more generally oriented towards victims, who are arguably its core consumers (Farrell, 2001).

(12) Efforts to prevent repeat victimization can lead to positive feedback from victims. This is still a relatively rare reward for police in the community. It may promote good community relations.

(13) Preventing repeat victimization is triggered by a crime being reported. Since victims can be asked about prior victimizations, a response does not necessarily require data analysis.

Figure 5-2. *(continued)*

---

(14) Preventing repeat victimization can sometimes — but not always — use off-the-shelf prevention tactics rather than requiring inventive problem solving.

(15) Preventing repeat victimization can be used to enhance the detection of serious and prolific offenders. Police officers like detecting offenders.

(16) Preventing repeat victimization presents possibilities for preventing and detecting organized crime and terrorism that focuses on vulnerable and, for offenders, lucrative victims and targets — including protection rackets, forced prostitution, loan-sharking, repeat trafficking via certain low-risk locations, art and other high-value thefts and robberies. (The 1993 terrorist attack on the World Trade Centre was a precursor of the 2001 attack.)

(17) Targeting repeat victimization can inform thinking on repeat crimes typically perceived as "victimless," where the repeatedly victimized target is the state or nation.

---

figure is not crime-specific and could include a range of specific types of violence, property, or disorder and nuisance offenses.

As Farrell and Sousa (2001) described, repeat victimization may occur either inside or outside buildings, and it can cluster into both hot spots and high-crime areas. It is also important to note that not all hot spots or high-crime areas will involve repeat victimization, not all high-crime areas will be made up of hot spots, and not all hot spots are located in high-crime areas (Farrell and Sousa, 2001). However, it does seem likely that there will be more repeat victimization in hot spots because repeat crimes may be committed by more prolific offenders, who tend to return sooner and more often to the same target while generally operating in the same area (Farrell and Sousa, 2001).

Integrating the concepts of crime hot spots and repeat victimization could lead to richer responses to crime problems. Farrell and Sousa (2001: 235) identified six points regarding the nature and benefits of such an integrated approach:

- Preventing repeat victimization is appropriate for some crimes, and policing hot spots for others, but for a significant third group a mixed or integrated preventive approach may be disproportionately rewarding.

Figure 5-3. Repeat Victimization, Hot Spots, and High-Crime Areas.
Source: Farrell and Sousa (2001: 230).

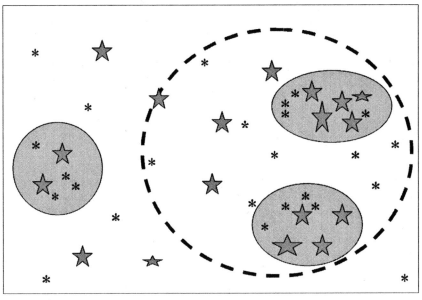

Legend:

* victimization	⬤ hot spot
☆ repeat victimization	(⌇) high-crime area

- Repeat victimization is already used as a mechanism to help police determine the strategic allocation of limited crime prevention resources. Targeting repeats within hot spots could further enhance the efficiency of this mechanism.

- Repeat victimization, hot spots and nuisance-call places can be used to focus offender detection tactics. If repeat victimization predicts the location of offenders who are more frequent and serious than the average, then repeat victimization in hot spots may predict where to find super-predators.

- Rates of repeat victimization, and of crime at hot spots and nuisance places, should be used as performance indicators for problem-oriented policing. Their use as performance indicators will increase the rate at which each is implemented.

- For many crimes, targeting repeat victimization for prevention and detection automatically places resources in hot spots and high crime areas. This also avoids the need for complex mapping or analysis.

- Necessity, driven by performance indicators for problem-oriented policing, will be mother of new and inventive ways of preventing repeats and policing hot spots and nuisance places.

Farrell and Sousa (2001) also comment that developing interventions to protect repeat victims may fit more readily than situational/problem-oriented policing into standard police practices because it does not necessitate problem analysis and a wide search for alternative responses. They suggest providing police with a fairly standard list of responses that can be tailored to the individual crime and its specific circumstances, which could include target-hardening to prevent a repeat by the same modus operandi, general security upgrades, "cocooning" of the victim by the watchful eyes of nearby neighbors, and extra investigative efforts to detect the repeat offender.

The Kirkholt Burglary Prevention Project

The Kirkholt Burglary Prevention Project served as a catalyst for research on and the development of crime prevention interventions to control repeat victimization (Forrester et al., 1988, 1990). The Kirkholt public housing estate was located in Rochdale in the northwest of England. As described in the introduction to this chapter, the Kirkholt public housing estate suffered from a burglary rate that was double the rate of similar high-crime housing estates. Further analyses revealed that nearly half of the households burglarized in December 1986 had been burglarized earlier in the year and that, once a home had been burgled its chance of a repeat burglary was four times the rate of homes that had not been burgled at all (Pease, 1991). The project research team believed that they could prevent a large portion of all burglaries if they could successfully prevent burglaries at repeatedly victimized homes.

The most obvious factor in Kirkholt burglaries was the taking of money from the coin-fed gas and electricity prepayment meters (Pease, 1991). Money was deposited in these meters in exchange for fuel or electricity dispensed; the utility company emptied the meters of deposited money once every month or three months. Nearly half of the burglaries on the estate involved the loss of meter cash. It was also discovered that some householders stole from their own meters and staged burglaries to cover their tracks. There was also a risk of coin collectors being robbed while collecting funds from meters in the housing estate. With the agreement of the householder, the utility boards agreed to replace the coin-fed meters with conventional billing meters.

Research also revealed that Kirkholt burglars entered a dwelling by the first route attempted (Pease, 1991). Accordingly, during the prevention project, when a house was burgled, it immediately received a security upgrade, during which any valuables in the home were property marked by unique identifiers. Instead of installing general security measures, the security upgrades were customized to the specific means of burglary that were described by both apprehended burglars and victims. An estate-wide burglary-monitoring program was also implemented so that any security upgrades could be revised to reflect any changes in burglary modus operandi (Pease, 1991). Small neighborhood watches called "cocoons" were also set up in which neighbors were enlisted to watch for burglars returning to the victimized household. As an incentive, participating neighbors also received security upgrades. A second phase of the burglary project, intended to secure community ownership of the program, involved a school-based crime prevention program, a provision for offenders from the Kirkholt area to attend groups to address their problems, a cheap savings and loan scheme for Kirkholt residents, and better informed probation officers (and better served courts in consequence; Pease, 1991).

As mentioned in the introduction, the strategy resulted in a 75 percent reduction in burglary for the entire Kirkholt estate, not just in the protected houses. Although coin-fed meters were removed from (and other project services were directed at) only a subgroup of homes, other households not protected by these initiatives experienced a diffusion of crime prevention benefits. Important lessons learned from the Kirkholt experience included that: (1) victimization often predicts further victimization, and (2) that victim support and crime prevention are two sides of the same coin (Pease, 1991). Reflecting on his experiences on the Kirkholt project, Pease (1991: 76-77) observed that:

- Attention to dwellings or people already victimized generates a higher "hit rate" of those likely to be victimized in the future.

- Preventing repeat victimization protects the most vulnerable social groups, without having to identify those groups as such, which can be socially divisive. Having been victimized already probably represents the least contentious basis for a claim to receive crime prevention attention.

- Repeat victimization is highest, both absolutely and proportionately, in the most crime-ridden areas, which are also the areas that suffer the most crime. The prevention of repeat victimization is thus commensurately more important in areas with more serious crime problems.

- Knowledge of the rate of victimization for repeat victims provides a realistic way to schedule routine crime prevention activities. As a result, crime prevention can be focused and paced at an appropriate level of effort (also known as "drip-feeding" crime prevention activities).

- Even accepting the unrealistic view that prevention causes crime to be displaced, avoiding repeat victimization at least shares the agony around.

Preventing Repeat Domestic Violence

Domestic violence often generates high levels of police calls-for-service (Sampson, 2007). For example, in West Yorkshire, United Kingdom, an analysis of police data revealed that 42 percent of domestic violence incidents within a one-year period were repeat offenses and that one-third of all domestic violence offenders generated two-thirds of all domestic violent incidents reported to the police (Hanmer, Griffiths, and Jerwood, 1999). The same study also found that the highest risk period for further assault was within the first four weeks of the last assault (Hanmer et al., 1999).

It is also important to note that the first police response to a domestic violence incident may not occur until an event is already part of a repeat series of violence. For repeated domestic violence, Millbank and Riches (2000) reported that between 6 and 20 prior assaults are likely to have taken place before the police were first notified.

The Minneapolis Domestic Violence Experiment

The well-known Minneapolis Domestic Violence Experiment and its subsequent replications offered firm evidence that police should take a problem-oriented approach to handling domestic violence incidents (Sherman, 1992b). The Minneapolis experiment was undertaken to determine the best way to prevent the risk of repeated violence by the suspect against the same victim in the future. Three approaches were tested. The traditional approach was to do very little because it was believed that the offenders would not be punished harshly by the courts and the arrest might provoke further violence against the victim. A second approach was for the police to undergo special training enabling them to mediate ongoing domestic disputes. The third approach was to treat violence as a criminal offense and arrest offenders in order to teach them that their conduct was serious and thereby to deter them from repeating it.

The experiment revealed that, in Minneapolis, arrest worked best: it significantly reduced repeat offenses relative to the other two approaches (Sherman and Berk, 1984). The results of the experiment were very influential as many police departments adopted mandatory arrest policies and a number of states adopted mandatory arrest and prosecution laws. However, replications of the Minneapolis domestic violence experiment in five other cities did not produce the same findings. In his review of those differing findings, Sherman (1992b: 19) identified four policy dilemmas for policing domestic violence:

(1) Arrest reduces domestic violence in some cities but increases it in others.

(2) Arrest reduces domestic violence among employed people but increases it among unemployed people.

(3) Arrest reduces domestic violence in the short run but can increase it in the long run.

(4) Police can predict which couples are most likely to suffer future violence, but our society values privacy too highly to encourage preventive action.

Clearly, the police need more options than simply mandatory arrest and subsequent prosecution. Sherman (1992b) suggested replacing mandatory arrest laws with structured police discretion that allows officers, after receiving training, to select from a range of approved options based on their assessment of the situation. Sherman (1992b) also advocated giving the police enhanced arrest powers in misdemeanor domestic violence cases that they did not witness;[1] issuing arrest warrants for domestic violence offenders who are not present or flee the scene; and developing special police units and policies that focus on chronically violent couples.

Arrest remains an important tool in controlling repeat domestic violence. A recent meta-analysis of the five NIJ spouse assault replication studies found a positive overall effect of arrest on the reduction of intimate violence (Maxwell, Garner, and Fagan, 2002).

The Merseyside and Killingbeck (UK) Projects

The Merseyside Domestic Violence Prevention Project, a demonstration program in England, focused on the prevention of repeated domestic assault (Lloyd et al., 1994). Merseyside project research revealed that domestic violence was very concentrated. A large proportion of calls-for-service came from a very small number of households that made repeat calls, and a repeat call was very likely to occur within a short time period after a call.

A package of preventive measures was provided to Merseyside's repeat victims that included two key components. First, borrowing technology already used for elderly people in sheltered housing, portable personal alarms were given to the repeat victims. These alarms were connected via telephone to local police stations. When the alarm was sounded, the police gave a priority response, and, via a computerized database, the responding officers received information on the history of violence at the victim's address before they arrived at the scene. As Farrell (1995) described, these alarms were given to victims based on certain criteria: the previous issuance of a court injunction, a recommendation by a police officer who had responded to an earlier domestic dispute, a referral from another agency, or a recommendation based on a history of violence as documented by analyses of police incident records. Alarms were loaned to victims for a period of 30 days, with the possibility of an extension depending on an assessment of the circumstances of the case.

The second component of the Merseyside project involved the assignment of a domestic violence prevention worker, who provided support and information to the domestic violence victims who had received the alarms. As Farrell (1995) described, the services provided by the prevention worker were crucial in developing a situation where the victim could feel safe and confident without the alarm.

Building on the Merseyside experience, the Killingbeck Division of the West Yorkshire Police Department implemented a repeat domestic violence prevention program that placed an equal focus on the victim and the offender (Hanmer et al., 1999). As the number of repeat incidents increased, the level of intervention moved from Levels 1 to 2 to 3 (Table 5-1). The intensity of the responses increased from supplying information and police watches, to cocoon watches and target-hardening at the victims'

Table 5-1. Domestic Violence Repeat Victimization Model

Intervention level	VICTIM	PERPETRATOR Common law offences	PERPETRATOR Criminal offences
Level 1	• Gather information • Information letter 1 • Police watch	• Reiterate force policy • First official warning • Information letter 1	• Magistrates – conditional bail/ checks • Police Watch • Information letter 1
Level 2	• Information letter 2 • Community constable visit • Cocoon and Police Watches • Target harden property	• Reiterate force policy • Second official warning • Police Watch • Information letter 2	• Magistrates – bail opposed/checks • Police Watch • Information letter 1
Level 3	• Information letter 3 • Police Watch • Domestic Violence Officer visit • Agency meeting • Panic button/vodaphone	• Reiterate force policy • Third official warning • Police Watch • Information letter 3	• Magistrates – bail opposed/checks • Police Watch increased • Information letter 3 • Crown Prosecution Service (CPS) file jacket and DV history and contact CPS
Emergency intervention	• Implement – log reasons for selection	• Not Applicable	• Implement and log level of action undertaken

Source: Hanmer et al. (1999: 4). Reprinted with permission.

residences, to supplying victims with a personal alarm. For the repeat offenders, arrests, when appropriate, were made for criminal and common law offenses (mostly breach of the peace) at all levels, and additional measures were implemented based on the nature of the situation. For example, if the victim was living independently of the perpetrator, the perpetrator might be barred from having an automatic right of entry to the victim's home, and burglary prevention measures were implemented to stop the offender from entering the home. This model also required continuing input and involvement from all officers in the police division to avoid limiting responsibility for any one domestic violence problem to one or two officers. Hanmer and her colleagues (1999) found this approach to be effective in reducing repeat domestic violence victimization and increasing the time intervals between repeat domestic violence incidents.

Violent Behavior by Repeat Domestic Violence Offenders

It is also important for problem-oriented police officers to recognize that domestic violence offenders are often generally violent people who assault strangers and non-strangers alike. For example, Fagan et al., (1983) examined 270 reports from abused women in intervention programs in five U.S. cities about their abusers. The researchers found that 46 percent of the abusers had been previously arrested for other violence. The men who had been arrested for violence against strangers were also the most frequent and violent abusers at home; the most violent husbands were also more likely to be involved in fights outside the home than the mildly or non-violent abusers. Therefore, police officers looking to halt particularly violent domestic abusers may be able to take advantage of this generally active criminal profile in controlling offender behavior.

Some of the techniques previously described in the earlier chapter on controlling high-activity offenders, such as the pulling-levers deterrence strategy, may be useful in preventing repeat domestic violence victimization. Some elements of a pulling levers strategy (Kennedy, 2002a) that may be useful in controlling highly active offenders who are also domestic violence offenders include:

- *Providing information to women*. Prior criminal histories and restraining orders for repeat adult domestic abusers are a matter of public record. It could be very useful to provide women with access to such information when they are considering entering a relationship or when trouble first arises in a new relationship.

- *Communicating existing enforcement actions to potential offenders*. Offenders are often ignorant of existing laws and their applications by law enforcement personnel. While law enforcement currently does a great deal to address domestic violence, unless other offenders and potential offenders know what is going on there is little deterrence generated by these actions. For example, in 2002, the U.S. Attorney for the District of Maine indicted 13 men and women on domestic violence-related firearms charges, either because they had a previous misdemeanor domestic violence conviction (which, under recent federal law prohibits them from firearms possession), or because they lied about such convictions in attempting to purchase firearms (Kennedy, 2002a). The deterrent value of this type of action could be increased by: explaining it to domestic violence offenders; mailings to individuals with the relevant prior convictions; in-person briefings by law enforcement personnel to men involved in treatment programs and on probation for domestic violence offenses; and as part of judicial statements to men sentenced for new domestic violence offenses, through posters in gun stores, and the like.

- *Developing "A Group" and "B Group" enforcement plans.* In any given jurisdiction, particular domestic violence offenders single themselves out as being especially dangerous, especially chronic, and deserving of removal from the street. These "A Group" offenders should be identified and, using the correct tools available to law enforcement, incarcerated. The tools used to incarcerate these individuals do not need to be directly related to their domestic violence offending; any actionable offense will do (e.g., drug offending, probation/parole violations, etc.). "B Group" offenders are a less serious and larger group to whom the actions targeted at the "A Group" can be communicated. If "B Group" offenders persist in domestic violence, they graduate to the "A Group."

- *Structuring information-gathering strategies to include friends, family, neighbors, and medical providers.* The more information that is received by police about the behavior of domestic violence offenders, the better these strategies will work. Useful information is clearly available through alternative channels. For example, two-thirds of the relatives of homicide victims knew of stalking prior to the killing (Kennedy, 2002a).

Comprehensive Approaches to Preventing Repeat Domestic Violence

In Cardiff, Wales, a coordinated community response to reducing repeat victimization among high-risk victims of domestic violence generated some promising results: both police and victim data revealed that six in ten victims who participated in the program had not been revictimized (Robinson, 2006). The Multi-Agency Risk Assessment Conference (MARAC) was an interagency forum for sharing information and action planning for domestic violence cases where there was a high risk that the survivor would be attacked again. Participating agencies included the police, probation, social services, housing services, education, specialist voluntary domestic violence advice services and a number of branches of the health service. Regular meetings discussed between 15 and 20 very high-risk cases per session. While any agency could bring a case to the MARAC, the majority of referrals were from the police, based on a risk assessment instrument. Some of the specific ways in which the MARAC streamlined the process of dealing with high-risk repeat victims were through (adapted from Robinson, 2006):

- Information sharing among agencies

- Identifying key contacts

- Making or modifying plans in the light of information shared (for example whether or not to recommend to go ahead with a prosecution)

- Holding agencies to account through minutes and when reviewing cases to ensure that agreed actions are taken

- Increased mutual understanding and use of risk assessment techniques

- Increased understanding of different agencies' ability to undertake action (and constraints thereon)

- Increased understanding of the success of different intervention strategies.

Rana Sampson's (2007a) recent review of responses to the problem of domestic violence also suggested taking comprehensive and collaborative approaches to prevent repeated domestic violence victimizations. Figure 5-4 presents a matrix of responses to domestic violence that can help problem solvers think about framing the strategic focus, goals, and timing of comprehensive and collaborative interventions.

As Lloyd, Farrell, and Pease (1994) suggested, single measures are unlikely to prevent complex problems like domestic violence. While some communities have adopted an integrated approach that engages advocates,

Figure 5-4. Matrix of Responses to Domestic Violence.

Source: Sampson (2007a: 25).

Strategic Focus	Strategic Times for Responses	Goal	Police Role	Other Agencies, Organizations, Group
At-risk population	Before incidents	Prevention; persuade those at risk that, if abused, call the police	Alert and educate at-risk victim population; educate/warn at-risk offending population	Public health organizations; domestic violence coalitions; schools and educators; medical professionals
Peers and neighbors of at-risk individuals	Ongoing	Getting peers and neighbors to call the police if they learn of domestic abuse	Educate these groups about the importance of calling the police to reduce the violence	Public health organizations; domestic violence coalitions; educators
Injured women and men	During medical care	Screen the injured for domestic violence; raise awareness of available services; provide medical care	Engage the medical profession and link medical professionals with appropriate referral organizations	Medical professionals
Individual incident	During	Violence cessation	Stop the violence; identify primary aggressor; accurately identify abuse history	Medical and public health professionals
Immediately after incident	After; ongoing	Prevent revictimization	Assist with victim safety; develop tailored strategies for victim and offender based on risk/physical violence history; increase focus on high-risk offenders; ensure victim is linked with needed resources; increase focus on high-risk victims; ongoing monitoring	Domestic violence victim advocates, victims' friends and family, shelters, victim services, criminal justice system, treatment services

social service providers, and the criminal justice system, recidivism generally remains high (Buzawa and Buzawa, 2003). To some observers, the small number of chronic batterers who generate repeat victimizations are resistant to these highly coordinated efforts and continue their generally violent behavior. However, there is some evidence that victims have high satisfaction levels when participating in these integrated approaches (Buzawa and Buzawa, 2003).

Preventing Repeat Fraud

Individuals may be victimized by fraud in a number of ways, such as telemarketing fraud, fraudulent acts involving consumer goods or services, or fraudulent acts involving financial advice on insurance coverage plans, investment packages, or business schemes. Titus and Gover (2001) provided examples of: scams involving credit assistance or loan consolidation; offers for free prizes that may not actually exist and/or may result in costs to victims; scams promising unnecessary or useless goods such as beauty products or home repairs; unauthorized use of bank or credit card numbers; and charity scams whereby victims make contributions to fraudulent institutions under the pretense of assisting a charity.

Fraud is surprisingly common, and there is a substantial proportion of individuals who are repeat victims of fraud. In the United States, a representative national telephone survey revealed that 58 percent of the respondents had been the victims of a fraudulent act or an attempted fraudulent act, and 8 percent of the sample reported victimization or attempted victimization in five or more fraud categories (Titus et al., 1995).

Personal fraud is often dependent upon victim cooperation or facilitation, ranging from no cooperation (e.g., identity theft), to some cooperation (e.g., making contributions to phony charity over the phone), to considerable cooperation (e.g., investing money in fraudulent investment opportunities for a number of years; Titus and Gover, 2001). Personal characteristics combined with demographics and life events affect the likelihood that an individual will succumb to a fraudulent solicitation if received. In contrast to popular images of the elderly as the most likely fraud victims, individuals aged 50 and older are less likely to be victims than younger people. Fraud victims are also more likely to be educated, informed, relatively affluent, and not socially isolated (Titus and Gover, 2001). When a person is victimized, however, s/he is much more likely to be approached again for both the same and different types of scam because con artists value such leads in identifying easy targets (Titus and Gover, 2001).

Titus and his colleagues (1995) found that fraud attempts were less likely to succeed if the offender was a stranger, the initial contact was by telephone or mail, the potential victim had heard of this type of fraud before, and the potential victim tried to investigate the person or proposition before responding. Thus, general public information campaigns clearly have a role in preventing fraud. However, since the best predictor of future victimization is past victimization, it also seems clear that fraud prevention strategies should be focused on repeat victims. As Titus and Gover (2001: 147-148) described:

> If the victim's actions helped the offender commit the crime, then changes in victim behavior should assist in preventing the crime. . . . One part of police and victim intake services should be to review with victims their daily activities and past fraud victimization history to assist them in assessing how they can reduce their risk of exposure to fraudulent solicitations. This would include a discussion of factors that research has identified as contributing to victimization and repeat victimization risk, an analysis of how these factors contribute to the victim's risk and a discussion of what changes the individual can make to reduce the risk. . . . By guiding the victim through the events that culminated in the crime, the victim may gain a more realistic idea of what changes in behavior could produce greater safety in the future, as well as an appropriate assessment of his involvement in the outcome.

Concluding Thoughts on the Prospects of Repeat Victimization Strategies

The reader of this chapter will undoubtedly note the overlap between problem-oriented approaches to preventing crime at hot spots, controlling high-activity offenders, and protecting repeat victims. A general concern is that police will see these approaches as being in competition. They are not. Repeat victims may be helped by apprehending and deterring chronic offenders and also by addressing high-crime place characteristics. When a crime hot spot is identified, attending to repeat victimization may be a good first move for police officers while they are analyzing the nature of the crime problems at the place and developing interventions to respond to the underlying conditions that caused the spot to become hot. Paying attention to repeat victims may also identify chronic offenders who merit focused police attention. The optimal form of response depends on the results of problem analysis. All methods should be available to the problem-oriented police officer and the resulting intervention to control a crime problem could contain elements that focus on offenders, victims, and places.

Strategies directed to aiding repeat victims also provide the police with a quick response to crime problems. Police may not be able to craft powerful interventions to address the underlying conditions of particular problems, such as repeat domestic violence. However, by taking a problem-oriented approach to repeat victimization, police can provide quick and temporary responses that could, in the least, provide victims with short-term relief from immediate harm. At best, since the timing of future victimizations depends upon the immediacy of past victimizations, these short-term solutions could set the victim on a different trajectory and spare him or her from becoming a repeat target.

NOTES

1. In general, police officers cannot make misdemeanor arrests for crimes they did not witness unless the victim asks for charges to be pressed. This can be problematic in domestic violence situations where the victim is afraid or doesn't want their spouse to be arrested.

6. FACILITATING PROBLEM-ORIENTED POLICING

This chapter highlights issues in three important areas that can greatly reduce deficiencies in the current practice of problem-oriented policing: improving crime analysis, measuring performance, and securing productive partnerships. This chapter does not attempt to tackle all the internal and external administrative arrangements necessary to facilitate effective problem-oriented policing. As such, important changes in management – such as redefining the role of line-level officers, exercising strong leadership, improving supervision, and decentralizing decision-making authority – are not discussed. Many other texts provide more than adequate coverage of these important issues (see, e.g., Eck and Spelman, 1987; Goldstein, 1990; Sparrow et al., 1990; Scott, 2000).

IMPROVING CRIME ANALYSIS

When knowledge about successful crime prevention programs in one field setting is disseminated to others, there is a tendency for police officers to blindly adopt these "proven" responses rather than conducting the necessary problem analysis to determine whether the program fits well with the nature of the crime problem as it manifests itself in the operational environments of their cities. According to Ekblom (1997), the fact that a crime prevention measure has proven successful in past circumstances does not guarantee its appropriateness in the future. On the surface, the problems may look similar. However, the circumstances may be different, and the causal mechanisms might be different; therefore, the resulting outcomes could be very different. For instance, in his examination of the Crime and Disorder Reduction Partnerships mandated by the 1998 Crime and Disorder Act in England and Wales, Hough (2006) suggested that mistaking tactics for strategy caused the failure of the local police and their partners to produce crime prevention gains.

As demonstrated in earlier chapters of this book, problem-oriented interventions may be composed of a package of specific tactics, and it may be unclear which is the active ingredient(s) among the various measures implemented. Finally, even if a particular measure has been shown to result in a strong reduction in crime, offenders may change tactics to overcome the implemented measure. For example, as Ekblom (1997) described, technological changes in the way safes are designed may be enough to thwart even the most skillful and well-organized safebreakers at any one time; however, this capacity to resist penetration may not last indefinitely because safebreakers are always learning new methods and developing new technologies. For problem-oriented police, the important lessons to be drawn from successful crime prevention case studies inhere in the guiding principles and underlying logic used in developing effective responses, rather than the specific interventions designed to tackle specific problems in specific settings.

Solid analyses of the underlying conditions that generated crime problems were the cornerstones of the successful prevention projects described in this text. Thus, police departments interested in improving their crime prevention capacities should work hard to improve their ability to analyze crime problems. As Nick Tilley (2002) observed, high-quality analysis for crime prevention is oriented directly to the formulation of preventive strategies. Such analysis identifies single offenses or concentrations of crime where there is potential for crime prevention gain; attempts to find the most efficient, effective, and, hopefully, equitable means of prevention; and can help forecast likely future crime problems with an eye toward developing preemptive strategies (Tilley, 2002).

Innovative crime analysis for prevention does not have to be complex to provide guidance to problem-oriented policing efforts. It simply has to provide grounded facts (i.e., true information derived from data) necessary to move the problem-oriented process forward. In the Boston "pulling levers" project, for instance, a simple analysis of the criminal histories of youth homicide victims and youth homicide offenders yielded the important insight that many of these individuals were chronic offenders who had been or were presently under criminal justice system control when they killed or were killed (Kennedy et al., 1996a). While many Boston practitioners knew this fact before the analysis was conducted, the information provided a rallying point within the working group assigned to harness the potential combined powers of the participating law enforcement agencies in preventing future acts of violence.

Clarke and Goldstein (2002) documented the vital role played by innovative crime analysis in a problem-oriented policing project undertaken by the Charlotte-Mecklenburg Police Department to address a sharp increase in the number of kitchen appliances stolen from new houses under construction. A detailed analysis was conducted of security practices and theft risks among 25 builders in one police service district. The analysis led to the recommendation that the installation of appliances should be delayed until the new owners moved into the residence. Removing the targets of theft was found to be an effective response: appliance theft declined markedly in the police service district and there was no evidence of displacement to surrounding district (Clarke and Goldstein, 2002).

A key moment in the analysis of the appliance theft problem in Charlotte-Mecklenburg occurred when the crime analyst discovered that a "certificate of occupancy" had to be issued by the county before a new owner could move into the residence. Building permits had been used in earlier iterations of the problem analysis, but the permits recorded only planned construction. Builders may obtain 100 permits to build houses, but only actually build a fraction in a given year. That is why building permit data could not be used to accurately assess the stage when a house was completed and, thus, at-risk for theft of newly installed appliances. In contrast, the certificates of occupancy provided a better measure of when a house was ready to be occupied and, therefore, a timelier basis for calculating the risk of theft.

Since most problem description exercises are based on analyses of official crime data, police departments need to be well aware of the limitations and difficulties of working with such data. The shortcomings of official data may be ignored, especially when presented through impressive mapping technologies, and potentially misleading results may gain an undeserved "scientific" aura. It is important to remember that official data are generated by human processes and therefore have inherent limitations. Harries (1999) covers a range of practical problems in mapping the locations of crime incidents that arise when working with address information contained in official records. Ambiguous, incorrect, and missing information are certainly found in the records, and not only in the address fields of official data. Crime analysts should expect to have to clean and massage the information contained in official records to make them useful for problem analysis.

Beyond data quality concerns, official data have some noteworthy substantive shortcomings. Arrest and investigation data are subject to both underreporting and enforcement bias (Black, 1970). Enforcement bias refers to the fact that police can exercise considerable discretion in deciding whether to arrest an offender or record a crime event as an official incident. In the case of measuring the extent of repeat victimization, police incident data are notoriously limited by underreporting that compounds with each additional incident generated by a specific address (Farrell and Pease, 1993, 2003):

> For example, a household suffers a burglary. A burglary has roughly a 70% (or 0.7) chance of featuring as a recorded crime in police statistics. The household suffers a second burglary. This too has a roughly 70% chance of featuring in police statistics. This means that the chance that the chance that they have been both recorded is 0.49 or 49% (that is, 0.7 × 0.7).... With three burglaries at the same address, given the chance of being recorded . . . [o]nly 34% will have all three burglaries recorded. (Farrell and Pease, 1993: 16)

While reports of citizen calls-for-service are not as affected by police discretion, these data are also subject to both underreporting (e.g., drug selling may be so commonplace in a socially disorganized area that no citizens call to complain) and overreporting (e.g., five separate callers may actually be identifying the same event rather than five separate events; Pierce et al., 1988; Sherman et al., 1989). In summary, the validity of the conclusions generated by analyses of official crime data depends on the application and on the care that is taken to correct for flaws in the data.

Clarke and Goldstein (2002) suggested that, at least for larger police departments, crime analysis units should be repositories for the research skills necessary for successful problem-oriented policing projects. Police officers charged with addressing particular crime problems may not have the special analytic and research skills necessary to conduct the fine-grained analyses needed for effective problem-oriented policing. Problem-solving and analysis guides have been helpful in providing officers with some basic understanding of the principles involved in conducting an innovative and thorough analysis, but such guides do not provide officers with the same level of expertise as is available from trained and experienced analysts (Scott, 2000). Clarke and Goldstein (2002) did not imply that line-level officers have little to offer in providing important insights on crime problems. Indeed, they strongly advocate that all police officers should be challenged to think about their work in terms of the problems they handle and the effectiveness of their methods to deal with them. However, crime analysts have the necessary analytic and technological background to benefit from training in problem-oriented policing, environmental criminology, and program evaluation.

Fortunately, the amount of guidance available to crime analysts and problem-oriented police officers has increased dramatically in recent years (Eck, 2006). There are now several general problem analysis guides available (e.g., Boba, 2003; Bynum, 2001). In their monograph *Crime Analysis for Problem Solvers in 60 Small Steps*, Ronald V. Clarke and John Eck (2005) presented a multitude of practical ideas and techniques from criminology, geography, psychology, mathematics, epidemiology, and other disciplines that can be used to enhance problem analysis. Via the Internet, a wealth of information is now available on crime problems and effective responses. With the support of funds from the federal government's Office of Community Oriented Policing Services (COPS), the Center for Problem-Oriented Policing offers printed and web site (www.popcenter.org) editions of its *problem-specific guides* to assist with diagnosing problems and developing responses to a wide range of issues, such as false burglary alarms (Sampson, 2007b), juvenile runaways (Dedel, 2006), prescription fraud (Wartell and La Vigne, 2004), and the robbery of convenience stores (Altizio and York, 2007). The Center also offers *response guides* that summarize available research on common police responses such as crackdowns (Scott, 2004b) and closing streets and alleys to reduce crime (Clarke, 2005). And the Center publishes *problem-solving tool guides* on general techniques such as researching crime problems (Clarke and Schultze, 2005) and analyzing repeat victimization (Lamm Weisel, 2005). The Popcenter web site also includes on-line problem analysis and response development simulations and a model problem-oriented policing training curriculum. Training opportunities and problem-oriented policing literature can also be found on the Police Executive Research Forum (www.policeforum.org) and Police Foundation (www.policefoundation.org) web sites. In the United Kingdom, the Jill Dando Institute for Crime Sciences web site (www.jdl.ucl.ac.uk) offers a wide variety of resources for problem solvers interested in more effective crime prevention. The Home Office Crime Reduction Unit (www.crimereduction.homeoffice.gov.uk) and the Australian Institute of Criminology (www.aic.gov.au) web sites also provide useful information on effective crime prevention practices.

Beyond training and ongoing exposure to the developing literature on problem analysis, crime analysts should be brought more directly into the management of police agencies. Clarke and Goldstein (2002) proposed that crime analysts within police departments could function much like analysts in the business world who report to executives on the quality of their end product. They suggested (2002: 119-120) that:

> Properly trained crime analysts, engaged in the systematic study of problems that the police handle, as contemplated in problem-oriented policing, should have direct access to the top police administrator; should be involved in management meetings; and should be routinely consulted for guidance on how to improve the effectiveness of police efforts. Fully developed, their unique contribution could go a long way toward increasing the effectiveness of the police and, as a consequence, the professional status of the police.

Crime Mapping and Beyond

Geographic mapping applications and their associated statistical tools can be used in support of problem-oriented policing by providing spatial and temporal information on: crime incidents, victims, and offenders; community and government resources; and community demographics (Weisburd and McEwen, 1997). Computerized crime mapping technology has spread significantly among law enforcement agencies in the United States and abroad, and it is now recognized as a readily accessible tool. There are many successful cases in which police departments have used crime mapping to good effect in dealing with crime and disorder problems (LaVigne and Wartell, 1998, 2000).

Harries (1999) observed that maps aid in visual thinking – that is, maps help generate ideas and hypotheses about the problem under investigation. Maps can help reveal relationships and correlations that may have otherwise gone unnoticed. Maps also aid in visual communication. A map that provides information that is germane to the question at hand can be highly persuasive (Harries, 1999). As MacEachern (1994: 9) suggested, "People believe maps." Readers interested in the details of crime mapping should acquire Harries's (1999) excellent text on the principle and practice of mapping crime and the recent volume by Eck, Chainey, and Cameron (2005) on mapping crime hot spots. They might also explore the U.S. National Institute of Justice Mapping and Analysis for Public Safety (MAPS) web site (http://www.ojp.usdoj.gov/nij/maps/).

As discussed in the chapter on the policing of problem places, a "hot spot" is a location where crime clusters. Crime mapping is an efficient and effective way to identify crime hot spots. While there is no standard definition of a crime hot spot, Lawrence Sherman (1995: 36) suggested that hot spots are "small places in which the occurrence of crime is so frequent that it is highly predictable, at least over a one year period." Harries (1999) observed that hot spot definition can vary considerably across jurisdictions, and that it is often influenced by scale (city, neighborhood, address, etc.). Mapping techniques to identify hot spots of crime have progressed greatly in recent years with software packages – such as the Illinois Criminal Justice Information Authority's Spatial and Temporal Analysis of Crime (STAC) program – that are easily available to law enforcement agencies (Block and Block, 1993). The CrimeStat III spatial statistics program, which can be downloaded free from the MAPS web site, contains a variety of analytic tools, including hot spot identification, space-time analysis (for understanding temporal and spatial interaction in offender behavior), and journey-to-crime estimation (for estimating the likely residence location of a serial offender).

The functionality and sophistication of crime mapping is continually being enhanced and expanded. Recent advances include the use of high definition or 3-D crime mapping to better understand the distribution of crimes across specific buildings, parking lots, and other facilities on a street block or the location of repeat crimes on specific floors and at specific units in multilevel buildings (Rengert et al., 2001). Research on repeat victimization has led to experimentation with "prospective mapping" to predict the location of future crimes based on the notion that future targets are likely to be people who live nearby or places with characteristics similar to the original target (Johnson and Bowers, 2004). A detailed discussion of defining hot spots and the various ways in which crime mapping technology can be deployed to identify hot spots, repeat victim addresses, and other identifiable risks is beyond the scope of this discussion (see Harries, 1999; Eck et al., 2005; Clarke and Eck, 2005). However, it is important to recognize that many of the successful place-oriented crime prevention projects described in Chapter 3 were supported by computerized mapping technology (e.g., Weisburd and Green, 1995a; Sherman and Weisburd, 1995; Braga et al., 1999).

COMPSTAT

One of the best known examples of the use of crime mapping in moving the problem-oriented policing process forward is the New York Police Department's (NYPD) system of regularly scheduled computerized statistics meetings. This program is known as "Compstat," which came from a computer file named "Compare Statistics" that was instituted in 1994 (Silverman, 1999). Compstat has been credited as a key ingredient in the NYPD's attack on crime in the 1990s (Bratton, 1998). It is important to note, however, that Compstat's effectiveness as a crime control strategy has not yet been confirmed (see, e.g. Eck and Maguire, 2000).

Compstat meetings grew from the need for a mechanism to ensure precinct commanders' accountability and the goal of improving performance in crime prevention. These routine strategy meetings require precinct commanders to discuss crime trends and crime fighting plans with the upper echelons of the NYPD hierarchy. Crime maps – as well as quantitative analyses of complaints, arrests, patterns and trends, and qualitative information about precinct-community relationships in effective crime fighting – were intensely scrutinized and discussed in the meetings (Silverman, 1999). The crime reduction principles embodied in the Compstat process are (from Harries, 1999: 79):

- *Accurate and Timely Intelligence.* This includes information describing how and where crimes are committed, as well as who criminals are. It must be available at all levels of policing.

- *Effective Tactics.* These are tactics designed to respond directly to facts discovered during the intelligence-gathering process. Tactics must be "comprehensive, flexible, and adaptable to the shifting crime trends we identify and monitor."

- *Rapid Deployment of Personnel and Resources.* Some problems may involve only patrol personnel, but "the most effective plans require that personnel from several units and enforcement functions work together as a team."

- *Relentless Follow Up and Assessment.* To ensure that appropriate outcomes occur, rigorous follow up is necessary.

The Compstat meetings are forums where new problem-solving approaches are presented, reviewed, reexamined, and circulated (Silverman, 1999). In these meetings, crime mapping is an indispensable way for the NYPD to portray crime data clearly and in a format that can be acted on quickly.

The Compstat process has rapidly spread across the country. A survey by Weisburd and his colleagues (2001) found that nearly 60 percent of police departments with 500 or more sworn officers have adopted the program. Compstat, unlike other recent innovations in American policing, does not challenge the traditional quasi-military model of police organization: it allows departments to adopt technological innovations while reinforcing the traditional hierarchical structure of police agencies (Weisburd et al., 2003). Indeed, the above-listed "crime reduction principles" make Compstat seem like a military operation, and there is nothing in the principles to encourage going beyond directed patrol and other traditional responses.

While departments engaging a Compstat process are more likely than other police forces to use data-driven problem identification and assessment, there is some evidence that Compstat, as currently practiced, is far from an ideal model of problem-oriented policing. Compstat departments, relative to police departments without a Compstat process, seem to find it more difficult to implement effective problem-solving tactics and are less successful in adopting innovations that demand significant change in the philosophy and practice of policing (Weisburd et al., 2003). (The importance of Compstat in driving organizational change is discussed below in the section on "Measuring Performance.")

Practitioners and scholars value computerized mapping as a powerful tool for identifying crime problems and developing crime control and prevention programs. However, police officers need to remember that examining the spatial distribution of official crime data is only one way to look at crime problems. To some observers, crime mapping can stifle creativity in analyzing problems. As Gloria Laycock suggested (as quoted in Scott, 2000: 104):

> Mapping, however, is actually a bit of a red herring. It can even be unhelpful. I worry that people are becoming obsessed with maps and their pretty colors, without thinking much about what information they contain or what can be learned from them. The technology itself becomes fascinating, rather than the knowledge gained from it. So technology can at times inhibit the development of problem-oriented policing because it stops people from thinking.

Additional Crime Mapping Applications

Other types of information can be incorporated in crime maps and mapping can be combined with other analytic techniques to provide greater insights on crime problems and develop a wider range of interventions. To date, mapping has been utilized mostly in support of place-focused diagnoses and interventions. The innate geographic character of maps has combined with interest in hot spots to generate this result. But as Kennedy and his colleagues (1997) observed, there is no logical reason that mapping applications should be limited to geographic phenomena, hot spot analyses, or hot spot/place-focused intervention strategies. For example, many cities have problems with delinquent groups, particularly youth violence fueled by conflicts between gangs (Curry et al., 1994). The resulting crime and disorder problems often exhibit geographic concentration, and mapping can identify such hot spots of youth violence. However, such analyses reveal nothing about the violent youth groups, or their conflict networks, that exist across the city. Identifying gangs and understanding the nature of their conflicts could be instrumental in preventing or responding to flare-ups of violence. As described earlier in this text, interventions focused on serious offenders, violent groups, patterns of conflict, and weapons all hold promise for reducing violence, including violence concentrated in hot spots.

Along with its focus on hot spots and place-focused interventions, mapping has largely relied on formal police data (Kennedy et al., 1997). For example, the designers of the Repeat Call Address Policing experiment in Minneapolis avoided using police officers to identify persistent problem addresses for three reasons: "(1) the potential criticism as discriminatory law enforcement; (2) its susceptibility to police officers' pet peeves to the exclusion of major consumers of police resources or major sources of bloodshed; (3) the potential for selection bias in evaluations, resulting from the picking of easier to solve problems" (Buerger, 1994a: footnote 3). The result has been that mapping techniques have been almost totally reliant on official police data. However, as described earlier, such data are known to have important shortcomings. Therefore, mapping techniques that rely exclusively on the analysis of official data have their own inherent biases and limits. They also run, to some extent, against the tide of community and problem-oriented policing, which seek to manage officer discretion rather than deny it, and to promote and benefit from line officers' creativity and problem-solving capacity (Goldstein, 1990; Sparrow et al., 1990; Kennedy and Moore, 1995). The ease of crime mapping, as well as other techniques that make searching and analyzing large volumes of data possible, often leads problem-oriented police to skip a more detailed analysis of the written narratives in police reports, which may contain many of the more useful insights about problems (Scott, 2000).

Mapping analyses have expanded to include data from non-police sources. The Illinois Criminal Justice Information Authority developed an extensive geographic database of both community and law enforcement data, known as the GeoArchive. The authority suggests that when combined with a community-oriented policing program, a GeoArchive can become an information foundation for community policing (Block, 1997). A variety of data are collected including: street map data, official crime data (calls-for-service, arrests, offender characteristics, victim characteristics), corrections data (the addresses of persons released on probation or parole), landmark data (parks, schools, public transportation), and population information (Block, 1997). The Chicago Police Department's Information Collection for Automated Mapping (ICAM) was a key part of its community policing program known as the Chicago Alternative Policing Strategy (CAPS). ICAM was connected to the city's mainframe computer and provided police officers with the locations of abandoned buildings, businesses, and liquor stores (Rich, 1995). Several multi-agency task forces, such as Denver's Pulling America's Communities Together (PACT) program, integrated and mapped data to identify risk factors for delinquency in crafting broad, multi-disciplinary solutions to reduce violence (Rich, 1995). The Redlands (CA) Police Department integrated cutting edge technology to map community, family, school, and peer group risk and protective factors. This enabled the department to focus limited community and police resources on the most problematic areas where the greatest potential for change existed (Harries, 1999). These types of information-gathering efforts can be invaluable to police officers and others in analyzing urban crime problems and developing appropriate interventions at the local, district, or citywide level.

Some of the richest information for describing public safety problems and driving problem-oriented policing efforts simply is not available from any official data systems. Qualitative research methods such as ethnography, interviews, focus groups, and survey research can supply valuable information for problem analysis. As described earlier in this text, interviews with offenders can provide important insights on the nature of crime problems. As Scott Decker (2005: 1) suggested:

> There is a long tradition in criminal justice research of interviewing active offenders, but very little of this research has focused specifically on police problem solving. This is unfortunate because active offenders provide substantial amounts of information about each of the elements of the crime triangle: victims, offenders, and places. Such information should prove useful for strategic problem-solving interventions, because it yields information about crime patterns in general that may not be obvious when examining one case at a time. The information from such interviews may enhance existing problem-

solving projects or generate new ones. The information can also improve officer safety.

In addition to qualitative data collection from offenders, the "experiential assets" of criminal justice practitioners and community members can also make powerful contributions to identifying and understanding crime problems (Kennedy et al., 1997).

Crime incident reviews, for example, provide a method of sharing detailed information on specific types of crime, usually homicides, in the local criminal justice system, and then using that information to develop strategic approaches to reduce that crime (Klofas and Hipple, 2006). These reviews are usually structured as focus group sessions, and they rely on input from front-line staff with street-level knowledge of the crimes being discussed. Representatives from across the criminal justice system – including law enforcement, prosecutors, probation and parole officers, and often others – participate in the review (Klofas and Hipple, 2006). The process involves researchers whose task it is to record the qualitative insights on the events and its participants, analyze these data, and identify patterns or other issues that may be useful in responding strategically to the crime problem. The Boston Gun Project used the crime incident review methodology to move the problem-solving process forward in a direction not possible by simply analyzing official crime data. Analysis of FBI Supplementary Homicide Report data, which are notoriously limited in documenting the circumstances of homicide incidents and the relationships between victims and offenders, suggested that Boston youth homicide in the 1990s was largely being committed by strangers against strangers for unknown reasons (Braga, Piehl, and Kennedy, 1999). Obviously, this picture of youth homicide did not lend itself to the development of strategic interventions. However, the crime incident review process revealed that Boston youth homicide was largely driven by retaliatory gang violence; this key insight was used to frame additional data collection efforts to better understand the nature of gang violence in Boston (Braga, Piehl, and Kennedy, 1999).

Cognitive Mapping

Particularly closely linked to crime mapping and hot spot approaches is cognitive mapping. Cognitive maps represent perceptions of spatial reality (see Smith and Patterson, 1980; Gould and White, 1974) by individuals on such dimensions as street gang territories, drug market areas, and other geographic phenomena. Criminologists have advocated the use of cognitive maps based on the perceptions of law enforcement personnel and community members to enhance community problem-solving efforts within neighborhoods and specific places (Block, 1997).

A key notion in cognitive mapping is that it is the perception of an individual (or perceptions of individuals) that is being mapped; the resulting construct may or may not have anything meaningful to say about reality. New knowledge, however, can be gained from the mapping exercise itself, and also from important consistencies and discrepancies between qualitative and official data (Rosenbaum and Lavrakas, 1995). These concepts have been sparsely used in support of crime prevention and problem-oriented policing exercises. Some notable exceptions have included the mapping of gang alliances and gang conflicts in Boston (Kennedy et al., 1997), the mapping of gang turf based on police officer perceptions in Chicago (Block and Block, 1993) and Los Angeles (Tita et al., 2004), and the identification of problem locations within buildings and common areas by housing project residents in Jersey City (Mazerolle and Terrill, 1997).

Network Analyses

Criminal network maps and analyses – which are graphic illustrations of the relationships among individual criminals, smaller crime groups, and larger criminal organizations – are obvious alternative applications of mapping technology in the problem-oriented policing process. For communities suffering from violence involving delinquent groups, for example, intelligence on social networks within groups and antagonisms between rival groups is important for addressing violent crime in affected neighborhoods. Qualitative methods are appropriate and desirable techniques to collect the relational data on contacts, ties, connections of groups, and group attachments of individuals within networks (Scott, 1991).

Applications of criminal network analyses can range from local youth gangs to narcotics organizations to terrorist groups. All represent significant challenges to law enforcement agencies. As Sparrow (1991) describes, there are a variety of analytic tools and concepts – ranging from simple analyses of telephone calls among criminals to sophisticated statistical analyses of relational data linking individuals within extended social networks – available to examine criminal organizations. These techniques can be potent tools for combating criminal groups, but are currently used primarily by federal law enforcement agencies with respect to more or less traditional organized crime and narcotics trafficking problems. They are underutilized by police agencies with regard to other crime problems. Further, the current state of the art is relatively unsophisticated. Criminal intelligence analysis can be improved by structural network analysis, and computerized network analysis programs hold much promise in identifying vulnerabilities, such as the identity of central players and weak links within criminal networks (see Sparrow, 1991).

Network analyses developed from practitioner knowledge have been used in several problem-oriented policing projects to better understand the relationships among gangs and gang members. In Stockton, California, qualitative data collection techniques were used to construct a network of gang conflicts and alliances (Figure 6-1). At the time the problem analysis work was completed, Stockton gangs had ongoing feuds that fell largely within particular racial groups: Asian gang conflicts, Hispanic gang conflicts, and African-American gang conflicts (Braga, 2005b). Within each broad set of ethnic antagonisms, particular gangs formed alliances with other gangs. For example, the Asian Boys and associates were united in their fight against the Asian Gangsters, Crazy Brother Clan, Tiny Rascal Gang, Moon Light Strangers, and associates. Conflicts among Hispanic gangs mainly involved a very violent rivalry between Norteno gangs (associated with criminal groups and gangs in Northern California) and Sureno gangs (associated with criminal groups and gangs in Southern California). However, while Norteno and Sureno gangs were united in their fight against their common rivals, they also had ongoing conflicts within their loose alliances. For instance, Stockton Police officers reported that the Norteno gangs South Side Stocktone and East Side Stocktone had a relatively long-standing feud, but they would help each other in their conflicts with the Sureno gangs. African-American gangs, such as the Westside Bloods and East Coast Crips, divided along Blood (red gang colors) and Crip (blue gang colors) lines. Stockton Police gang officers reported an uneasy alliance among these groups involving street-level drug sales. However, violent disputes occasionally developed among these groups when drug business conflicts arose.

In Newark, New Jersey, a network analysis of individual gang members found that street gangs were loosely organized with pockets of cohesion (McGloin, 2005). There was also variation in the "connectedness" of individuals within gangs, with certain members emerging as "cut-points": i.e., the only connection point among gang members or groups of gang members. These insights were drawn from data collected from semi-structured interviews with law enforcement officials (McGloin, 2004). The results of this

Figure 6-1. Conflicts Among Active Stockton Street Gangs.

Source: Braga (2005b: 27).

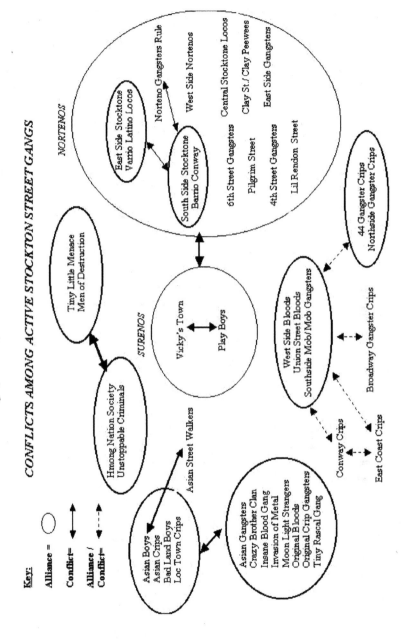

analysis suggested that particular groups of gang members might be more amenable to collective interventions, such as the pulling levers strategy discussed in Chapter 4, while other groups might become more cohesive as a consequence of such focused attention (McGloin, 2005). The cut-points were regarded as particularly worthy of attention for their capacity to act of communication agents of a deterrence message and for their vulnerability to a pulling levers strategy (McGloin, 2005).

Data from Practitioners

Both academics and police practitioners have been reluctant to incorporate the knowledge of front-line personnel into easily used mapping approaches and computer applications. Some argue that the subjective assessments of practitioners are not accurate. For example, psychiatrists' ability to predict "dangerous" persons has been found to be minimal (Monahan, 1981; Ennis and Litwack, 1974). Mainstream police administrators, and many academics in police and public safety research, have long discounted the views of line officers as partial, biased, and of no great utility (Goldstein, 1990; Sparrow et al., 1990). At the same time, many police feel that their knowledge and expertise are essentially ineffable – that, in the words of James Fyfe, "It's just something you learn over time, is all" (as quoted in Toch and Grant, 1991: 41). Neither attitude – that police officers know nothing, or that police knowledge is irredeemably particular and incommunicable – lends itself to collecting, testing, and analyzing practitioner knowledge (Kennedy et al., 1997).

Others feel that practitioners, particularly police officers, develop rich pictures of their environment and can provide accurate assessments of area characteristics, crime problems, and criminal activity (Bittner, 1970; Braga et al., 1994). These perceptions sharpen and improve as police mature in their careers and gain experience (Rubinstein, 1973; Muir, 1977). For example, a rigorous examination of the assessments of experienced narcotics officers relative to other, more formal, measures of drug activity found that the officers were highly capable of identifying street drug activity based on quite brief exposures (Braga et al., 1994). To date, though, most mapping exercises, geographic/hot spot focused or otherwise, have not relied heavily on the systematic gathering, analysis, and application of information from practitioner or community sources. This is an important, but largely unexplored, frontier (Toch and Grant, 1991).

The Process of Crime Analysis

This section has described a variety of methods to enrich the quality of problem analysis in problem-oriented policing projects. Equally important, however, is the observation that the *process* of analyzing crime problems needs to be better developed. In a recent paper, Deborah Lamm Weisel (2003) suggested a logical sequence of steps in the analysis of crime problems that can enhance the quality of work done by analysts and officers alike (Figure 6-2). The first phase involves the *documentation* of the crime problem and its major steps include: parsing – reducing the identified problem to a manageable subset: e.g., reducing commercial burglary to the theft of appliances from construction sites; enumeration – developing a baseline count of a specific type of problem during a given time period: e.g. the number of reported thefts from a construction site over six months or an average nightly count of prostitutes working in a four-block area in a particular month; and, establishing prevalence – developing a denominator to determine whether the prevalence of an event constitutes a problem: e.g. the number of dwellings under construction as a denominator for the number of thefts).

After the problem has been documented, delimited, and verified, the analysis process then turns to the data collection and analytic phases (Lamm Weisel, 2003). It is critical that data collection tasks and protocols be designed for each problem-oriented venture. Conducting a literature review of research on similar problems and then, based on this review, identifying key contextual variables (e.g., security practices at construction sites, or the placement of cash registers in convenience stores) will shed important light on the causal sequencing of the problem being examined. A working, or provisional, hypothesis that explains the causes of the problem can then be established (e.g., the width of aisles in grocery stores facilitates pursue snatching as offenders bump patrons without causing suspicion) and appropriate data collection tasks designed. There will, of course, be a sequencing of data collection and analysis tasks that will start with the acquisition and analysis of existing data (e.g. spatial and temporal analyses of incident, arrest, and calls-for-service data), which will inform the collection and analysis of primary data on the nature of the problem (Lamm Weisel, 2003). Primary data collection can include unobtrusive measures, such as traffic counters and environmental surveys of facilities and site features (e.g., creating a map of grocery store aisle widths), and intrusive measures such as surveys, interviews, and focus groups (e.g., interviewing known

Figure 6-2. The Sequence of Analysis.

Source: Lamm Weisel (2003: 120).

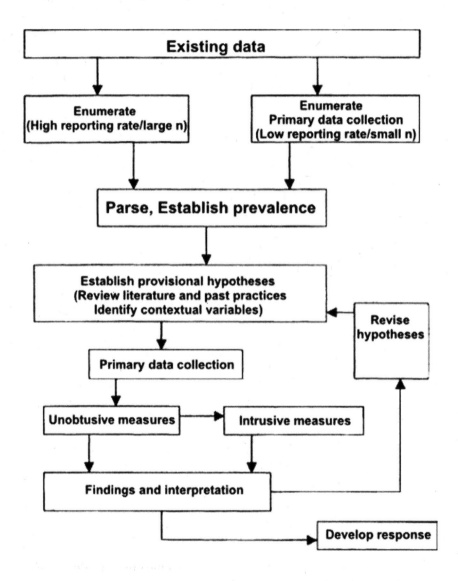

purse snatchers on attractive opportunities and targets). After these data are analyzed, using the appropriate methods (ranging from simple counts to more complicated statistical analyses), the working hypothesis can be tested (is it true that narrow aisles are associated with increase purse snatching?), and revised if necessary (and the process repeated).

MEASURING PERFORMANCE IN PROBLEM-ORIENTED POLICING

The historically accepted, and still enshrined, key measures of police performance are: reported crime rates, overall arrests, clearance rates, and response times (Alpert and Moore, 1993). Examining official data on crime, particularly data disaggregated from citywide or district-wide figures, remains an important way to measure police effectiveness. However, the paradigm shift from traditional policing to community and problem-oriented policing expands the police mandate to include a wider range of community concerns. Dimensions other than crime (e.g., safe and orderly neighborhoods, civil behavior, fair play, and prompt response) are important in recognizing the value that police departments contribute to cities (Kennedy and Moore, 1995; Wilson, 1993). The production of safer and more orderly neighborhoods is a primary goal of the new paradigm of policing, and police officers need ways to assess neighborhood conditions before and after various interventions (Kelling, 1992; Wilson, 1993).

What to Measure

One of the key issues in using performance measurement for internal management purposes has been whether the measures should focus on: (1) the ultimate results of policing, such as reduced crime and enhanced security (*outcomes*); or (2) police efforts to produce these results (*processes*); or (3) the investments made in the police (*inputs*); for a discussion, see Moore (2002). Recently, those advising police departments about how to improve their accountability and performance have emphasized the use of *outcome* measures rather than *process* measures. Outcomes are direct measures of the value that the police seek to produce. Unless the value of police actions can be assessed, citizens cannot be sure that police efforts are worthwhile. In this respect, outcomes are closer to a true "bottom line" for policing (Moore, 2002). In addition, the measurement of outcomes also allows police departments to test existing operational theories to find out "what works" in policing. Without outcome measures, it would also be very difficult to guide police departments toward the reliable creation of public value.

However, in policing, there are many important reasons to pay attention to processes as well as to outcomes. Society as a whole has expectations about how the police will do their work, as well as what the results of their work will be. This is particularly true when discussing how the police use the authority of their office: the powers to stop, to detain, to arrest, and to use force to accomplish these goals. This is also true when discussing the use of money. As Moore (2002) notes, police departments have long been reviewed in terms of how complete their policies and procedures were, what kind of training they provided to officers, how much overtime they used, and the extent to which they had "civilianized" their work force. They have also long been evaluated in terms of how efficiently and effectively their staffing patterns matched the times and places where crime was likely to occur. These processes and activities are things that the police can measure easily and are well within their control. Moreover, the police cannot learn much about whether a particular operational approach worked or not unless the police can measure what they did to ensure that the operational approach was actually implemented. As such, it is important to measure process activities as well as outcomes.

Given these observations, police managers should not restrict themselves to simply one outcome measure to use as the bottom line for policing. It probably makes sense for them to take guidance from the idea of a "balanced scorecard," and develop a battery of measurements that include: (1) outcome measures, both as ultimate measures of value created, and as ways of testing whether innovative programs work or not; (2) process measures to focus managerial attention on the way they are using authority and money to accomplish their results; and (3) measures of inputs such as expenditures and investments to help organizations manage the transition from traditional styles of policing to the new style more effectively (Moore, 2002). Multi-dimensional performance evaluation, from processes to outcomes to the investments being made in the organization is probably the best way to conceptualize an effective performance measurement system. As Moore (2002) observes, this is to be preferred to one that focuses only on outcomes, or only on processes.

The Importance of Measurement in Driving Organizational Change

As police departments evolved from the professional model of policing towards a strategy of community and problem-oriented policing, it became clear that the traditional measures of police performance had become outdated and needed to be changed (Kelling, 1992; Langworthy, 1999). Performance measurement systems based on response times, clearance rates, and numbers of arrests offer little in the evaluation of police efforts to address community needs and problems. Measurement systems based entirely on these indicators offer no way to hold police departments externally accountable for addressing community concerns and no way to hold particular officers internally accountable for engaging in community problem-solving activities (Moore and Braga, 2003). As such, in the absence of relevant measurement systems, police executives experience difficulty motivating their managers and line-level officers to change their approach towards policing.

A number of departments have made considerable progress in developing performance measurement systems that both address community concerns and drive their organizations towards a community problem-solving strategy. The most famous example is the previously mentioned NYPD Compstat system which holds police managers accountable for preventing crime in their precincts. The Compstat system has become a highly influential administrative innovation in police departments. Indeed, it seems to be setting the standard for police management generally, and particularly for the use of performance measurement in systems of internal accountability. Moore and Braga (2003) identify some of the features that make this measurement system behaviorally powerful in driving the NYPD:

- The measurement system aligns with organizational units so that the managers of those units can be held accountable for their performance.

- The measures are simple, objective, reliably calculated and continuous so that changes in performance can be observed over time within an operational unit, and across units that are roughly similar.

- The measures are closely aligned with what external overseers want and expect from the organization, with any important value that the organization is trying to produce, and with a goal that the organization itself wants to produce.

- The system holds managers to account frequently enough to capture their attention.

- The managers think that their current standing and pay as well as their future promotional opportunities, depend on performing well with respect to these measures.

- The reviews of performance are public so that everyone can see how well a particular manager has done.

- There are many managers in comparable situations so that comparisons can be made across managers as well as for a particular manager over time.

These features combine to give the Compstat system great behavioral power. The managers in the department work hard, and demand that others work hard, to produce results that the system will record as favorable. Given the power of the system, Moore (2002) observes that it is particularly important that one pay close attention to what the system recognizes as valuable, what it ignores, and how managers subject to the system are likely to respond, since that will determine whether the system drives the organization towards high levels of performance or not.

Each precinct commander is held publicly accountable for levels of serious crime in his precinct. The precinct commander's crime statistics are reviewed in the context of crime rates in immediately adjacent precincts so that he cannot reduce crime in his precinct simply by driving it to neighboring precincts. Special attention is also focused on particular crime problems that seem to be troublesome within the larger overall pattern of serious crime. If the Compstat system reveals a crime problem that is getting worse in a precinct, or not improving as much as top management thinks it should, the precinct commander is questioned about his *plans* for dealing with the problem. He is often peppered with questions about whether he is or is not making use of particular activities such as the use of warrant squads, or increased use of fingerprinting, or arrests for weapons offenses that top management thinks might be helpful in dealing with the problem. The system seems to hold managers accountable for an *outcome* of policing as well as *processes*.

As Moore (2002) observes, this part of the system has two important features. First, to some degree, it softens the harsh "strict liability" aspects of the system. Precinct commanders are held accountable for reducing crime. However, they can also get credit if they have a thoughtful plan for dealing with crime problems that have not been resolved. A thoughtful plan is one that makes sense, and/or one that takes advantage of processes and activities that are favored by top management (Moore, 2002). In essence, the Compstat system was constructed to enforce tightly aligned internal and external accountability. The system followed the organizational structure so that individual managers could be called to account for specific results, and the results they achieved were believed to be important to their career prospects. Second, because the system focuses some attention on plans and processes for achieving results as well as the results themselves, the system has some capacity to support innovation and organizational learning about what works to produce outcomes as well as the outcomes themselves (Moore, 2002). If a manager's plan for dealing with a problem is innovative, and if it works, there is come capacity for the system to capture that idea for the future. If a manager is faced with a problem that he can't seem to solve, top management has a chance to suggest ideas, and through that device, to spread innovations through the department.

Moore (2002) also notes some of the potential weaknesses of Compstat in driving organizational change. First, even though the system is capturing one important dimension of value to be produced by the police, it is not capturing all the relevant valued dimensions. It does not, for instance, capture levels of fear in the community, or their perceptions of the quality of service they receive. Second, while the system focuses on results, it does not concentrate much attention on the resources used to produce those results. In this regard, the system equates the crime reduction effect of policing with the "profit" earned by policing. The "profitability" of policing cannot be observed until the value of the resources used in policing is subtracted from the value of the effects produced (Moore, 2002). Third, although the system allows precinct commanders to talk about their special efforts to deal with serious crime problems, it provides little room for them to talk about problem-solving efforts focused on non-crime problems, and the quality of the engagement between the police and community groups in identifying and responding to the concerns of the community. No system can do everything that is valuable, of course. Skilled management often depends on making choices about what particular things to concentrate on, and then living with a system that is at best an imperfect reflection of what one is really trying to achieve (Moore, 2002).

As described earlier, by reinforcing the hierarchical organizational structure of policing, Compstat may itself inhibit innovation and creativity in the problem-oriented policing process (see Braga and Weisburd, 2006). In their close examination of Compstat, Willis, Mastrofski, and Weisburd (2004) found that, while the program holds out the promise of allowing police agencies to adopt innovative technologies and problem-solving techniques, it actually hindered innovative problem solving while strengthening the existing hierarchy through the added pressure of increased internal accountability. Officers were reluctant to brainstorm problem-solving approaches during Compstat meetings for fear of undermining authority or the credibility of their colleagues. Moreover, the danger of "looking bad" in front of superior officers discouraged middle managers from pursuing more creative crime strategies with a higher risk of failure.

It is also important to recognize that the organizational culture of policing is resistant to problem-oriented policing ideals. The community policing movement that emerged in the 1980s stressed greater police recognition of the role of the community and emphasized "decentralization" and "debureaucratization" to empower rank and file officers to make decisions about how to better serve the neighborhoods to which they were assigned (Mastrofski, 1998; Skolnick and Bayley, 1986). Weisburd and his colleagues (2003) suggest that the popularity and rapid diffusion of Compstat programs across larger police departments in the United States during the 1990s could be interpreted as an effort to maintain and reinforce traditional police structures rather than an attempt to truly reform American policing. The rapid rise of Compstat within police agencies did not enhance their strategic problem solving capacity at the beat level as Compstat departments were found to be reluctant to relinquish power that would decentralize some key elements of decision making such as allowing middle managers to determine beat boundaries and staffing levels, enhancing operational flexibility, and risk going beyond the standard tool kit of police tactics and strategies (Weisburd et al., 2003). The overall effect of the spread of Compstat, whether intended or not, was to reinforce the traditional bureaucratic model of command and control.

More generally, the type of in-depth problem solving that Goldstein and other problem-oriented policing advocates have proposed seems unrealistic in the real world of policing, especially at the street level where it is often envisioned. In the real world of police organizations, community and problem-oriented police officers rarely have the latitude necessary to assess and respond to problems creatively. As William Bratton (1998: 199) observed in his assessment of community policing in New York City at the beginning of his tenure, "street-level police officers were never going to be empowered to follow through." Compstat was offered as a solution to this problem, but the ability of the rank and file officer to make decisions changed little as middle managers were held accountable for achieving organizational goals of successful crime control (Willis et al., 2004). Of course, decentralizing decision making power to line-level officers does not guarantee effective problem solving. In their assessment of problem solving in Chicago, a police department well known for its efforts to decentralize their organization to facilitate community policing, Skogan and his colleagues (1999) gave a failing grade ranging from "struggling" to "woeful" for problem solving efforts in 40 percent of the beats they studied (231). Inadequate management, poor leadership and vision, lack of training, and weak performance measures were among the operational problems identified as affecting problem solving in the poorly performing beats (Skogan et al., 1999).

Measuring the Effects of Crime Prevention Strategies

As described in Chapter 2, it is critically important to conduct both process and impact evaluations of problem-oriented policing projects. A process evaluation focuses on the resources that were employed by the response (inputs) and the activities accomplished with these resources (results), but it does not examine whether the response was effective at reducing the problem (outcomes) (Clarke and Eck, 2005: 90; Moore, 2002). Figure 6-3 presents the relationship between process and impact evaluations. In general, it is important to understand whether any observed declines in the targeted problem can be associated with the response that was implemented. If the response was properly implemented and there was no observable decline in the problem, it would suggest that the problem-oriented policing project was not effective. Similarly, if the response was implemented as planned and the problem declined, this could be considered credible evidence that the problem-oriented policing project had preventive value.

Measuring the impact of implemented responses on crime problems is a key to the problem-oriented policing process. Evaluating programs designed to influence human behavior in field settings is a very complex task. Many problem-oriented policing interventions are multifaceted and, as such, it is complicated to evaluate a single strategy within a varied bundle of tactics because it is difficult to isolate each response's effects (Eck, 1997).

Figure 6-3. Focus of Process and Impact Evaluations.

Source: Clarke and Eck (2005: Step 46).

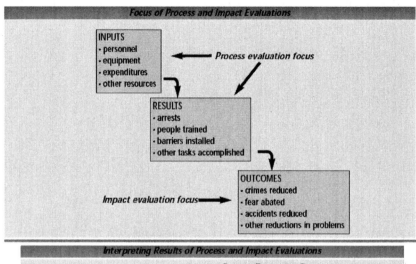

In general, the assessment of implemented problem-oriented responses is rare and, when undertaken, it is usually cursory and limited to anecdotal or impressionistic data (Scott and Clarke, 2000).

Certainly there is ample room for improvement in the current state-of-the-art in impact evaluations of problem-oriented policing interventions. However, as Scott (2000) observes, there is considerable disagreement over evaluation methodology and standards of proof in determining what works. Some scholars, such as Herman Goldstein and Ronald V. Clarke, recommend a flexible, eclectic approach to evaluating problem-oriented responses. They suggest that the degree of rigor applied to evaluation should be commensurate with the consequences of being wrong about whether something works (Scott, 2000). Other scholars, primarily Larry Sherman (1997), find only rigorous methods, such as randomized controlled experiments, acceptable in determining what works in policing crime. However, clear conclusions about policy do not always flow from rigorous evaluations. Sherman (1992) himself found a multitude of policy dilemmas arising from the replications of his Minneapolis Domestic Violence experiment. Moreover, Kennedy and Moore (1995) argue that this type of evaluative framework may hinder the full development of problem-oriented police departments as learning organizations since police agencies can't always wait for the results of rigorous evaluations when faced with some new kind of urgent crime problem, such as carjacking or an epidemic of youth gun violence.

In contrast to current practices, the effectiveness of problem-oriented policing responses should be measured with a more appropriate standard of proof in mind. Since police officers generally are not trained to apply program evaluation methods in field settings, academic partners and police crime analysis units can be helpful. Nick Tilley (1999: 267) observes that most crime prevention evaluations suffer from "the use of simple before/after comparisons, use of short and arbitrary before-and-after periods, neglect of benchmark statistics, failure to consider other (nonintervention) causes of the changes observed, failure to test for displacement or diffusion effects, and uncritical promotion of success stories." Crime prevention evaluations also rarely use controls (similar groups, places, and individuals that did not experience the preventive measure) to rule out alternative explanations for observed decreases (Clarke, 1998). Controls reveal to the evaluator what would have happened to the target protected by the crime prevention strategy if it had not received the intervention. For instance, if crime decreases in the targeted area and remains the same or increases in the control area, it provides credible evidence that the implemented strategy actually produced the desired effect.

Not all assessments of problem-solving efforts require consideration of these evaluation issues. Nonetheless, police departments developing a knowledge base on effective methods of crime prevention should be aware of the limits of responses assessed as "effective" and consider whether these limits are relevant to their performance objectives in handling problems. The landmark problem-oriented policing project in Newport News, Virginia (Eck and Spelman, 1987) set forth a set of alternative performance objectives that provide a reasonable framework for the assessment of problem-solving responses (Scott, 2000: 80):

1. totally eliminate a problem;

2. substantially reduce a problem;

3. reduce the harm created by a problem;

4. deal with a problem better (e.g., treat people more humanely, reduce costs or increase effectiveness); and

5. remove the problem from police consideration.

Removing a problem from police consideration does not suggest that police should work to absolve themselves from responsibility for the handling of a problem; rather it means that, if the problem is shifted to another entity that handles the problem more effectively, police can claim some success in dealing with it (Scott, 2000).

Problem-oriented police often target physical and social incivilities in neighborhoods because they generate fear and cause residents to withdraw from their communities by adopting avoidance and defensive behaviors such as staying indoors and not frequenting public spaces In turn, these withdrawals from community involvement erode the neighborhood's ability to exert informal social control (Skogan, 1990; Ferraro, 1995). The diversity of potential community problems that problem-oriented police may have to address suggests that a wide array of data must be collected on a number of different dimensions to detect changes that would otherwise elude police statistics. The level of fear in a community can be monitored by victimization surveys and focus groups. While police can easily borrow questions from the numerous victimization surveys that have developed items about fear of crime, the costs associated with this form of data collection, on a large scale, may be prohibitive for many police departments (Langworthy, 1999). Focus groups, which can range from elaborate well-modulated discussions to informal meetings with citizens, may be a cost-effective way to gain insight on crime problems, but should be carefully constructed to produce information appropriate for monitoring programs. Langworthy (1999) also suggests a number of unobtrusive measures to measure fear, such as monitoring self-protective crime prevention measures like handgun sales, burglar alarm installations, and calls to the police for prevention tips.

There are also numerous methods available to monitor physical and social incivilities, such as surveys of perceptions of disorder, systematic social observation, on-site assessments (physical surveys), and archival data (Skogan, 1999; Taylor, 1999). Systematic social observation and on-site assessments involve collecting site-specific information on physical disorder (e.g., the numbers of vacant lots, abandoned buildings, and trash on the streets) and social disorder (e.g., the numbers of people loitering, drinking in public, and playing loud music). Since these methods can also be costly, Langworthy (1999) suggests mobilizing area service personnel who routinely observe communities (such as postal workers and trash collectors) to document disorder as part of their routine. Finally, archival data, such as U.S. Bureau of Census statistics and information held by planning/zoning departments, can provide indicators of decay associated with disorder, such as vacancy rates, plumbing, and ownership (Langworthy, 1999).

Several evaluations of place-oriented policing strategies have recognized the need to supplement official crime statistics and have advanced new technologies to measure disorder at specific places. For example, the Jersey City Problem-Oriented Policing in Violent Crime Places experiment used multiple indicators to assess the effects of the intervention on the problems of a place (Braga et al., 1999). Multiple indicators are often used in evaluations where program effectiveness can be complex to measure (Rossi and Freeman, 1993). These data were collected for the following purposes (see Braga, 1997 for a full methodological discussion):

1. *Emergency calls-for-service and crime incident data* to measure the program's impact on levels of violent crime and overall crime in the hot spots.

2. *Physical observations* to detect changes in physical incivilities at the place, such as vacant lots, trash, graffiti, and broken windows. The physical characteristics of the treatment locations were videotaped, coded into a computerized database and analyzed.

3. *Systematic social observations* to examine variations of social incivilities (e.g., drinking in public, loitering, and the like) in the hot spots via trained observers recording behaviors during times when these places were "hot."

4. *Interviews with key community members* to gain qualitative insight into the dynamics of the places before and after the intervention. Key community members were selected based on their unique insights on the problems of targeted places. For example, the resident manager of an elderly housing complex suffering from robberies of its residents was interviewed, rather than any one resident since he would be more aware of the general problems of the property.

These multiple indicators permitted the effectiveness of the Jersey City problem-oriented policing program to be assessed in terms of crime prevention, the abatement of social and physical disorder, reduction of fear, and citizen satisfaction with the police response.

Finally, in preventing repeat victimization, the "time-window effect" is a key issue in measuring the performance of crime prevention measures. This term is used to describe the proportion of crimes committed against particular targets within a specified period of observation. The length of the "time window" directly affects the proportion of repeat victimization that is captured (Farrell et al., 2002). Repeat victimization studies with short time windows will under-count repeat events and over-count single incident crimes (Farrell and Pease, 1993). For example, Farrell and his colleagues (2002) analyzed data on residential burglaries in Baltimore, Dallas, and San Diego for a three-year period, and compared rates of repeat victimization captured using different periods of time. They found that a one-year window captured 42 percent more repeats than a six-month window, and a three-year window captured 57 percent more repeats than a one-year window. Farrell and his colleagues (2002) argue that the typical one-year time window used by most analyses may measure at least 50 percent less repeat victimization than actually occurs. The implication of their research is that, for crime analysts measuring repeat victimization or the performance of a crime prevention intervention, longer time windows were better.

SECURING PRODUCTIVE PARTNERSHIPS

Police responses to crime problems can be greatly enhanced by securing productive partnerships with community members, other government agencies, other criminal justice agencies, and academic researchers. As Tilley (1999) observed, police are not the only custodians of data on crime and are not the only agency that can make contributions to understanding crime patterns or developing effective responses. Often, without the help of partners, police are not in the position to implement many potentially powerful crime prevention measures. Unfortunately, partnerships are often difficult to establish, and maintaining partnerships requires hard work and sensitivity. Figure 6-4 presents some key points in maintaining effective partnerships.

Figure 6-4. Keys to Effective Partnerships.

If the rhetoric of partnership is to be converted to reality, and partnerships are to deliver the promised benefits, partnerships need to be nurtured. For many agencies, ceding authority may seem threatening. Apparent additional claims on already scarce human and financial resources will be unwelcome. In many cases, the time spent on partnership work will be viewed as time spent away from the agency's "real" work. Practitioners at the sharp end will be apt to ask, "what's in it for us?" and unless there is a good answer, their enthusiasm will wane and subversion will set in. Here are some suggestions for initiating a virtuous circle of increasing reward, trust, achievement, and commitment, drawn mainly from the early experience of Britain's Safer Cities Program (Tilley, 1992). Though they may sound both pious and somewhat obvious, unsuccessful partnerships are notable for ignoring these simple strategies.

1. Begin with "quick wins" from which individual workers and agencies benefit.

2. Take opportunities to bestow "gifts" on partners in the form of funds, recognition, publicity, or expressions of appreciation.

3. Avoid individual agency (mis)appropriation of credit for collective achievements.

4. Make efforts to understand the circumstances of your potential partners – their problems, aims, traditional ways of working, and the like – and try to adapt them.

5. Avoid taking umbrage.

6. Take part in joint training.

7. Show up to meetings.

8. Avoid malicious gossip about partners.

9. Recognize problems when they arise and take advantage of helpful outsiders to help sort them out.

Source: Tilley (1999: 266). Reprinted with permission.

Community Partners

Advocates of problem-oriented policing argue that community involvement can be an important ingredient in success (Goldstein, 1990; Eck and Spelman, 1987). However, despite its acknowledged importance, community involvement remains a problem area in the development of these programs. True police-community partnerships are scarce in community and problem-oriented policing programs,in part because there are numerous difficulties in stimulating community involvement (see, e.g., Grinc, 1994; Rosenbaum, 1994; Buerger, 1994b; Weisburd and McElroy, 1988).

Maintaining order within communities is an important outcome of informal social processes beyond formal social control activities such as policing (see Bursik and Grasmick, 1993; Byrne and Sampson, 1986); thus, it is important to stimulate community involvement in problem-oriented activities. Among other benefits, citizen participation in crime prevention efforts can improve police-community relations, increase the legitimacy of police operations, reduce fear, and decrease crime and disorder (Eck and Rosenbaum, 1994). More indirectly, community and problem-oriented policing can help rebuild the social and organizational fabric of neighborhoods that previously been given up for lost, enabling residents to contribute to maintaining order in their community (Sampson, Raudenbush and Earls, 1997; Skogan, 2006). Moreover, residents involved in problem-oriented policing efforts can increase the level of guardianship in communities (Cohen and Felson, 1979), discourage crime by properly managing places (Felson, 1995), and maintain conditions and crime control gains once the police have ceased active problem-solving efforts.

Citizen Involvement in POP Programs

Unfortunately, experience has revealed that it is very difficult to get citizens involved in problem-oriented community efforts. This is especially true in disadvantaged neighborhoods that could benefit the most from such partnerships. Sadd and Grinc (1994) suggested that a lack of community involvement in poorer neighborhoods arises from generations of residents who have faced the brunt of police abuse and past experiences with seemingly endless government programs designed to improve the quality of their lives. Thus, in their examination of the Community Patrol Officer Program in New York City, Weisburd and McElroy (1988) noted that community police officers were often confronted with settings of severe social disorganization, and that such disorganization was not easily transformed into the kind of community organization envisioned by the community problem-solving philosophy.

Wesley Skogan (2006), however, reported some encouraging findings from a 13-year study of community policing in Chicago. After community policing was implemented in 1993, crime and fear dropped in the city's predominately African-American neighborhoods. Skogan (2006) also found that residents in black-majority communities were very enthusiastic about community policing and turned out in large numbers for beat meetings, neighborhood problem-solving projects, and supportive rallies. Unfortunately, by most measures, things grew worse for the city's growing Latino population. Long-time Latino residents in racially-integrated neighborhoods did well, but residents of predominately Spanish-speaking neighborhoods experienced higher levels of crime and disorder problems (Skogan, 2006). Very few residents of Latino-majority communities participated in beat meetings and other community problem-solving initiatives.

In many problem-oriented policing projects, community members serve as an information source rather than as "partners" or "co-producers" of public safety (see, e.g., Capowich and Roehl, 1994; Sadd and Grinc, 1994; Braga, 1997). Buerger (1994b: 271) suggested that the "police establishment assigns to the community a role that simply enhances the police response to crime and disorder." Often, problem-oriented officers gain extra sets of "eyes and ears" on illegal street activities, while the officers' authority and sovereignty over service provision remain essentially unchanged from their traditional role in police-citizen transactions (Braga, 1997). Research, however, suggests that many citizens are comfortable in these less prominent roles. For example, the evaluators of the eight-city Innovative Neighborhood Oriented Policing (INOP) programs collected data strongly suggesting that community members did not want to become involved in community problem-solving efforts (Sadd and Grinc, 1994). Across all eight INOP cities, the most frequently reported explanation for a lack of citizen involvement in community policing efforts was fear of retaliation from local drug dealers and gang members. Similarly, at three violent crime hot spots in the Jersey City experiment, community members who were perceived by local drug sellers and illicit loiterers as too cooperative with the police had multiple threats made on their lives (Braga, 1997). As "information sources" rather than "partners," citizens seem to reap the benefits of having a mechanism to address their concerns without changing their routine activities. In other words, they are able to go about their daily business without additional tasks or suffering the repercussions of being perceived as a community activist or working with the police.

In practice, problem-oriented police tackling a particular problem should strive to develop the level of community involvement that facilitates the development and implementation of an effective response. Sometimes, key community members will not want to participate in police efforts to control crime. In these situations, police may want to consider the use of civil remedies to induce some participation. Civil remedies are procedures and sanctions specified by civil statutes and regulations that can be used to prevent crime and disorder problems. As Green Mazerolle and Roehl (1998) described, civil remedies generally aim to persuade or coerce non-offending third parties to take responsibility and action to prevent or end criminal or nuisance behavior. Also known as "third party" policing (see Chapter 3 in this book), such approaches can include using nuisance and drug abatement statutes to require landlords and property owners to maintain drug- and nuisance-free properties through repair requirements, fines, padlocks, securing entries/exits, and property forfeiture (Green Mazerolle and Roehl, 1998).

Fortunately, community members often do want to assist the police in some capacity. For very serious crime problems that threaten the viability of a community, organized groups may be quite aggressive in seeking appropriate police action. For example, the Ten Point Coalition of activist black clergy played an important role in organizing Boston communities suffering from gang violence (see Winship and Berrien, 1999; Braga and Winship, 2006). In 1992, the Ten Point Coalition formed after gang members invaded the Morningstar Baptist Church, where a slain rival gang member was being memorialized, and the intruders attacked mourners with knives and guns. In the wake of that watershed moment, the Ten Point Coalition decided to respond to violence in their community by reaching out to drug-involved and gang-involved youth and by organizing within Boston's black community. The Ten Point clergy came to work closely with the Boston Centers for Youth and Families streetworkers program to provide at-risk youth with opportunities such as summer and after-school jobs, job skills training, educational assistance, and substance abuse counseling. Although the Ten Point coalition was initially very critical of Boston law enforcement, the two groups eventually forged a strong working relationship. Ten Point clergy and others involved in this faith-based organization accompanied police officers on home visits to the families of troubled youth and also acted as advocates for youth in the criminal justice system. These home visits and street work by the clergy were later incorporated into Operation Ceasefire's portfolio of interventions. Ten Point clergy also provided a strong moral voice at the gang forums in the presentation of Operation Ceasefire's anti-violence message.

Although they were not involved in Operation Ceasefire until after the strategy had been designed and implemented, the Ten Point Coalition played a crucial role in framing a discussion that made it much easier to speak directly about the nature of youth violence in Boston. Members of the Ceasefire Working Group could speak with relative safety about the painful realities of minority male offending and victimization, "gangs," and chronic offenders. The Ten Point clergy also made it possible for Boston's minority community to have an ongoing conversation with Boston's law enforcement agencies on legitimate and illegitimate means to control crime in the community. The clergy supported Operation Ceasefire's tight focus on violent youth. but condemned any indiscriminate, highly aggressive law enforcement sweeps that put non-violent minority youth at risk of being swept into the criminal justice system. Before the Ten Point developed its role as an intermediary, Boston's black community viewed past attempts of law enforcement agencies to monitor violent youth as illegitimate. As Christopher Winship and Jenny Berrien (1999) observed, the Ten Point Coalition evolved into an institution that provides an umbrella of legitimacy for the police to work under. With the Ten Point's approval of and involvement in Operation Ceasefire, the community supported the approach as a legitimate youth violence prevention campaign.

The Key Role of Police Legitimacy

Legitimacy is a property of legal authorities that, when it exists, leads people to feel that the actions of the police and courts are appropriate, proper, and/or just and ought to be voluntarily deferred to and followed (Tyler, 2006). In contrast to compliance based upon the fear of sanctions or the promise of rewards, legitimacy-based deference is motivated by people's internal values, and occurs irrespective of the immediate presence of legal authorities (Tyler, 1990). In particular, people are motivated to follow "legitimate" legal rules and decisions even when their behavior is not under surveillance by legal authorities. Kelman and Hamilton (1989) referred to legitimacy as "authorization," in order to emphasize the idea that a person permits an authority to determine appropriate behavior within some situation and then feels obligated to follow the directives or rules that the authority establishes. The importance of legitimacy to securing adherence to rules and deference to the decisions of legal authorities has been increasingly recognized as the limits of deterrence-based approaches to order maintenance have become more evident (Meares, 2000; Meares and Skogan, 2004).

Recent discussions of policing acknowledge the important role that policing strategies have in shaping crime, but argue that attention needs to be given to a larger framework within which the influence of police actions on police legitimacy in the eyes of the public is also studied (Skogan and Frydl, 2004). As described in Chapter 1, such concerns have fueled a series of reforms in the manner in which the police act, including community and problem-oriented policing. Research suggests that the public does not evaluate the police only in terms of their ability to fight crime. People are also sensitive to the manner through which the police exercise their authority. As a consequence, the procedural justice, or fairness, of police actions is central to police legitimacy. Practices such as racial profiling, which are viewed as unjust by many citizens, undermine police legitimacy and reduce community participation in police crime prevention efforts (Tyler and Wakslak, 2004). While the work is difficult, long-term community engagement efforts can pay large dividends in improving the quality of police-community relationships and collaborative crime prevention efforts.

For instance, in their recent article on the relationship between the Chicago Police Department and predominately African-American churches on the West Side of Chicago, Meares and Brown Corkran (2007) noted the significance of this collaboration in building the community's capacity to resist crime. Moreover, the integration of key community institutions into the partnership with police enabled the combined entities to complete other community-building goals and urban renewal projects. As in Boston, the initial relationship between the black community and the police was tense and characterized by mistrust. However, the ongoing connection between the police and church leaders led to noteworthy improvements in West Side residents' perceptions of the legitimacy of the local police in particular and local government in general (Meares and Brown Corkran, 2007). While churches played key roles in the Boston and Chicago experiences, other community institutions can also be engaged to build public trust, reduce crime, and support urban renewal.

Working Cooperatively with the Private Sector

Problem-oriented police should keep a broad conception of "community" in mind when thinking about possible partners in dealing with crime problems. In-depth case studies have revealed that, time and again, specific segments of the private sector have been very helpful in preventing crime and reducing the load on the police. Productive partnerships with the private sector have been shown to be effective in controlling a wide range of problems – from security alarm companies helping to deal with false burglar alarms in Salt Lake City, Utah (Sampson, 2007b), to contractors assisting with reducing the theft of kitchen appliances from new homes in Charlotte-Mecklenburg, North Carolina (Clarke and Goldstein, 2002), to pub and club owners helping reduce alcohol-related violence in Surfers Paradise, Queensland, Australia (Homel et al., 1997).

The International Association of Chiefs of Police estimated that there are some two million private security personnel working for nearly 90,000 individual security companies in the United States (Chamard, 2006). While private security personnel protect about 85 percent of the nation's critical infrastructure, only 5 to 10 percent of police departments are believed to have partnerships with private security (Chamard, 2006). Through partnerships with private security companies, police can gain new information about particular crimes and access specialized knowledge and technology. Police-private security partnerships can provide joint security for business improvement districts in high-crime areas and undertake joint efforts to prevent business crimes such as check fraud, shoplifting, and robbery (Chamard, 2006).

Finally, private sector advertising agencies can be very helpful in designing and implementing crime prevention publicity campaigns. As part of their Project Safe Neighborhoods gang violence reduction initiative (see Chapter 3), the U.S. Attorney's Office and the Lowell, Massachusetts Police Department hired a private company to assist in setting up a series of public service announcements, billboards, and fliers to explain both the harsh penalties for gun crimes and the social services available to gang members who wanted to change their lifestyles (Braga et al., 2006). More generally, when designed properly, crime prevention publicity campaigns can be a helpful tool in reducing crime. These efforts can help remove crime opportunities by teaching and encouraging the public to adopt better self-protection measures, or they can warn offenders of increased police vigilance or improved police practices (see Barthe, 2006 and Figure 6-5). For example, in their evaluation of burglary prevention publicity campaigns in England, Johnson and Bowers (2003) found that the effectiveness of burglary prevention strategies was significantly enhanced by publicity and that promoting prevention plans prior to their implementation produced an anticipatory reduction in burglary before the strategies were actually in place.

Partnerships with Other Agencies

One of the least discussed and least well-implemented components of community and problem-oriented policing around the country is inter-agency involvement. The cooperation of other municipal, state, and federal agencies is a key to implementing alternative responses to crime and disorder problems. Local government agencies, such as public works departments, can be very helpful in implementing problem-oriented interventions. Problem-oriented police departments should develop general resource books that explain the functions of the different governmental agencies, describe what services each has to offer, and outline the proper protocol for making service requests (Braga, 1997). The knowledge developed by problem-oriented officers in working with these city agencies should be documented, ideally with participation of the various agencies, and disseminated to all officers in the department.

Obtaining many responses from city agencies, such as razing abandoned buildings and cleaning vacant lots, takes time. These delays result from the substantial amount of time it takes to identify and contact property owners, to handle legalities, to plan the specifics of the job (e.g., rerouting water lines or electrical systems), and to allocate the resources. These delays should be expected, and officers need to develop both short-term and longer-term responses to crime problems that require advanced situational responses. For example, if the long-term plan to alleviate crime within a city block is to raze an abandoned building that serves as a magnet for illicit activity, then the officers should also implement short term responses such as boarding the doors and windows shut or initiating an aggressive order-maintenance patrol of the property. These actions can provide immediate relief to suffering communities until the longer-term plan is fulfilled.

Criminal justice agencies work largely independently of each other, often at cross-purposes, often without coordination, and often in an atmosphere of distrust and dislike (Kennedy, 2002b). This is also often true of

Figure 6-5. Best Practices in Victim-Oriented and Offender-Oriented Crime Prevention Publicity Campaigns.

Source: Barthe (2006: 6, 8 and 11).

Publicity directed at **VICTIMS** can advertise:

- self-protection techniques
- new ways to report crime
- locations of police facilities or resources
- dangerous areas
- offenders living in the area (e.g., sex offenders)
- neighborhood crime problem

Summary of Victim-Oriented Campaigns

- Victim-oriented campaigns work best when carried out in small geographic areas.
- Victim campaigns should focus on specific crime types.
- General victim campaigns are rarely successful in changing prevention behaviors.
- Many victim campaigns fail to reach the intended audiences with the message.
- Timeliness and relevance are key to campaign success.
- The campaign may have an indirect positive effect of warning offenders.

Publicity directed at **OFFENDERS** can advertise:

- police techniques or future police crackdowns
- penalties or the risk of apprehension for certain crimes
- results of past crackdowns or police operations
- knowledge or an illicit market or drug trade
- legislative changes

Summary of Offender-Oriented Campaigns

- Advertise increased risks and reduced rewards.
- Avoid moral appeals; instead, focus on the likelihood of immediate detection and arrest.
- The message should be publicized when and where offenders can see it.
- Offender-oriented campaigns work best when carried out in small geographic areas.
- Offender campaigns should focus on specific crime types.
- Timeliness and relevance are key to campaign success.

different units operating within agencies. The ability of Boston (as well as other cities experimenting with the "pulling levers" approach to controlling violent offenders) to deliver a meaningful violence prevention intervention was based on convening an interagency working group of line-level personnel with decision-making power that could assemble a wide range of incentives and disincentives (Braga et al., 2002). Since all criminal justice agencies were represented, the working group could customize its responses to violent behavior by considering a varied menu of possible interventions, such as changes in probation and parole conditions, the reopening of "cold" cases, and the use of intensified career criminal prosecutions. It was also important to place a locus of responsibility for reducing violence on the group. Prior to the creation of the working groups, no one in these cities was responsible for developing and implementing an overall strategy for reducing violence.

In recent years, the prosecutor's role in the larger enterprise of promoting public safety has been reconsidered as federal, state, and local prosecutors' offices have been experimenting with the "community prosecution" model (Coles and Kelling, 1999; Glazer, 1999). Under this model, prosecutors are assigned to a specific geographic area and have responsibility for prosecuting all or most of the crimes in that area. Prosecutors are expected to learn about the crime and disorder concerns of the community in their areas and are challenged to move beyond simply prosecuting individual cases by functioning as a solver of public safety problems (Goldstock, 1991). Such an orientation by prosecutors toward larger community concerns would provide obvious benefits to problem-oriented police. Unfortunately, this movement is still in its infancy. As Scott (2000: 125) suggested:

> Prosecutors' failure to fully engage in a problem-oriented approach to reducing crime, disorder and fear is unfortunate for two related reasons. First, without prosecutors, a valuable perspective on crime problems is missing from many police-led initiatives. Prosecutors are better aware of how cases are processed through the court system and, accordingly, are more aware of the effectiveness of existing means for disposing of cases. Prosecutors also are more aware of the range of legal responses that might be used to address a particular problem, as well as some of the risks of alternative approaches. Prosecutors have access to data and judges, and research skills the police often lack. When prosecutors are open-minded and take a broad perspective on their role, they can greatly facilitate problem-oriented policing. The second reason it is unfortunate that prosecutors are not more engaged in problem-oriented policing is that their absence conveys a powerful signal to the police that problem-solving is not

valued as highly as criminal investigation. This can discourage the police from investing more fully in problem solving. Detectives are especially sensitive to prosecutors' signals. Prosecutors' general disengagement with problem-oriented policing partially explains why so few police detectives have engaged in the concept, as well.

Partnerships with Academic Researchers

Many of the successful problem-oriented policing projects described in this book benefited from partnerships between police agencies and academic researchers. Often, partnerships between academics and police practitioners have been characterized by role conflicts, such as researchers reporting the "bad news" that an evaluated program was not effective in preventing crime. For academic researchers, success or failure matters less than commitment to the development of knowledge on what does or doesn't work in preventing crime (Weisburd, 1994). For the police, this news could be interpreted as accusing them of personal failure, and the skepticism of academics may be found irritating (Weisburd, 1994).

In recent years, partnerships between police and academics have become much more collaborative and focused on working together in addressing crime problems. Academics have much to offer in the advancement of problem analysis. In addition to providing training in analytic methods and concepts and developing a body of problem-analysis literature, academics can conduct problem analyses and high-quality action research evaluations in partnership with criminal justice agencies. While police departments should position themselves to internally support problem-oriented efforts with well-functioning crime analysis units, collaborations with outside researchers can be quite potent and should be encouraged. For example, in Charlotte-Mecklenburg, North Carolina Clarke and Goldstein (2002: 118-119) used their experience and knowledge to move the theft-reduction project forward by drawing attention to:

1. having realistic expectations about the results of enforcement efforts;

2. focusing the project on a highly specific problem, or form of crime (i.e., appliance theft);

3. supplementing the most common form of "hot spot" mapping with carefully developed information about the environment being mapped (i.e., the stage of construction reached and the identity of the different builders operating in the subdivisions);

4. relating the absolute numbers of appliance thefts to the number of vulnerable homes, thereby producing suitable measures of risks before reaching conclusions about trends or patterns in these thefts;

5. using acquired data to compare security practices and theft risks among builders, and to engage builders in assuming some responsibility for solving the problem;

6. assuring that, in the language of routine activity theory, there are capable guardians of vulnerable targets;

7. being alert to the possibility of diffusion of benefits, and not being deterred from preventive action by the threat of displacement;

8. monitoring closely the process of implementation; and,

9. utilizing an evaluation design that would permit definitive conclusions about the value of the response.

In the Boston "pulling levers" project, the research conducted by Harvard University researchers helped support the working group process in important ways (Kennedy et al., 2001). The activities of the research team departed from the traditional research and evaluation roles usually played by academics (see, e.g., Sherman, 1991). The integrated research/practitioner partnerships in the working group closely resembled policy analysis exercises that blend research, policy design, action, and evaluation (Kennedy and Moore, 1995). The Harvard team essentially provided "real-time" social science aimed at: refining the working group's understanding of the problem; creating information products for both strategic and tactical use; testing – often in very elementary, but nevertheless valid ways – prospective intervention ideas; and maintaining a focus on clear outcomes and the evaluation of performance (Braga et al., 2002). None of the research was terribly sophisticated methodologically. But the ability to pin down key issues – such as where guns were coming from, what guns gang members favored, who was killing and being killed, and what role was played by gangs and gang conflict – kept the working group moving on solid ground, helped participating agencies understand the logic of the proposed intervention (and the relative illogic of at least some competing interventions), and helped justify the intervention to the public.

Unfortunately, the number of academics with the experience and expertise in working with police departments on problem analysis and response development is relatively small (Boba, 2003). The challenge to the field is to increase these collaborations by educating police departments on the benefits of working with academics and to encourage uninvolved academics to learn more about and participate in problem analysis and problem-oriented policing projects. Establishing new and more productive relationships will require flexibility and openness among both parties. Academics cannot be condescending in their relationships with the police; they must demonstrate a genuine interest in helping the police to be more effective, and must select research methodologies that produce credible results but are not disproportionately demanding, given the limits of available data and the nature of the strategy being evaluated (Goldstein, 2003). The police must recognize that quality research takes time and patience, that researchers must be objective and that they require facts to support conclusions, and that evaluations may produce results that could be interpreted as critical of past and current operations (Goldstein, 2003).

7. THE PROBLEM OF DISPLACEMENT

Displacement is the notion that efforts to eliminate crimes at specific places or that are generated by specific situations will simply cause criminal activity to move elsewhere, be committed in another way, or even be manifested as another type of crime, thus negating any crime control gains (Repetto, 1976). This perspective on the crime prevention effectiveness of police efforts to control crime problems developed from dispositional theories of criminal motivations, and the views of these skeptics were supported by early studies of opportunity-reducing measures (Gabor, 1990; Clarke, 1980). For instance, although exact fare systems reduced the number of robberies on New York City buses, a corresponding increase in robberies occurred in the subways (Chaiken et al., 1974). And Mayhew et al. (1980) found that reductions in the theft of newer cars after the implementation of a new law in England – which required all new domestic and imported cars to be fitted with steering column locks – were offset by displacement to older, unprotected autos. After a successful police crackdown on street crimes in one New York City precinct, Press (1971) found that street crimes had increased in surrounding precincts. Finally, traditional police efforts to control street level drug markets have been found to be quite susceptible to spatial, temporal, and tactical displacement. Offenders have been found to change the time and place they sell drugs and use different tactics to sell drugs, such as hiring lookouts to detect police surveillance, wearing disguises, and inventing complex transaction schemes (see Eck, 1993b; Sherman, 1990; Caulkins, 1992).

These perspectives have been challenged by recent research studies suggesting that crime displacement is not an inevitable outcome of focused police efforts to prevent crime problems. Many evaluations have found crime displacement to be limited or completely absent (Hesseling, 1994). There is also a growing body of evidence suggesting that these strategies can actually reduce crime in the areas surrounding the target places; this phenomenon is termed "diffusion of crime control benefits" (Clarke and Weisburd, 1994). This chapter briefly discusses the importance of measuring displacement and diffusion effects when evaluating problem-oriented policing initiatives and examines the existing research that suggests displacement is not an unavoidable outcome of crime prevention strategies.

The Importance of Measuring Displacement and Diffusion Effects

Displacement can take many different forms (Gabor, 1990), and it is a complex phenomenon to measure (see Barr and Pease, 1990). Most studies of crime prevention efforts are designed to measure main effects, so the measurement of displacement is often neglected until it is time to defend claims of crime control gains. Some researchers suggest that evaluations should be planned to study both main effects and possible displacement or diffusion effects (Weisburd and Green, 1995b). Others argue that anticipating and measuring displacement could be an import tool in optimizing crime prevention gains by maximizing the amount of disruption that potentially displaced offenders experience (Barnes, 1995).

The research literature identifies six types of displacement:

- *spatial* – offenders move away from protected areas to new locations where crime is easier to commit;

- *temporal* – offenders perpetrate crimes at time that are less risky;

- *target* – difficult targets are given up in favor of those that are easily hit;

- *tactical* – tactics are changed to get around crime prevention measures;

- *perpetrator* – new offenders take the place of those who move, quit, or are apprehended; and,

- *type of crime* – offenders commit another type of crime if one type becomes too difficult to commit (Barnes, 1995).

Due to data limits, the current state-of-the-art in assessing displacement has focused mostly on spatial displacement, which means figuring out if crime was simply moved elsewhere. However, even measuring spatial displacement is quite difficult. While it seems very straightforward to establish an intervention target area and surrounding displacement area, the ability to measure displacement is affected by the impact of the intervention as well as the size of both the target area and the displacement zone and their existing crime levels (Harries, 1999). In their examination of spatial displacement associated with the Minneapolis Hot Spots Patrol Experiment, Weisburd and Green (1995b: 354) explained:

> We decided upon a two-block radius for the "catchment" area because we felt it a reasonable compromise between competing problems of washout of displacement impact and a failure to provide adequate distance to identify immediate spatial displacement. While we recognized at the outset that we would miss the movement of crime more than two blocks away from a hot spot, given our measure of crime as a general rather than specific indicator we did not think it practical to identify all potential places that might provide opportunity for displaced offenders.

In their evaluation of the Jersey City Drug Markets Analysis Program, Weisburd and Green (1995a) pioneered another approach known as measuring "offender movement patterns," which involved examining the time sequencing of offender arrest locations to determine whether specific individuals were arrested for selling drugs in locations outside of the targeted drug markets. Weisburd and Green (1994) also found offender movement analysis to be a robust method of creating boundaries around drug markets due to the sellers' high degree of territoriality with respect to drug turf. While measuring displacement is more complex than one might think, it is certainly a worthwhile pursuit that analysts should consider on a case-by-case basis (Harries, 1999). Nonetheless, as Weisburd and Green (1995b: 358) concluded: "one must be extraordinarily cautious in analyzing and interpreting data on immediate spatial displacement. Statistics that appear solid on paper may reflect the difficulties of analyzing this process as much as any real substantive findings."

Empirical studies also point to the difficulty of detecting displacement effects because the potential manifestations of displacement are quite diverse. As Barr and Pease (1990: 293) suggested:

> If, in truth, displacement is complete, some displaced crime will probably fall outside the areas and types of crime being studied or be so dispersed as to be masked by background variation. In such an event, the optimist would speculate about why the unmeasured areas or types of crime probably escaped displaced crime, while the pessimist would speculate why they probably did not. No research study, however massive, is likely to resolve the issue. The wider the scope of the study in terms of types of crimes and places, the thinner

the patina of displaced crime could be spread across them; thus disappearing into the realm of measurement error.

Different forms of displacement can also occur in combination. As Hesseling (1994: 198) observed: " . . . a burglar may move to a different neighborhood, employ new tactics, *and* offend at a different time of day. . . . it may be impossible to confirm empirically the existence or magnitude of displacement." Hesseling further argued that researchers must be aware of factors independent of the crime control intervention that could produce what appears to be a displacement effect, such as changes in offender populations, opportunity structures, and overall crime rate trends. While diffusion effects are likely to be difficult to assess, a failure to examine diffusion effects may mean that program evaluators are underestimating the crime control benefits of interventions (Clarke and Weisburd, 1994). Although measurement of displacement and diffusion effects is very complex, evaluations of crime control strategies must assess the possibility of displacement and diffusion before any conclusions can be made about the overall effectiveness of the intervention.

Detecting displacement effects after the implementation of a crime prevention strategy should not necessarily be viewed as a "failure." The elimination of one easy opportunity and the identification of another can represent important steps in dealing with multifaceted and complex crime problems. For instance, Boston's Operation Ceasefire strategy to disrupt illegal gun sales to criminals and youth resulted in a significant reduction in the recovery of new handguns in crime (discussed in Chapter 4 on controlling high-rate offenders). However, the evaluation also found that, when it became difficult to acquire new handguns, criminals tended to acquire older handguns to commit their crimes (Braga and Pierce, 2005). Illegal gun traffickers sought to avoid detection by diverting older, second-hand guns recently purchased through less-regulated primary and secondary market sources. The substitution effect suggested that the problem-oriented gun market disruption strategy had a significant impact on one mode of illegal gun acquisition and law enforcement agencies needed to shut down other supply lines to reduce the overall prevalence of guns on Boston streets. As a result of the evaluation, local, state, federal law enforcement agencies started analyzing Massachusetts firearms purchase and sales data to identify illegal diversions of secondhand guns from Massachusetts licensed dealers and private residents (Braga and Pierce, 2005).

Displacement is Not an Unavoidable Outcome of Crime Prevention Efforts

Recent studies have indicated that the purported inevitability of displacement was very much overestimated. Several reviews of situational crime prevention measures have concluded that crime displacement was either absent or incomplete (Gabor, 1990; Clarke, 1992; Hesseling, 1994). A recent review of hot spots policing initiatives revealed that, when displacement was measured, surrounding areas often experienced unintended crime reductions rather than crime increases (Braga, 2001, 2005a). In another example, Matthews (1990) reported that prostitutes were not displaced to other locations in London after the "red-light" district was cleaned up by police officers. Neither the Jersey City Problem-Oriented Policing in Violent Places project (Braga et al., 1999), the Lowell Policing Crime and Disorder Hot Spots project (Braga and Bond, 2007), nor the Kansas City Gun project (Sherman and Rogan, 1995b) discussed in Chapter 3, resulted in the significant displacement of crime to surrounding areas. Even when displacement is present, it is rarely complete. For example, in New York City's crackdown on street crimes, the estimate of displaced crime was less than the reduction of crime in the targeted precinct (Press, 1971).

Offenders are most likely to displace when other crime targets share the same "choice-structuring properties" as the original crime opportunity structure (Cornish and Clarke, 1987). But as Clarke (1995) suggested, the easy and/or profitable criminal opportunities of the targeted offenses may not be available elsewhere. Moreover, the level of displacement may be dependent on the offender's familiarity with alternative tactics, places, times and targets. As Bennett and Wright's (1984) interview research on residential burglars revealed, only 40 percent of their respondents would seek targets elsewhere if their original opportunities were blocked. Similarly, in a study of armed robberies, a lack of displacement from newly protected banks to alternative targets, such as convenience stores and gas stations, was attributed to smaller cash bounties that were not as attractive to organized robbery gangs (Clarke et al., 1991). Likewise, the reductions in suicides from the detoxification of domestic gas in England and Wales were not followed by substantial increases in other suicide techniques (Clarke and Mayhew, 1988) because the alternative methods were not as readily available, painless, or lethal. Hesseling's (1994) review of ethnographic studies of serious offenders (imprisoned robbers, burglars, and drug addicts) and blocked criminal opportunities suggested that between one-half and two-thirds of these offenders were likely to displace. However, he also argued that these committed offenders were not representative of general criminal populations; it is very probable that less committed offenders would be less likely to displace.

Beyond the absence of complete displacement, Barr and Pease (1990) argued that displacement could be "benign" if it was to lesser crimes, such as from burglary to shoplifting, or if victimization became more evenly distributed so that a few victims would not suffer disproportionate amounts of crime. In support of these assertions, Gabor et al.'s (1987) study of imprisoned inmates found that criminals who desisted from armed robbery had shifted their focus to lesser forms of criminality such as fraud and drug selling.

Hesseling (1994) reviewed 55 studies on crime prevention measures that had examined evidence of displacement. Thirty-three studies reported some form of displacement. No study reported complete crime displacement; in fact, most studies observed that the displacement was very limited in scope. The forms of displacement that were most likely to occur were temporal, target, and spatial – the types that required the least amount of effort on the part of the offender. Hesseling (1994) suggested that the costs associated with these types of displacement were lower than the costs associated with changes in offense or tactics. Twenty-two of the studies did not report any evidence of displacement, and six of the studies reported unexpected beneficial effects of reducing crime in adjacent areas.

Diffusion of Crime Control Benefits

Several scholars have suggested that crime prevention efforts may result in the complete opposite of displacement – that anticipated crime control benefits may be greater than expected and "spill over" into places beyond the target areas. Generally referred to as "diffusion of benefits" (Clarke and Weisburd, 1994), these unexpected benefits have been reported by a number of studies on crime prevention measures. For example, Chaiken et al. (1974) found that sharp increases in police patrol in the New York City subway between the hours of 8:00 pm and 4:00 am decreased robbery rates during both the day and night hours. Poyner's (1988) evaluation of the use of closed-circuit television to combat vandalism and graffiti in a fleet of 80 double-deck buses in northern England reported that vandalism and graffiti declined for the entire fleet – even though only two buses were protected by live cameras and three buses had dummy cameras installed. The Jersey City Drug Market Analysis Experiment revealed that drug-related calls-for-service declined in two-block buffer zones constructed around experimental hot spots as compared to catchment zones surrounding the control locations (Weisburd and Green, 1995a). Similarly, Green (1996) found improvements in the physical appearance and reductions in the number of police contacts in housing units surrounding "nuisance" addresses targeted by the Oakland Beat Health Program.

Using a rational choice framework, Clarke and Weisburd (1994) classified diffusion effects into two processes – deterrence and discouragement. In the deterrent diffusion process, offenders may overestimate the reach of the crime control measure and believe that they face a greater risk of arrest than is the case. Sherman (1990) described this effect as the "free bonus" of deterrence beyond the period that a police crackdown is actually in force. Poyner's (1988) evaluation of the use of CCTV on buses to prevent graffiti and vandalism exemplifies the deterrent diffusion process: "the children have learned . . . that the cameras will enable misbehaving individuals to be picked out and that action will be taken. However, what they do not know is how extensive the risk is. They appear to believe that most buses have cameras, or at least they are uncertain about which buses have cameras" (Poyner, 1988: 50).

Alternatively, discouragement of offenders may cause crime control benefits to diffuse to other places, targets and times. According to the rational choice perspective, offenders consider effort and reward, in addition to the risk of apprehension. Offenders may become discouraged from crime if the amount of effort is not commensurate with the reward. Thus, the replacement of coin-fed gas and electricity meters with ordinary billed meters in residences that suffered repeat victimization caused a reduction in burglary in the protected homes as well as other homes across the Kirkholt estate (Pease, 1991). The burglars were uncertain which homes in the estate still had the profitable coin-fed meters; the increased amount of effort necessary to locate a residence that still had the coin-fed version outweighed the rewards of finding the device. Similarly, Decker's (1972) evaluation of slug-rejecter devices on parking meters found a decline in slug use in control areas where the devices had not been installed on the meters. This effect was presumably explained by the inability of prospective offenders to distinguish easily between parking meters that had the device and those that did not.

A recent controlled study of displacement and diffusion effects generated by intensive police interventions in two hot spots areas in Jersey City found that the most likely outcome of focused crime prevention efforts was a diffusion of crime control benefits to the surrounding areas (Weisburd, Wyckoff, Ready, Eck, Hinkle, and Gajewski, 2006). Qualitative data collected by Weisburd and his colleagues suggested that spatial movement from the targeted crime sites involved substantial effort and risk by offenders. Offenders interviewed in the study described factors that inhibited spatial displacement, including a) the importance to offenders of operating in familiar territory, and b) the social organization of illicit activities at hot spots, which often precluded easy movement to other areas that offer crime opportunities. Prostitutes, for example, were found to work near to their homes, and they were described as being uncomfortable moving to other areas where different types of people worked and different types of clients were found. Prostitutes and drug dealers in the study said it was important that a place be familiar to their clients, and some offenders also talked of the dangers of encroaching on the territories of offenders in other hot spots. Eck (1993a) described this phenomenon as "familiarity decay," arguing that offenders will avoid areas that they are unfamiliar with. According to a dealer arrested at a drug crime place, it was difficult to move because "the money won't be the same," he "would have to start from scratch," and it "takes time to build up customers" (Weisburd et al., 2006: 578). Commenting on the importance of having regular customers in maintaining personal safety and the difficulty of changing locations, a prostitute interviewed at the high-activity prostitution area stated:

> If they aren't regulars, I try to feel them out. I use precautions. I never will get into a car with two men. I always check the doors to make sure that I can get out if I need to, like if an emergency arises, like a guy trying to hurt me. I will always go into an area I know. This way, if I need help, I know that somehow I can find someone or get someone's attention. But, in the same way, I don't go into an area that would give away what I am doing and get me arrested. I basically don't let guys take me where they want to go. If they insist on this, then I make them pay me up front, before the zipper goes down.

> I walked over to the cemetery and I didn't think I'd make money. It was unfamiliar to me . . . I didn't know the guys (clients). On Cornelison you recognize the guys. I know from being out there everyday (on Cornelison), the cars, the faces. It's different. In my area, I know the people. Up on "the hill" – I don't really know the people at that end of town (Weisburd et al., 2006: 578-579).

These perspectives suggest why offenders may not simply move around the corner, or possibly to other areas, in response to a police intervention.

Summary. Research reveals that problem-oriented policing interventions at places do not inevitably lead to the displacement of crime problems to other places, times, or crime commission techniques. In fact, unintended crime prevention benefits may be extended to unprotected targets. Police officers designing crime prevention strategies should measure displacement and diffusion effects to determine the true crime prevention effects of their initiatives. In the planning of the problem-oriented interventions, officers should also consider and anticipate the likely avenues for displacement to occur. For instance, when dealing with crime hot spots, nearby places with criminal opportunities similar to that of the targeted place should be monitored closely and received focused police attention if crime problems develop.

8. FINAL THOUGHTS

The substance and implementation of many problem-oriented policing projects are limited due to shortcomings in the linkages between analysis and response. Environmental criminology and other selected perspectives on offending and criminal opportunities (see Chapters 1 and 3) have a lot to offer the police in thinking about crime problems and developing effective responses. It is important to recognize, however, that the problem-oriented policing approach does not depend on any one crime prevention theory for its viability. The practice of problem-oriented policing is essentially about insight, imagination, and creativity. Assembling crime theories, research evidence, and practical case studies in a transparent way is one method of moving the problem-oriented process closer to the original concept as envisioned by Herman Goldstein (1979). Unfortunately, criminological research is usually conducted outside police agencies and is often inaccessible to the police.

This book represents one attempt to bring this knowledge to problem-oriented police personnel. While it breaks some new ground in the depth of coverage of theoretical concepts, it certainly isn't the first volume to try to connect crime prevention research to the practice of policing. Problem-oriented policing advocates such as Ronald Clarke, John Eck, Herman Goldstein, Peter Homel, David Kennedy, Johannes Knutsson, Gloria Laycock, Rana Sampson, Michael Scott, Nick Tilley, and Deborah Lamm Weisel, have made a concerted effort to disseminate research methodologies, theoretical insights, and research findings to the police and the communities they serve. Much has changed since the publication of the first edition of this book. As described in Chapter 6, through Internet searches, crime prevention scholars and police practitioners can now easily access insightful research that provides evidence-based guidance in identifying and analyzing problems, developing and implementing responses, and evaluating crime prevention strategies.

The research evidence presented in this book underscores the promise that problem-oriented policing holds as a fundamentally sound approach to controlling crime and disorder problems. Indeed, the pioneers of this young and evolving field have accomplished much since Herman Goldstein first presented the concept in 1979. Yet, it is important to recognize that problem-oriented policing is still in its formative stages and much work still needs to be done. Our knowledge about the most effective and economical ways in which to address problems is very limited, and often primitive. We are still only at the beginning in testing the value of specific strategies for dealing with specific crime problems. The problem-oriented policing movement is at a stage where, through greater involvement of the police and those working closer with them, its practice can be further honed and developed by improved conceptualization of crime and disorder problems and greater creativity in the search for effective responses.

While our knowledge about the effects of problem-oriented interventions on specific crime problems is still developing, there is much reason for optimism about the future of problem-oriented policing. The last two decades represented a period of innovation which demonstrated that police can prevent crime and can improve their relationships with the communities they serve. In the near future, we shouldn't anticipate the dramatic strategic innovations that characterized the 1980s and 1990s. Rather, we should expect further refinement of our knowledge of "what works" in policing, under what circumstances particular strategies may work, and why these strategies are effective in improving police performance. The challenge for the future of problem-oriented policing is to continue making progress in further developing and implementing promising crime prevention strategies, while simultaneously addressing the new problems of public safety that have been created by the post-9/11 threat of terrorism and the need for police commitment to homeland security.

REFERENCES

Abrahamse, A., P. Ebener, P. Greenwood, N. Fitzgerald and T. Kosin. (1991). "An Experimental Evaluation of the Phoenix Repeat Offender Program." *Justice Quarterly* 8: 141-168.

Alpert, G., and M.H. Moore. (1993). "Measuring Police Performance in the New Paradigm of Policing." In: Princeton Study Group on Criminal Justice Performance Measures (ed.), *Performance Measures for the Criminal Justice System.* Washington, DC: Bureau of Justice Statistics.

Altizio, A., and D. York. (2007). *The Problem of Robbery of Convenience Stores.* (Problem-Oriented Guides for Police Series,no. 49.) Washington, DC: U.S. Department of Justice, Office of Community Oriented Policing Services.

Anderson, D., and K. Pease. (1997). "Biting Back: Preventing Repeat Burglary and Car Crime in Huddersfield." In: R.V. Clarke (ed.), *Situational Crime Prevention: Successful Case Studies.* (2nd ed.). Monsey, NY: Criminal Justice Press.

Barnes, G. (1995). "Defining and Optimizing Displacement." In: J. Eck and D. Weisburd (eds.), *Crime and Place.* (Crime Prevention Studies, vol. 4.) Monsey, NY: Criminal Justice Press.

Barr, R., and K. Pease. (1990). "Crime Placement, Displacement, and Deflection." In: M. Tonry and N. Morris (eds.), *Crime and Justice: A Review of Research,* vol. 12. Chicago, IL: University of Chicago Press.

Barthe, E. (2006). *Crime Prevention Publicity Campaigns.* (Problem-Oriented Guides for Police, Response Guides Series, no. 49.) Washington, DC: U.S. Department of Justice, Office of Community Oriented Policing Services.

Beha, J.A. (1977). " 'And Nobody Can Get You Out:' The Impact of a Mandatory Prison Sentence for the Illegal Carrying of a Firearm on the Use of Firearms and on the Administration of Criminal Justice in Boston - Part I." *Boston University Law Review* 57: 96-146.

Bennett, T., and R. Wright. (1984). *Burglars on Burglary.* Franborough, Hants, UK: Gower.

Benson, B.L., B.D. Mast and D. Rasmussen. (2000). "Can Police Deter Drunk Driving?" *Applied Economics* 32: 357-366.

Bichler, G., and R.V. Clarke. (1996). "Eliminating Pay Phone Toll Fraud at the Port Authority Bus Terminal in Manhattan." In: R.V. Clarke (ed.), *Preventing Mass*

Transit Crime. (Crime Prevention Studies, vol. 6.) Monsey, NY: Criminal Justice Press.

Bittner, E. (1970). *The Functions of the Police in Modern Society.* New York: Aronson.

Black, D. (1970). "The Production of Crime Rates." *American Sociological Review* 35: 733-748.

Block, C.R. (1997). "The GeoArchive: An Information Foundation for Community Policing." In: D. Weisburd and J.T. McEwen (eds.), *Crime Mapping and Crime Prevention*. (Crime Prevention Studies, vol. 8.) Monsey, NY: Criminal Justice Press.

Block, C.R., and R. Block. (1993). *Street Gang Crime in Chicago.* (Research in Brief series.) Washington, DC: National Institute of Justice, U.S. Department of Justice.

Block, R., and C. Block. (1995). "Space, Place and Crime: Hot Spot Areas and Hot Places of Liquor-Related Crime." In: J. Eck and D. Weisburd (eds.), *Crime and Place*. (Crime Prevention Studies, vol. 4.) Monsey, NY: Criminal Justice Press.

Blumstein, A. (1995). "Youth Violence, Guns, and the Illicit Drug Industry." *Journal of Criminal Law and Criminology* 86: 10-36.

Blumstein, A., J. Cohen and D. Nagin (eds.), (1978). *Deterrence and Incapacitation: Estimating the Effects of Criminal Sanctions on Crime Rates.* Washington, DC: National Academy of Sciences.

Blumstein, A., J. Cohen, J. Roth and C. Visher (eds.), (1986). *Criminal Careers and Career Criminals.* Washington, DC: National Academy Press.

Boba, R. (2003). *Problem Analysis in Policing.* Washington, DC: Police Foundation.

Bowling, B. (1999). "The Rise and Fall of New York Murder: Zero Tolerance or Crack's Decline?" *British Journal of Criminology* 39: 531-554.

Boydstun, J., R. Mekemson, M. Minton and W. Keesling. (1981). *Evaluation of the San Diego Police Department's Career Criminal Program.* San Diego, CA: Systems Development Corporation.

Braga, A.A. (1997). "Solving Violent Crime Problems: An Evaluation of the Jersey City Police Department's Pilot Program to Control Violent Places." Doctoral dissertation, Rutgers University. Ann Arbor, MI: University Microfilms International.

———— (2001). "The Effects of Hot Spots Policing on Crime." *Annals of the American Academy of Political and Social Science* 455: 104-125.

———— (2005a). "Hot Spots Policing and Crime Prevention: A Systematic Review of Randomized Controlled Trials." *Journal of Experimental Criminology* 1: 317-342.

———— (2005b). "Analyzing Homicide Problems: Practical Approaches to Developing a Policy-relevant Description of Serious Urban Violence." *Security Journal* 18: 17-32.

———— (2008, forthcoming). "Pulling Levers Focused Deterrence Strategies and the Prevention of Gun Homicide." *Journal of Criminal Justice* 36.

Braga, A.A., and B.J. Bond. (2007). *Policing Crime and Disorder Hot Spots: A Randomized Controlled Trial.* Final report submitted to the Massachusetts Executive Office of Public Safety. Cambridge, MA: Harvard University, John F. Kennedy School of Government.

Braga, A.A., and R.V. Clarke. (1994). "Improved Radios and More Stripped Cars in Germany: A Routine Activities Analysis." *Security Journal* 5: 154-159

Braga, A.A., P.J. Cook, D.M. Kennedy and M.H. Moore. (2002a). "The Illegal Supply of Firearms." In: M. Tonry (ed.), *Crime and Justice: A Review of Research*, vol. 29. Chicago, IL: University of Chicago Press.

Braga, A.A., L. Green, D. Weisburd and F. Gajewski. (1994). "Police Perceptions of Street-level Narcotics Activity: Evaluating Drug Buys as a Research Tool." *American Journal of Police* 13: 37-58.

Braga, A.A., and D.M. Kennedy. (2002). "Reducing Gang Violence in Boston." In: W.L. Reed and S.H. Decker, *Responding to Gangs: Evaluation and Research*. Washington, DC: National Institute of Justice, U.S. Department of Justice.

Braga, A.A., D.M. Kennedy and G. Tita. (2002b). "New Approaches to the Strategic Prevention of Gang and Group-Involved Violence." In: C.R. Huff (ed.), *Gangs in America*. (3rd ed.). Newbury Park, CA: Sage Publications.

Braga, A.A., D.M. Kennedy, E.J. Waring and A.M. Piehl. (2001). "Problem-Oriented Policing, Deterrence, and Youth Violence: An Evaluation of Boston's Operation Ceasefire." *Journal of Research in Crime and Delinquency* 38: 195-225.

Braga, A.A., J. McDevitt, and G.L. Pierce. (2006). "Understanding and Preventing Gang Violence: Problem Analysis and Response Development in Lowell, Massachusetts." *Police Quarterly* 9: 20-46.

Braga, A.A., A. M. Piehl, and D. M. Kennedy. (1999). "Youth Homicide in Boston: An Assessment of Supplementary Homicide Reports." *Homicide Studies* 3: 277-299.

Braga, A.A., and G. L. Pierce. (2005). "Disrupting Illegal Firearms Markets in Boston: The Effects of Operation Ceasefire on the Supply of New Handguns to Criminals." *Criminology and Public Policy* 4: 717-748.

Braga, A.A., G. L. Pierce, J. McDevitt, B. J. Bond, and S. Cronin. (2008, forthcoming). "The Strategic Prevention of Gun Violence Among Gang-Involved Offenders." *Justice Quarterly* 25.

Braga, A.A., and D.L. Weisburd. (2006). "Problem-Oriented Policing: The Disconnect Between Principles and Practice." In: D.L. Weisburd and A.A. Braga (eds.), *Police Innovation: Contrasting Perspectives*. New York: Cambridge University Press.

Braga, A.A., D.L. Weisburd, E.J. Waring, L. Green Mazerolle, W. Spelman and F. Gajewski. (1999). "Problem-Oriented Policing in Violent Crime Places: A Randomized Controlled Experiment." *Criminology* 37: 541-580.

Braga, A.A., and C. Winship. (2006). "Partnership, Accountability, and Innovation: Clarifying Boston's Experience with Pulling Levers." In: D.L. Weisburd and A.A. Braga (eds.), *Police Innovation: Contrasting Perspectives*. New York: Cambridge University Press.

Brantingham, P.J., and P.L. Brantingham (eds.), (1991a). *Environmental Criminology*. (2nd ed.). Prospect Heights, IL: Waveland Press.

——— (1991b). "Notes on the Geometry of Crime." In: P.J. Brantingham and P.L. Brantingham (eds.), *Environmental Criminology.* (2nd ed.). Prospect Heights, IL: Waveland Press.

Bratton, W. (1998). *Turnaround: How America's Top Cop Reversed the Crime Epidemic.* New York, NY: Random House.

Bright, J.A. (1969). *The Beat Patrol Experiment.* (Unpublished paper.) London, UK: Home Office Police Research and Development Branch.

Buerger, M. (1994a). "The Problems of Problem-Solving: Resistance, Interdependencies, and Conflicting Interests." *American Journal of Police* 13: 1-36.

——— (1994b). "The Limits of Community." In: D. Rosenbaum (ed.), *The Challenge of Community Policing: Testing the Promises.* Thousand Oaks, CA: Sage Publications.

Buerger, M., and L. Green Mazerolle. (1998). "Third-Party Policing: A Theoretical Analysis of an Emerging Trend." *Justice Quarterly* 15: 301-328.

Bursik, R., and H. Grasmick. (1993). *Neighborhoods and Crime: The Dimensions of Effective Community Control.* Lexington, MA: Lexington Books.

Buzawa, E., and C. Buzawa. (2003). *Domestic Violence: The Criminal Justice Response.* (3rd ed.). Thousand Oaks, CA: Sage Publications.

Byrne, J., and R. Sampson (eds.), (1986). *The Social Ecology of Crime.* New York: Springer-Verlag.

Callahan, C., F. Rivara, and T. Koepsell. (1994). "Money for Guns: Evaluation of the Seattle Gun Buy-Back Program." *Public Health Reports* 109: 472-477.

Cameron, S. (1988). "The Economics of Crime Deterrence: A Survey of Theory and Evidence." *Kyklos* 41: 301-323.

Capone, D.L., and W. Nichols. (1976). "Urban Structure and Criminal Mobility." *American Behavioral Scientist* 20: 199-213.

Capowich, G., and J. Roehl. (1994). "Problem-Oriented Policing: Actions and Effectiveness in San Diego." In: D. Rosenbaum (ed.), *The Challenge of Community Policing: Testing the Promises.* Thousand Oaks, CA: Sage Publications.

Capowich, G., J. Roehl and C. Andrews. (1995). *Evaluating Problem-Oriented Policing Outcomes in Tulsa and San Diego.* (Final Report to the National Institute of Justice.) Alexandria, VA: Institute for Social Analysis.

Caulkins, J. (1992). "Thinking About Displacement in Drug Markets: Why Observing Change of Venue Isn't Enough." *Journal of Drug Issues* 22: 17-30.

Chaiken, J., M. Lawless and K. Stevenson. (1974). *The Impact of Police Activity on Crime: Robberies on the New York City Subway System.* Santa Monica, CA: Rand Corporation.

Chaiken, J., and M. Chaiken. (1982). *Varieties of Criminal Behavior.* Santa Monica, CA: Rand Corporation.

Chamard, S. (2006). *Partnering with Businesses to Address Public Safety Problems.* (Problem-Oriented Guides for Police, Problem-Solving Tools No. 5.) Washington, DC: U.S. Department of Justice, Office of Community Oriented Policing Services.

Chin, K. (1996). *Chinatown Gangs: Extortion, Enterprise, and Ethnicity.* New York: Oxford University Press.

Clarke, R.V. (1980). "Situational Crime Prevention: Theory and Practice." *British Journal of Criminology* 20: 136-147.

—— (1983). "Situational Crime Prevention: Its Theoretical Basis and Practical Scope." In: M. Tonry and N. Morris (eds.), *Crime and Justice: An Annual Review of Research,* vol. 4. Chicago, IL: University of Chicago Press.

—— (1990). "Deterring Obscene Phone Callers: Preliminary Results of the New Jersey Experience." *Security Journal* 1: 143-148.

—— (ed.), (1992). *Situational Crime Prevention: Successful Case Studies.* Albany, NY: Harrow and Heston.

—— (1995). "Situational Crime Prevention." In: M. Tonry and D. Farrington (eds.), *Building a Safer Society: Strategic Approaches to Crime Prevention.* Chicago, IL: University of Chicago Press.

—— (ed.), (1997). *Situational Crime Prevention: Successful Case Studies.* (2nd ed.). Monsey, NY: Criminal Justice Press.

—— (1998). "Defining Police Strategies: Problem Solving, Problem-Oriented Policing and Community-Oriented Policing." In: T. O'Connor Shelley and A.C. Grant (eds.), *Problem-Oriented Policing: Crime-Specific Problems, Critical Issues, and Making POP Work.* Washington, DC: Police Executive Research Forum.

—— (2005). *Closing Streets and Alleys to Reduce Crime: Should You Go Down This Road?.* (Problem-Oriented Guides for Police, Response Guide Series, Number 2.) Washington DC: U.S. Department of Justice, Office of Community Oriented Policing Services.

Clarke, R.V., and J. Eck. (2003). *Become a Problem-Solving Crime Analyst in 55 Small Steps.* London: Jill Dando Institute of Crime Science.

—— (2005). *Crime Analysis for Problem Solvers in 60 Small Steps.* Washington, DC: U.S. Department of Justice, Office of Community Oriented Policing Services.

—— (2007). *Understanding Risky Facilities.* (Problem-Oriented Guides for Police, Problem Solving Tools Series, no. 6.) Washington, DC: U.S. Department of Justice, Office of Community Oriented Policing Services.

Clarke, R.V., and M. Felson. (1993). "Introduction: Criminology, Routine Activity, and Rational Choice." In: R.V. Clarke and M. Felson (eds.), *Routine Activity and Rational Choice.* (Advances in Criminological Theory, vol. 5.) New Brunswick, NJ: Transaction Press.

Clarke, R.V., S. Field and G. McGrath. (1991). "Target Hardening of Banks in Australia and the Displacement of Robberies." *Security Journal* 2: 84-90.

Clarke, R.V., and H. Goldstein. (2002). "Reducing Theft at Construction Sites: Lessons from a Problem-Oriented Project." In: N. Tilley (ed.), *Analysis for Crime Prevention.* (Crime Prevention Studies, vol. 13.) Monsey, NY: Criminal Justice Press.

—— (2003). "Thefts From Cars in Center-City Parking Facilities: A Case Study in Implementing Problem-Oriented Policing." In: J. Knutsson (ed.), *Problem-*

Oriented Policing: From Innovation to Mainstream. (Crime Prevention Studies, vol. 15.) Monsey, NY: Criminal Justice Press.

Clarke, R.V., and P. Mayhew. (1988). "The British Gas Suicide Story and Its Criminological Implications." In: M. Tonry and N. Morris (eds.), *Crime and Justice: A Review of Research*, vol. 10. Chicago, IL: University of Chicago Press.

Clarke, R.V., and P. Schultze. (2005). *Researching a Problem.* (Problem-Oriented Guides for Police, Problem Solving Tools Series, no. 2.) Washington, DC: U.S. Department of Justice, Office of Community Oriented Policing Services.

Clarke, R.V., and D. Weisburd. (1994). "Diffusion of Crime Control Benefits: Observations on the Reverse of Displacement." *Crime Prevention Studies* 2: 165-184.

Cohen, L.E., and M. Felson. (1979). "Social Change and Crime Rate Trends: A Routine Activity Approach." *American Sociological Review* 44: 588-605.

Coleman, V., W.C. Holton, K. Olson, S. Robinson and J. Stewart. (1999). "Using Knowledge and Teamwork to Reduce Crime." *National Institute of Justice Journal* October: 16-23.

Coles, C., and G. Kelling. (1999). "Prevention through Community Prosecution." *The Public Interest.* (Summer): 69-84.

Cook, P.J. (1977). "Punishment and Crime: A Critique of Current Findings Concerning the Preventive Effects of Punishment." *Law and Contemporary Problems* 41: 164-204.

——— (1980). "Research in Criminal Deterrence: Laying the Groundwork for the Second Decade." In: N. Morris and M. Tonry (eds.), *Crime and Justice: An Annual Review of Research*, vol. 2. Chicago, IL: University of Chicago Press.

Cook, P.J., and A.A. Braga. (2001). "Comprehensive Firearms Tracing: Strategic and Investigative Uses of New Data on Firearms Markets." *Arizona Law Review* 43(2): 277-309.

Cook, P.J., and J. Ludwig. (2000). *Gun Violence: The Real Costs.* New York, NY: Oxford University Press.

Cook, P.J., S. Molliconi, and T. Cole. (1995). "Regulating Gun Markets." *Journal of Criminal Law and Criminology* 86: 59-92.

Cordner, G. (1998). "Problem-Oriented Policing vs. Zero Tolerance." In: T. O'Connor Shelley and A.C. Grant (eds.), *Problem-Oriented Policing: Crime-Specific Problems, Critical Issues, and Making POP Work.* Washington, DC: Police Executive Research Forum.

Cordner, G., and E.P. Biebel. (2005). "Problem-Oriented Policing in Practice." *Criminology and Public Policy* 4: 155-180.

Corman, H., and N. Mocan. (2005). "Carrots, Sticks, and Broken Windows." *Journal of Law and Economics* 48: 235-262.

Cornish, D. (1994). "The Procedural Analysis of Offending and Its Relevance for Situational Prevention." In: R.V. Clarke (ed.), *Crime Prevention Studies*, vol. 3. Monsey, New York: Criminal Justice Press.

Cornish, D., and R.V. Clarke (eds.), (1986). *The Reasoning Criminal: Rational Choice Perspectives on Offending.* New York, NY: Springer-Verlag.

——— (1987). "Understanding Crime Displacement: An Application of Rational Choice Theory." *Criminology* 25: 933-947.

——— (2003). "Opportunities, Precipitators and Criminal Decisions: A Reply to Wortley's Critique of Situational Crime Prevention." In: M.J. Smith and D.B. Cornish (eds.), *Theory for Practice in Situational Crime Prevention*. (Crime Prevention Studies, vol. 16.) Monsey, NY: Criminal Justice Press.

Crow, W.J., and J.L. Bull. (1975). *Robbery Deterrence: An Applied Behavioral Science Demonstration-Final Report*. La Jolla, CA: Western Behavioral Sciences Institute.

Crowell, N., and A. Burgess (eds.), (1996). *Understanding Violence Against Women*. Washington, DC: National Academy Press.

Curry, G.D, R. Ball, and R. Fox. (1994). *Gang Crime and Law Enforcement Record Keeping*. Washington, DC: National Institute of Justice.

Curry, G.D., and S. H. Decker. (1998). *Confronting Gangs: Crime and Community*. Los Angeles: Roxbury Press.

Dalton, E. (2002). "Targeted Crime Reduction Efforts in Ten Communities: Lessons for the Project Safe Neighborhoods Initiative." *U.S. Attorney's Bulletin* 50: 16-25.

Decker, J. (1972). "Curbside Deterrence: An Analysis of the Effect of a Slug Rejectory Device, Coin View Window, and Warning Labels on Slug Usage in New York City Parking Meters." *Criminology* 10: 127-142.

Decker, S.H. (1996). "Gangs and Violence: The Expressive Character of Collective Involvement." *Justice Quarterly* 11: 231-250.

——— (2005). *Using Offender Interviews to Inform Police Problem Solving*. (Problem-Oriented Guide for Police, Problem Solving Tools Series no. 3.) Washington, DC: U.S. Department of Justice, Office of Community Oriented Policing Services.

Decker, S.H., and R. Rosenfeld. (2004). *Reducing Gun Violence: The St. Louis Consent-to-Search Program*. Washington, DC: U.S. Department of Justice, National Institute of Justice.

Dedel, K. (2006). *Juvenile Runaways*. (Problem-Oriented Guides for Police, Series, no. 37.) Washington, DC: U.S. Department of Justice, Office of Community Oriented Policing Services.

Eck, J.E. (1983). *Solving Crimes: The Investigation of Burglary and Robbery*. Washington, DC: Police Executive Research Forum.

——— (1993a). "The Threat of Crime Displacement." *Criminal Justice Abstracts* 25: 527-546.

——— (1993b). "Alternative Futures for Policing." In: D. Weisburd and C. Uchida (eds.), *Police Innovation and Control of the Police*. New York, NY: Springer-Verlag.

——— (1994). "Drug Markets and Drug Places: A Case-Control Study of the Spatial Structure of Illicit Dealing." Unpublished Ph.D. Dissertation, University of Maryland, College Park.

——— (1997). "Preventing Crime at Places." In: University of Maryland, Department of Criminology and Criminal Justice (eds.), *Preventing Crime: What Works, What Doesn't, What's Promising*. Washington, DC: Office of Justice Programs, U.S. Department of Justice

———— (2000). "Problem-Oriented Policing and It's Problems: The Means Over Ends Syndrome Strikes Back and the Return of the Problem-Solver.". (Unpublished manuscript.) Cincinnati, OH: University of Cincinnati.

———— (2002). *Assessing Responses to Problems: An Introductory Guide for Police Problem Solvers.* (Problem-Oriented Guides for Police, Problem Solving Tools Series, no. 1.) Washington, DC: U.S. Department of Justice, Office of Community Oriented Policing Services.

———— (2003). "Police Problems: The Complexity of Problem Theory, Research and Evaluation." In: J. Knutsson (ed.), *Problem-Oriented Policing: From Innovation to Mainstream.* (Crime Prevention Studies, vol. 15.) Monsey, NY: Criminal Justice Press.

———— (2006). "Science, Values, and Problem-Oriented Policing: why Problem-Oriented Policing?" In: D.L. Weisburd and A.A. Braga (eds.), *Police Innovation: Contrasting Perspectives.* New York: Cambridge University Press.

Eck, J.E., S. Chainey, and J. Cameron. (2005). *Mapping Crime: Understanding Hot Spots.* Washington, DC: U.S. Department of Justice, National Institute of Justice.

Eck, J.E., and R.V. Clarke. (2003). "Classifying Common Police Problems: A Routine Activity Approach." In: M.J. Smith and D.B. Cornish (eds.), *Theory for Practice in Situational Crime Prevention.* (Crime Prevention Studies, vol. 16.) Monsey, NY: Criminal Justice Press.

Eck, J.E., and E. Maguire. (2000). "Have Changes in Policing Reduced Violent Crime? An Assessment of the Evidence." In: A. Blumstein and J Wallman (eds.), *The Crime Drop in America.* New York: Cambridge University Press.

Eck, J.E., and D. Rosenbaum. (1994). "The New Police Order: Effectiveness, Equity, and Efficiency in Community Policing." In: D. Rosenbaum (ed.), *The Challenge of Community Policing: Testing the Promises.* Thousand Oaks, CA: Sage Publications.

Eck, J.E., and W. Spelman. (1987). *Problem-Solving: Problem-Oriented Policing in Newport News.* Washington, DC: National Institute of Justice.

Eck, J.E., and D. Weisburd. (1995). "Crime Places in Crime Theory." In: J. Eck and D. Weisburd (eds.), *Crime and Place.* (Crime Prevention Studies, vol. 4.) Monsey, NY: Criminal Justice Press.

Ekblom, P. (1997). "Gearing Up Against Crime: A Dynamic Framework to Help Designers Keep Up with the Adaptive Criminal in a Changing World." *International Journal of Risk, Security, and Crime Prevention* 2: 249-265.

Ennis, B., and T. Litwack. (1974). "Psychiatry and the Presumption of Expertise: Flipping Coins in the Courtroom." *California Law Review* 62: 693-752.

Fagan, J. (2002). "Policing Guns and Youth Violence." *The Future of Children* 12: 133-151.

Fagan, J., D. Stewart and K. Hansen. (1983). "Violent Men or Violent Husbands?" In: D. Finkelhor, R. Gelles, G. Hotaling and M. Straus (eds.), *The Dark Side of Families.* Beverly Hills, CA: Sage Publications.

Fagan, J., F.E. Zimring and J. Kim. (1998). "Declining Homicide in New York City: A Tale of Two Trends." *Journal of Criminal Law and Criminology* 88: 1277-1324.

Farrell, G. (1995). "Preventing Repeat Victimization." In: M. Tonry and D. Farrington (eds.), *Building a Safer Society: Strategic Approaches to Crime Prevention.* (Crime and Justice series, vol. 19.) Chicago, IL: University of Chicago Press.

———— (2005). "Progress and Prospects in the Prevention of Repeat Victimization." In: N. Tilley (ed.), *Handbook of Crime Prevention and Community Safety.* London: Willan Publishing.

Farrell, G., W. Buck and K. Pease. (1993). "The Merseyside Domestic Violence Prevention Project." *Studies on Crime and Crime Prevention,* vol. 2. Stockholm, SWE: Scandinavian University Press.

Farrell, G., and K. Pease. (1993). *Once Bitten, Twice Bitten: Repeat Victimization and its Implications for Crime Prevention.* (Crime Reduction Research Series Paper Number 5.) London, UK: Home Office.

———— (2003). "Measuring and Interpreting Repeat Victimization Using Police Data: An Analysis of Burglary Data and Policy for Charlotte, North Carolina." In: M.J. Smith and D.B. Cornish (eds.), *Theory for Practice in Situational Crime Prevention.* (Crime Prevention Studies, vol. 16.) Monsey, NY: Criminal Justice Press.

Farrell, G., and W. Sousa. (2001). "Repeat Victimization and Hot Spots: The Overlap and Its Implication for Crime Control and Problem-Oriented Policing." In: G. Farrell and K. Pease (eds.), *Repeat Victimization.* (Crime Prevention Studies, vol. 12.) Monsey, NY: Criminal Justice Press.

Farrell, G., W. Sousa and D. Lamm Weisel. (2002). "The Time-Window Effect in the Measurement of Repeat Victimization: A Methodology for its Examination, and an Empirical Study." In: N. Tilley (ed.), *Analysis for Crime Prevention.* (Crime Prevention Studies, vol. 13.) Monsey, NY: Criminal Justice Press.

Felson, M. (1994). *Crime and Everyday Life.* Thousand Oaks, CA: Pine Forge Press.

———— (1995). "Those Who Discourage Crime." In: J. Eck and D. Weisburd (eds.), *Crime and Place.* (Crime Prevention Studies, vol. 4.) Monsey, NY: Criminal Justice Press.

———— (2003). "The Process of Co-Offending." In: M. Smith and D. Cornish (eds.), *Theory for Practice in Situational Crime Prevention.* (Crime Prevention Studies, vol. 16.) Monsey, NY: Criminal Justice Press.

———— (2006). *Crime and Nature.* Thousand Oaks, CA: Sage Publications.

Felson, M., and many others. (1996). "Redesigning Hell: Preventing Crime and Disorder at the Port Authority Bus Terminal." In: R.V. Clarke (ed.), *Preventing Mass Transit Crime.* (Crime Prevention Studies, vol. 6.) Monsey, NY: Criminal Justice Press.

Felson, M., and R.V. Clarke. (1998). *Opportunity Makes the Thief: Practical Theory for Crime Prevention.* (Crime Prevention and Detection Series Paper 98.) London, UK: Home Office.

Felson, M., R. Berends, B. Richardson and A. Veno. (1997). "Reducing Pub Hopping and Related Crime." In: R. Homel (ed.), *Policing for Prevention: Reducing Crime, Public Intoxication, and Injury.* (Crime Prevention Studies, vol. 7.) Monsey, NY: Criminal Justice Press.

Ferraro, K. (1995). *Fear of Crime: Interpreting Victimization Risk.* Albany, NY: State University of New York Press.

Forrester, D., M. Chatterton and K. Pease. (1988). *The Kirkholt Burglary Prevention Project.* (Home Office Crime Prevention Unit Paper 13.) London, UK: Home Office.

Forrester, D., S. Frenz, M. O'Connell and K. Pease. (1990). *The Kirkholt Burglary Prevention Project: Phase II.* (Home Office Crime Prevention Unit Paper 23.) London, UK: Home Office.

Frabutt, J., M.J. Gathings, E.D. Hunt, and T.J. Loggins. (2004). *High Point West End Initiative: Project Description, Log, and Preliminary Impact Analysis.* Greensboro, NC: Center for Youth, Family, and Community Partnerships.

Gabor, T. (1990). "Crime Displacement and Situational Prevention: Toward the Development of Some Principles." *Canadian Journal of Criminology* 32: 41-74.

Gabor, T., M. Baril, M. Cusson, E. Elie, M. Le Blanc and A. Normandeau. (1987). *Armed Robbery: Cops, Robbers, and Victims.* Springfield, IL: Charles C. Thomas.

Garofalo, J. (1979). "Victimization and the Fear of Crime." *Journal of Research in Crime and Delinquency* 16: 80-97.

——— (1987). "Reassessing the Lifestyle Model of Criminal Victimization." In: M. Gottfredson and T. Hirschi (eds.), *Positive Criminology.* Newbury Park, CA: Sage Publications.

Gibbs, J.P. (1975). *Crime, Punishment, and Deterrence.* New York, NY: Elsevier.

Gill, M., and K. Pease. (1998). "Repeat Robbers: How Are They Different?" In: M. Gill (ed.), *Crime at Work: Studies in Security and Crime Prevention.* Leicester, UK: Perpetuity Press.

Glazer, E. (1999). "How Federal Prosecutors Can Reduce Crime." *The Public Interest,* (Summer): 85-99.

Goldstein, H. (1979). "Improving Policing: A Problem-Oriented Approach." *Crime & Delinquency* 25: 236-258.

——— (1990). *Problem-Oriented Policing.* Philadelphia, PA: Temple University Press.

——— (2003). "On Further Developing Problem-Oriented Policing: The Most Critical Need, the Major Impediments, and a Proposal." In: J. Knutsson (ed.), *Problem-Oriented Policing: From Innovation to Mainstream.* (Crime Prevention Studies, vol. 15). Monsey, NY: Criminal Justice Press.

Goldstein, H., and C. Susmilch. (1982). "The Drinking-Driver in Madison: A Study of the Problem and the Community's Response." Madison, WI: University of Wisconsin Law School.

Goldstock, R. (1991). *The Prosecutor as Problem-Solver.* New York, NY: Center for Research in Crime and Justice, New York University Law School.

Golub, A., B.D. Johnson, and E. Dunlap. (2007). "The Race/ethnicity Disparity in Misdemeanor Marijuana Arrests in New York City." *Criminology and Public Policy* 6: 131-164.

Gottfredson, M., and T. Hirschi. (1990). *A General Theory of Crime.* Stanford, CA: Stanford University Press.

Gould, P., and R. White. (1974). *Mental Maps.* New York, NY: Penguin Books.

Green, L. (1996). *Policing Places With Drug Problems.* Thousand Oaks, CA: Sage Publications.

Green Mazerolle, L., and J. Roehl. (1998). "Civil Remedies and Crime Prevention: An Introduction." In: L. Green Mazerolle and J. Roehl (eds.), *Civil Remedies and Crime Prevention.* (Crime Prevention Studies, vol. 9.) Monsey, NY: Criminal Justice Press.

Greene, J.A. (1999). "Zero Tolerance: A Case Study of Police Practices and Policies in New York City." *Crime & Delinquency* 45: 171-181.

Greene, J.R. (2000). "Community Policing in America: Changing the Nature, Structure and Function of the Police." In: J. Horney, R. Peterson, D. MacKenzie, J. Martin and D. Rosenbaum (eds.), *Policies, Processes and Decisions of the Criminal Justice System.* (Criminal Justice 2000 series, vol. 3.) Washington, DC: U.S. National Institute of Justice.

Greene, J.R., and S. Mastrofski (eds.), (1988). *Community Policing: Rhetoric or Reality?* New York, NY: Praeger.

Greenwood, P., J. Chaiken and J. Petersilia. (1977). *The Investigation Process.* Lexington, MA: Lexington Books.

Grinc, R. (1994). " 'Angels in Marble:' Problems in Stimulating Community Involvement in Community Policing." *Crime & Delinquency* 40: 437-468.

Hale, C., C. Harris, S. Uglow, L. Gilling, and A. Netten. (2004). *Targeting the Market for Stolen Goods: Two Targeted Policing Initiative Project.* (Home Office Development and Practice Report 17.) London: Home Office

Hanmer, J., S. Griffiths and D. Jerwood. (1999). *Arresting Evidence: Domestic Violence and Repeat Victimization.* (Police Research Series Paper 104.) London, UK: Home Office.

Harcourt, B. (1998). "Reflecting on the Subject: A Critique of the Social Influence of Deterrence, the Broken Windows Theory, and Order-Maintenance Policing New York Style." *Michigan Law Review* 97: 291-389.

—— (2001). *Illusion of Order: The False Promise of Broken Windows Policing.* Cambridge, MA: Harvard University Press.

Harcourt, B., and Jens Ludwig. (2006). "Broken Windows: New Evidence from New York City and a Five-city Experiment." *University of Chicago Law Review* 73: 271-320.

—— (2007). "Reefer Madness: Broken Windows Policing and Misdemeanor Marijuana Arrests in New York City, 1989-2000." *Criminology and Public Policy* 6: 165-182.

Harries, K. (1999). *Mapping Crime: Principle and Practice.* Washington, DC: National Institute of Justice, U.S. Department of Justice.

Hartmann, F. (1988). "Debating the Evolution of American Policing." *Perspectives on Policing.* Washington, DC: National Institute of Justice, U.S. Department of Justice.

Hawken, A., and M.A.R. Kleiman. (2007). "H.O.P.E. for Reform: What a Novel Probation Program in Hawaii Might Teach Other States." *American Prospect,* April 10 (http://www.prospect.org/cs/articles?articleId=12628).

Hawley, A. (1944). "Ecology and Human Ecology." *Social Forces* 23: 398-405.

——— (1950). *Human Ecology: A Theory of Urban Structure.* New York, NY: Ronald Press.

Hesseling, R. (1994). "Displacement: A Review of the Empirical Literature." *Crime Prevention Studies* 3: 197-230.

Hindelang, M., M. Gottfredson and J. Garofalo. (1978). *Victims of Personal Crime: An Empirical Foundation for a Theory of Personal Victimization.* Cambridge, MA: Ballinger.

Homel, R. (1990). "Random Breath Testing and Random Stopping Programs in Australia." In R. Wilson and R. Mann (eds.), *Drinking and Driving: Advances in Research and Prevention.* New York, NY: Guilford.

Homel, R., and J. Clark. (1994). "The Prevention of Violence in Pubs and Clubs." *Crime Prevention Studies* 3: 1-46.

Homel, R., M. Hauritz, R. Wortley, G. McIlwain and R. Carvolth. (1997). "Preventing Alcohol-Related Crime Through Community Action: The Surfers Paradise Safety Action Project." In: R. Homel (ed.), *Policing for Prevention: Reducing Crime, Public Intoxication, and Injury.* (Crime Prevention Studies, vol. 7.) Monsey, NY: Criminal Justice Press.

Hope, T. (1994). "Problem-Oriented Policing and Drug Market Locations: Three Case Studies." *Crime Prevention Studies* 2: 5-32.

Hough, M. (2006). "Not Seeing the Wood for the Trees: Mistaking Tactics for Strategy in Crime Reduction Initiatives." In: J. Knutsson and R.V. Clarke (eds.), *Putting Theory to Work: Implementing Situational Prevention and Problem-Oriented Policing.* (Crime Prevention Studies, vol. 20.) Monsey, NY: Criminal Justice Press.

Hough, M., and N. Tilley. (1998). *Getting the Grease to Squeak: Research Lessons for Crime Prevention.* (Crime Detection and Prevention Series Paper 85.) London, UK: Home Office.

Hunter, R., and C.R. Jeffrey. (1992). "Preventing Convenience Store Robbery through Environmental Design." In: R. Clarke (ed.), *Situational Crime Prevention: Successful Case Studies.* Albany, NY: Harrow and Heston.

Jacobs, J.B. (1988). *Drunk Driving: An American Dilemma.* Chicago, IL: University of Chicago Press.

Jang, S. J., and B. Johnson. (2001). "Neighborhood Disorder, Individual Religiosity, and Adolescent Use of Illicit Drugs: A Test of Multilevel Hypotheses." *Criminology* 39: 109-144.

Johnson, S., and K. Bowers. (2003). "Opportunity is in the Eye of the Beholder: The Role of Publicity in Crime Prevention." *Criminology and Public Policy* 3: 497-524.

—— (2004). "The Burglary as Clue to the Future: The Beginnings of Prospective Hot-spotting." *European Journal of Criminology* 1: 237-255.

—— (2007). "Burglary Prediction: The Roles of Theory, Flow, and Friction." In: G. Farrell, K. Bowers, S. Johnson, and M. Townsley (eds.), *Imagination for Crime Prevention: Essays in Honour of Ken Pease.* (Crime Prevention Studies, vol. 21.) Monsey, NY: Criminal Justice Press.

Kansas City Police Department. (1978). *Response Time Analysis: Executive Summary.* Washington, DC: U.S. Department of Justice.

Katz, C., V. Webb, and D. Schaefer. (2001). "An Assessment of the Impact of Quality-of-life Policing on Crime and Disorder." *Justice Quarterly* 18: 825-876.

Karmen, A. (2000). *New York Murder Mystery: The True Story Behind the Crime Crash of the 1990s.* New York: New York University Press.

Kelling, G. (1992). "Measuring What Matters: A New Way of Thinking About Crime and Public Order." *City Journal.* (Autumn): 34-45.

Kelling, G., and C. Coles. (1996). *Fixing Broken Windows: Restoring Order and Reducing Crime in Our Communities.* New York, NY: Free Press.

Kelling, G., and M.H. Moore. (1988). "From Political to Reform to Community: The Evolving Strategy of Police." In: J. Greene and S. Mastrofski (eds.), *Community Policing: Rhetoric or Reality?* New York, NY: Praeger.

Kelling, G., T. Pate, D. Dieckman and C. Brown. (1974). *The Kansas City Preventive Patrol Experiment: A Technical Report.* Washington, DC: Police Foundation.

Kelling, G., and W. Sousa. (2001). *Do Police Matter? An Analysis of the Impact of New York City's Police Reforms.* (Civic Report No 22.) New York, NY: The Manhattan Institute.

Kelman, H.C., and V. L. Hamilton. (1989). *Crimes of Obedience.* New Haven, CT: Yale University Press.

Kennedy, D.M. (1993). *Closing the Market: Controlling the Drug Trade in Tampa, Florida.* (National Institute of Justice Program Focus series.) Washington, DC: U.S. Department of Justice.

—— (1994). "Can We Keep Guns Away From Kids?" *American Prospect* 18: 74-80.

—— (1997). "Pulling Levers: Chronic Offenders, High-Crime Settings, and a Theory of Prevention." *Valparaiso University Law Review* 31: 449-484.

—— (1998). "Pulling Levers: Getting Deterrence Right." *National Institute of Justice Journal* July: 2-8.

—— (2002a). "Controlling Domestic Violence Offenders." Working Paper, Program in Criminal Justice Policy and Management. Cambridge, MA: John F. Kennedy School of Government, Harvard University.

—— (2002b). "A Tale of One City: Reflections on the Boston Gun Project." In: G. Katzmann (ed.), *Managing Youth Violence.* Washington, DC: Brookings Institution Press.

———— (2006). "Old Wine in New Bottles: Policing and the Lessons of Pulling Levers." In: D.L. Weisburd and A.A. Braga (eds.), *Police Innovation: Contrasting Perspectives.* New York: Cambridge University Press.

Kennedy, D.M., A.A. Braga, and A.M. Piehl. (1997). "The. (Un)Known Universe: Mapping Gangs and Gang Violence in Boston." In: D. Weisburd and J. T. McEwen (eds.), *Crime Mapping and Crime Prevention.* (Crime Prevention Studies, vol. 8.) Monsey, NY: New York: Criminal Justice Press.

———— (2001). "Developing and Implementing Operation Ceasefire." In: *Reducing Gun Violence: The Boston Gun Project's Operation Ceasefire.* Washington, DC: National Institute of Justice, U.S. Department of Justice.

Kennedy, D.M., and M.H. Moore. (1995). "Underwriting the Risky Investment in Community Policing: What Social Science Should Be Doing to Evaluate Community Policing." *Justice System Journal* 17(3): 271-290.

Kennedy, D.M., A.M. Piehl and A.A. Braga. (1996a). "Youth Violence in Boston: Gun Markets, Serious Youth Offenders, and a Use-Reduction Strategy." *Law and Contemporary Problems* 59: 147-197.

———— (1996b). "Gun Buy-Backs: Where Do We Stand and Where Do We Go?" In: M.R. Plotkin (ed.), *Under Fire: Gun Buy-Backs, Exchanges, and Amnesty Programs.* Washington, DC: Police Executive Research Forum.

Kleck, G. (1991). *Point Blank: Guns and Violence in America.* New York, NY Aldine de Gruyter.

Kleiman, M. (1988). "Crackdowns: The Effects of Intensive Enforcement on Retail Heroin Dealing." In: M. Chaiken (ed.), *Street-Level Drug Enforcement: Examining the Issues.* Washington, DC: National Institute of Justice.

———— (1997). "Coerced Abstinence: A Neopaternalist Drug Policy Initiative." In: L. Mead (ed.), *The New Paternalism: Strategic Approaches to Poverty.* Washington, DC: Brookings Institution.

Klein, M. (1993). "Attempting Gang Control by Suppression: The Misuse of Deterrence Principles." *Studies on Crime and Crime Prevention* 2: 88-111.

———— (1995). *The American Street Gang: Its Nature, Prevalence, and Control.* New York and London: Oxford University Press.

Klein, M., and C. Maxson. (1989). "Street Gang Violence." In: N.A. Weiner (ed.), *Violent Crimes, Violent Criminals.* Beverly Hills, CA: Sage.

Klockars, C. (1980). "Jonathan Wild and the Modern Sting." In: J. Inciardi and C. Faupel (eds.), *History and Crime: Implications for Criminal Justice Policy.* Beverly Hills, CA: Sage Publications.

———— (1985). "Order Maintenance, the Quality of Urban Life, and Police: A Different Line of Argument." In: W. Geller (ed.), *Police Leadership in America: Crisis and Opportunity.* New York: Praeger.

Klofas, J., and N.K. Hipple. (2006). *Crime Incident Reviews.* (Project Safe Neighborhoods: Strategic Interventions Case Study No. 3.) Washington, DC: U.S. Department of Justice.

References

Koper, C. (1995). "Just Enough Police Presence: Reducing Crime and Disorderly Behavior by Optimizing Patrol Time in Crime Hot Spots." *Justice Quarterly* 12: 649-672.

LaGrange, R., K. Ferraro and M. Supancic. (1992). "Perceived Risk and Fear of Crime: Role of Social and Physical Incivilities." *Journal of Research in Crime and Delinquency* 29: 311-334.

Lamm Weisel, D. (2003). "The Sequence of Analysis in Solving Problems." In: J. Knutsson (ed.), *Problem-Oriented Policing: From Innovation to Mainstream.* (Crime Prevention Studies, vol. 15.) Monsey, NY: Criminal Justice Press.

—— (2004). *Analyzing Repeat Victimization.* (Problem-Oriented Guides for Police, Problem-Solving Tools no. 4.) Washington, DC: U.S. Department of Justice, Office of Community Oriented Policing Services.

—— (2007). *Bank Robbery.* (Problem-Oriented Guides for Police, no. 48.) Washington, DC: U.S. Department of Justice, Office of Community Oriented Policing Services.

Lane, R. (1971). *Policing the City: Boston 1822-1855.* New York, NY: Antheneum.

Langworthy, R. (1999). "What Matters Routinely?" In: R. Langworthy (ed.), *Measuring What Matters: Proceedings from the Policing Research Institute Meetings.* Washington, DC: National Institute of Justice, U.S. Department of Justice.

Laub, J., and R. Sampson. (2003). *Shared Beginnings, Divergent Lives: Delinquent Boys to Age 70.* Cambridge, MA: Harvard University Press.

Lauritsen, J., R. Sampson and J. Laub. (1991). "The Link Between Offending and Victimization Among Adolescents." *Criminology* 29: 265-292.

LaVigne, N., and J. Wartell (eds.), (1998). *Crime Mapping Case Studies: Successes in the Field.* Washington, DC: Police Executive Research Forum.

—— (2000). *Crime Mapping Case Studies: Successes in the Field,* vol. 2. Washington, DC: Police Executive Research Forum.

Laycock, G., and C. Austin. (1992). "Crime Prevention in Parking Facilities." *Security Journal* 3: 154-60.

Laycock, G., and G. Farrell. (2003). "Repeat Victimization: Lessons for Implementing Problem-Oriented Policing." In: J. Knutsson (ed.), *Problem-Oriented Policing: From Innovation to Mainstream.* (Crime Prevention Studies, vol. 15.) Monsey, New York: Criminal Justice Press.

Leigh, A., T. Read and N. Tilley. (1996). *Problem-Oriented Policing: Brit POP.* (Crime Prevention and Detection Series Paper 75.) London, UK: Home Office.

Levitt, S. (2004). "Understanding Why Crime Fell in the 1990s: Four Factors that Explain the Decline and Six that Do Not." *Journal of Economic Perspectives* 18: 163-190.

Lewin, K. 1947. "Group Decisions and Social Change." In T. Newcomb and E. Hartley (eds.), *Readings in Social Psychology.* New York: Atherton Press.

Lloyd, S., G. Farrell and K. Pease. (1994). *Preventing Repeated Domestic Violence: A Demonstration Project on Merseyside.* (Home Office Crime Prevention Unit Paper 48.) London, UK: Home Office.

Ludwig, J. (2005). "Better Gun Enforcement, Less Crime." *Criminology and Public Policy* 4: 677-716.

MacEachern, A.M. (1994). *Some Truths with Maps: A Primer on Symbolization and Design.* Washington, DC: Association of American Geographers.

Martin, S., and L. Sherman. (1986). "Selective Apprehension: A Police Strategy for Repeat Offenders." *Criminology* 24: 155-73.

Marx, G.T. (1988). *Undercover: Police Surveillance in America.* Los Angeles, CA: University of California Press.

Mastrofski, S.D. (1998). "Community Policing and Police Organization Structure." In: J.P. Brodeur (ed.), *How to Recognize Good Policing: Problems and Issues.* Thousand Oaks, CA: Sage Publications.

Matthews, R. (1990). "Developing More Effective Strategies for Curbing Prostitution." *Security Journal* 1: 182-187.

Mawby, R.I. (2001). "The Impact of Repeat Victimization on Burglary Victims in East and West Europe." In: G. Farrell and K. Pease (eds.), *Repeat Victimization.* (Crime Prevention Studies, vol. 12.) Monsey, NY: Criminal Justice Press.

Mayhew, P., R.V. Clarke and J.M. Hough. (1980). "Steering Column Locks and Car Theft." In: R.V. Clarke and P. Mayhew (eds.), *Designing Out Crime.* London, UK: Her Majesty's Stationery Office.

Maxwell, C., J. Garner, and J. Fagan. (2002). "Research, Policy and Theory: The Preventive Effects of Arrest on Intimate Partner Violence." *Criminology and Public Policy* 2: 51-80.

Mazerolle, L., J.F. Price and J. Roehl. (2000). "Civil Remedies and Drug Control: A Randomized Field Trial in Oakland, California." *Evaluation Review* 24: 212-241.

Mazerolle, L., and J. Ransley. (2006). *Third-Party Policing.* Cambridge, UK: Cambridge University Press.

Mazerolle, L., and W. Terrill. (1997). "Problem-Oriented Policing in Public Housing: Identifying the Distribution of Problem Places." *Policing: An International Journal of Police Strategies and Management,* 20: 235-255.

McElroy, J., C. Cosgrove and M. Farrell. (1981). *Felony Case Preparation: Quality Counts.* New York, NY: Vera Institute of Justice.

McGarrell, E., S. Chermak, J. Wilson, and N. Corsaro. (2006). "Reducing Homicide through a 'Lever-Pulling' Strategy." *Justice Quarterly* 23: 214-229.

McGloin, J.M. (2004). *Street Gangs and Interventions: Innovative Problem Solving with Network Analysis.* Washington, DC: U.S. Department of Justice, Office of Community Oriented Policing Services.

——— (2005). "Policy and Intervention Considerations of a Network Analysis of Street Gangs." *Criminology and Public Policy* 4: 607-636.

Meares, T.L. (2000). "Norms, Legitimacy, and Law Enforcement." *Oregon Law Review* 79: 391-415.

Meares, T.L., and K. Brown Corkran. (2007). "When 2 or 3 Come Together." *William and Mary Law Review* 48: 1315-1387.

Meares, T.L., and W. Skogan. (2004). "Lawful Policing." *Annals of the American Academy of Political and Social Science* 593: 66-83.

Messner, S.F., S. Galea, K.J. Tardiff, M. Tracy, A. Bucciarelli, T. Markham Piper, V. Frye, and D. Vlahov. (2007). "Policing, Drugs, and the Homicide Decline in New York City in the 1990s." *Criminology* 45: 385-414.

Millbank, S., and M. Riches. (2000). "Reducing Repeat Victimization of Domestic Violence: The NDV Project." Paper presented at the Reducing Criminality: Partnerships and Best Practice convened by the Australian Institute of Criminology, Perth, Australia, July 31.

Miller, W.B. (1975). *Violence by Youth Gangs and Youth Groups as a Crime Problem in Major American Cities.* Washington, DC: U.S. Government Printing Office.

Monahan, J. (1981). *Predicting Violent Behavior: An Assessment of Clinical Techniques.* Beverly Hills, CA: Sage Publications.

Moore, M.H. (1973). "Achieving Discrimination on the Effective Price of Heroin." *American Economic Review* 63: 270-77.

——— (1976). *Buy and Bust: The Effective Regulation of an Illicit Market in Heroin.* Lexington, MA: Heath.

——— (1980). "The Police and Weapons Offenses." *Annals of the American Academy of Political and Social Science* 455: 92-109.

——— (1983a). "Invisible Offenses: A Challenge to Minimally Intrusive Law Enforcement." In: G.M. Kaplan (ed.), *ABSCAM Ethics: Moral Issues and Deception in Law Enforcement.* Washington, DC: Police Foundation.

——— (1983b). "The Bird in Hand: A Feasible Strategy for Gun Control." *Journal of Policy Analysis and Management* 2: 185-188.

——— (1992). "Problem-Solving and Community Policing." In: M. Tonry and N. Morris (eds.), *Modern Policing.* Chicago, IL: University of Chicago Press.

——— (2002). *Recognizing Value in Policing.* Washington, DC: Police Executive Research Forum.

Moore, M.H., and A.A. Braga. (2003). "Measuring and Improving Police Performance: The Lessons of Compstat and its Progeny." *Policing: An International Journal of Police Strategies and Management* 26: 439-453.

Moore, M.H., S. Estrich, D. Gillis and W. Spelman. (1984). *Dangerous Offenders: Elusive Targets of Justice.* Cambridge, MA: Harvard University Press.

Muir, W.K. (1977). *Police: Streetcorner Politicians.* Chicago, IL: University of Chicago Press.

Novak, K., J. Hartman, A. Holsinger, and M. Turner. (1999). "The Effects of Aggressive Policing of Disorder on Serious Crime." *Policing: An International Journal of Police Strategies and Management* 22: 171-190.

O'Connor Shelly, T., and A. Grant (eds.), (1998). *Problem-Oriented Policing: Crime-Specific Problems, Critical Issues, and Making POP Work.* Washington, DC: Police Executive Research Forum.

Papachristos, A., T. Meares, and J. Fagan. (2007). "Attention Felons: Evaluating Project Safe Neighborhoods in Chicago." *Journal of Empirical Legal Studies* 4: 223-272.

Pate, A., R. Bowers and R. Parks. (1976). *Three Approaches to Criminal Apprehension in Kansas City: An Evaluation Report.* Washington, DC: Police Foundation.

Pate, A., W. Skogan, M.A. Wycoff, and L. Sherman. (1986). *Reducing Fear of Crime in Houston and Newark: A Summary Report.* Washington, DC: Police Foundation.

Paternoster, R. (1987). "The Deterrent Effect of the Perceived Certainty and Severity of Punishment: A Review of the Evidence and Issues." *Justice Quarterly* 4: 173-217.

Pease, K. (1991). "The Kirkholt Project: Preventing Burglary on a British Public Housing Estate." *Security Journal* 2: 73-77.

Pease, K., and G. Laycock. (1996). *Repeat Victimization: Reducing the Heat on Hot Victims.* Washington, DC: National Institute of Justice, U.S. Department of Justice.

——— (1998). *Repeat Victimization: Taking Stock.* (Crime Prevention and Detection Series Paper 89.) London, UK: Home Office.

Piehl, A.M., S.J. Cooper, A.A. Braga, and D.M. Kennedy. (2003). "Testing for Structural Breaks in the Evaluation of Programs." *Review of Economics and Statistics,* 85: 550-558.

Pierce, G. L., A.A. Braga, R.R. Hyatt, and C. S. Koper. (2004). "The Characteristics and Dynamics of Illegal Firearms Markets: Implications for a Supply-Side Enforcement Strategy." *Justice Quarterly* 21: 391-422.

Pierce, G.L., S. Spaar and L. Briggs. (1988). *The Character of Police Work Strategic and Tactical Implications.* Boston, MA: Center for Applied Social Research.

Police Foundation. (1981). *The Newark Foot Patrol Experiment.* Washington, DC: author.

Polvi, N., T. Looman, C. Humphries and K. Pease. (1990). "Repeat Break-and-Enter Victimization: Time-Course and Crime Prevention Opportunity." *Journal of Police Science and Administration* 17: 8-11.

——— (1991). "The Time-Course of Repeat Burglary Victimization." *British Journal of Criminology* 31: 411-414.

Poyner, B. (1988). "Video Cameras and Bus Vandalism." *Security Administration* 11: 44-51.

——— (1991). "Situational Prevention in Two Car Parks." *Security Journal* 2: 96-101.

Poyner, B., and B. Webb. (1991). *Crime Free Housing.* Oxford, UK: Butterworth-Architecture.

——— and B. Webb. (1997). "Reducing Theft from Shopping Bags in City Center Markets." In R.V. Clarke (ed.), *Situational Crime Prevention: Successful Case Studies.* (2nd ed.). Monsey, NY: Criminal Justice Press.

Press, J.S. (1971). "Some Effects of an Increase in Police Manpower in the 20th Precinct of New York City." New York, NY: Rand Institute.

Read, T., and N. Tilley. (2000). *Not Rocket Science? Problem-Solving and Crime Reduction.* (Crime Reduction Series Paper 6.) London, UK: Policing and Crime Reduction Unit, Home Office.

Ready, J., L. Green Mazerolle and E. Revere. (1998). "Getting Evicted from Public Housing: An Analysis of the Factors Influencing Eviction Decisions in Six Public Housing Sites." In: L. Green Mazerolle and J. Roehl (eds.), *Civil Remedies and Crime Prevention.* (Crime Prevention Studies, vol. 9.) New York, NY: Criminal Justice Press.

Rengert, G., M. Mattson, and K. Henderson. (2001). *Campus Security: Situational Crime Prevention in High-Density Environments.* Monsey, NY: Criminal Justice Press.

Rengert, G., and J. Wasilchick. (1990). "Space, Time, and Crime: Ethnographic Insights into Residential Burglary." Report submitted to U.S. Department of Justice, National Institute of Justice.

Reiss, A. (1980). "Victim Proneness in Repeat Victimization by Type of Crime." In S. Fienberg and A. Reiss (eds.), *Indicators of Crime and Criminal Justice: Quantitative Studies.* Washington, DC: Bureau of Justice Statistics, U.S. Department of Justice.

—— (1988) "Co-Offending and Criminal Careers." In: M. Tonry and N. Morris (eds.), *Crime and Justice: A Review of Research,* vol. 10. Chicago: University of Chicago Press.

Reiss, A. and J. Roth (eds.), (1993). *Understanding and Preventing Violence.* Washington, DC: National Academy Press.

Repetto, T. (1976). "Crime Prevention and the Displacement Phenomenon." *Crime & Delinquency* 22: 166-177.

Rhodes, W., and C. Conley. (1991) "Crime and Mobility: An Empirical Study." In: P.J. Brantingham and P.L. Brantingham (eds.), *Environmental Criminology.* (2nd ed.). Newbury Park, CA: Sage Publications.

Rich, J., and D. Stone. (1996). "The Experience of Violent Injury for Young African-American Men: The Meaning of Being a 'Sucker'." *Journal of General Internal Medicine* 11: 77-82.

Rich, T. (1995). "The Use of Computerized Mapping in Crime Control and Prevention Programs." *Research in Action.* Washington, DC: National Institute of Justice, U.S. Department of Justice.

Ridgeway, G., G. L. Pierce, A.A. Braga, G. Tita, G. Wintemute, and W. Roberts. (2007). *Understanding Illegal Firearms Markets in Los Angeles: Developing Information Resources, Analytic Capacity, and Interventions.* Santa Monica, CA: Rand Corporation.

Riley, K.J., G.L. Pierce, A.A. Braga and G.J. Wintemute. (2001). "Strategic Disruption of Illegal Firearms Markets: A Los Angeles Demonstration Program.". (Funded proposal to the National Institute of Justice.) Santa Monica, CA: Rand Corporation.

References

Robinson, A. L. (2006). "Reducing Repeat Victimization Among High-Risk Victims of Domestic Violence: The Benefits of a Coordinated Community Response in Cardiff, Wales." *Violence Against Women* 12: 761-788.

Rolph, J., J. Chaiken and R. Houchens. (1981). *Methods for Estimating the Crime Rates of Individuals.* Santa Monica, CA: Rand Corporation.

Roncek, D., and P. Meier. (1991). "Bar Blocks and Crimes Revisited: Linking the Theory of Routine Activities to the Empiricism of 'Hot Spots'." *Criminology* 29: 725-755.

Rosenbaum, D. (ed.), (1994). *The Challenge of Community Policing: Testing the Promises.* Thousand Oaks, CA: Sage Publications.

Rosenbaum, D., and P. Lavrakas. (1995). "Self Reports About Place: The Application of Survey and Interview Methods to the Study of Small Areas." In: J. Eck and D. Weisburd (eds.), *Crime and Place.* (Crime Prevention Studies, vol. 4.). Monsey, NY: Criminal Justice Press.

Rosenfeld, R., and S. Decker. (1996). "Consent to Search and Seize Firearms: Evaluating an Innovative Youth Firearms Suppression Program." *Law and Contemporary Problems* 59: 197-220.

Rosenfeld, R., R. Fornango, and E. Baumer. (2005). "Did Ceasefire, Compstat, and Exile Reduce Homicide?" *Criminology and Public Policy* 4: 419-450.

Rosenfeld, R., R. Fornango, and A.F. Renfigo. (2007). "The Impact of Order-maintenance Policing on New York City Homicide and Robbery Rates." *Criminology* 45: 355-384.

Ross, H.L. (1992). "The Law and Drunk Driving." *Law and Society Review* 26: 219-230.

———— R. McCleary and G. LaFree. (1990). "Can Mandatory Jail Laws Deter Drunk Driving? The Arizona Case." *Journal of Criminal Law and Criminology* 81: 156-170.

Roth, J., J. Ryan, S. Gaffigan, C. Koper, M. Moore, J. Roehl, C. Johnson, G. Moore, R. White, M. Buerger, E. Langston and D. Thacher. (2000). *National Evaluation of the COPS Program – Title I of the 1994 Crime Act.* Washington, DC: National Institute of Justice, U.S. Department of Justice.

Rubinstein, J. (1973). *City Police.* New York, NY: Farrar, Straus, and Giroux.

Sadd, S., and R. Grinc. (1994). "Innovative Neighborhood Oriented Policing: An Evaluation of Community Policing Programs in Eight Cities." In: D. Rosenbaum (ed.), *The Challenge of Community Policing: Testing the Promises.* Thousand Oaks, CA: Sage Publications.

Sampson, A., and C. Philips. (1992). *Multiple Victimization: Racial Attacks on an East London Estate.* (Home Office Crime Prevention Unit Paper 36.) London, UK: Home Office.

Sampson, R. (2007a). *Domestic Violence.* (Problem-Oriented Guides for Police Series, Number 45.) Washington, DC: U.S. Department of Justice, Office of Community Oriented Policing Services.

———— (2007b). *False Burglar Alarms* (2nd ed.). (Problem-Oriented Guides for Police Series, Number 5.) Washington, DC: Office of Community Oriented Policing Services, U.S. Department of Justice.

Sampson, R. and M. Scott. (2000). *Tackling Crime and Other Public-Safety Problems: Case Studies in Problem Solving.* Washington, DC: Office of Community Oriented Policing Services, U.S. Department of Justice.

Sampson, R.J., and J. Cohen. (1988). "Deterrent Effects of the Police on Crime: A Replication and Theoretical Extension." *Law and Society Review* 22: 163-89.

Sampson, R.J., and S. Raudenbush. (1999). "Systematic Social Observation of Public Spaces: A New Look at Disorder in Urban Neighborhoods." *American Journal of Sociology* 105: 603-651.

Sampson, R.J., S. Raudenbush, and F. Earls. (1997). "Neighborhoods and Violent Crime." *Science* 277: 918-924.

Schnelle, J., R. Kirchner, J. Casey, P. Uselton and P. McNees. (1977). "Patrol Evaluation Research: A Multiple-Baseline Analysis of Saturation Police Patrolling During Day and Night Hours." *Journal of Applied Behavior Analysis* 10: 33-40.

Scott, J. (1991). *Social Network Analysis: A Handbook.* Newbury Park, CA: Sage Publications.

Scott, M. (2000). *Problem-Oriented Policing: Reflections on the First 20 Years.* Washington, DC: Office of Community Oriented Policing Services, U.S. Department of Justice.

———— (2004a). *Burglary of Single Family Houses in Savannah Georgia.* (Final Report to the U.S. Department of Justice, Office of Community Oriented Policing Services). Washington, DC.

———— (2004b). *The Benefits and Consequences of Police Crackdowns.* (Problem-Oriented Guides for Police, Response Guide Series, Number 1.) Washington DC: U.S. Department of Justice, Office of Community Oriented Policing Services.

———— (2006a). "Implementing Crime Prevention: Lessons Learned from Problem-Oriented Policing Projects." In: J. Knuttson and R.V. Clarke (eds.), *Putting Theory to Work: Implementing Situation Prevention and Problem-Oriented Policing.* (Crime Prevention Studies, vol. 20). Monsey, NY: Criminal Justice Press.

———— (2006b). *Drunk Driving.* (Problem-Oriented Guides for Police Series, Number 36.) Washington DC: U.S. Department of Justice, Office of Community Oriented Policing Services.

Scott, M., and R.V. Clarke. (2000). "A Review of Submission for the Herman Goldstein Excellence in Problem-Oriented Policing." In: C. Sole Brito and E. Gratto (eds.), *Problem Oriented Policing: Crime-Specific Problems, Critical Issues, and Making POP Work,* vol. 3. Washington, DC: Police Executive Research Forum.

Shaw, C., and H. McKay. (1942). *Juvenile Delinquency in Urban Areas.* Chicago, IL: University of Chicago Press.

Shaw, J. (1995). "Community Policing Against Guns: Public Opinion of the Kansas City Gun Experiment." *Justice Quarterly* 12: 695-710.

Shaw, M. (2001). "Time Heals All Wounds?" In: G. Farrell and K. Pease (eds.), *Repeat Victimization*. (Crime Prevention Studies, vol. 12.). Monsey, NY: Criminal Justice Press.

Sherman, L. (1987). "Repeat Calls to Police in Minneapolis." *Crime Control Reports Number 4*. Washington, DC: Crime Control Institute.

——— (1990). "Police Crackdowns: Initial and Residual Deterrence." In: M. Tonry and N. Morris (eds.), *Crime and Justice: A Review of Research*, vol. 12. Chicago, IL: University of Chicago Press.

——— (1991). "Herman Goldstein: Problem-Oriented Policing [book review]." *Journal of Criminal Law and Criminology* 82: 693-702.

——— (1992a). "Attacking Crime: Police and Crime Control." In M. Tonry and N. Morris (eds.) *Modern Policing*. (Crime and Justice series, vol. 15.) Chicago, IL: University of Chicago Press.

——— (1992b). *Policing Domestic Violence: Experiments and Dilemmas*. New York, NY: The Free Press.

——— (1995). "Hot Spots of Crime and Criminal Careers of Places." In: J. Eck and D. Weisburd (eds.), *Crime and Place*. (Crime Prevention Studies, vol. 4.) Monsey, NY: Criminal Justice Press.

——— (1997). "Policing for Crime Prevention." In: University of Maryland, Department of Criminology and Criminal Justice (eds.), *Preventing Crime: What Works, What Doesn't, What's Promising*. Washington, DC: Office of Justice Programs, U.S. Department of Justice.

Sherman, L., and R. Berk. (1984). "The Specific Deterrent Effects of Arrest for Domestic Assault." *American Sociological Review* 49: 261-72.

Sherman, L., P. Gartin and M. Buerger. (1989). "Hot Spots of Predatory Crime: Routine Activities and the Criminology of Place." *Criminology* 27: 27-56.

Sherman, L., and D. Rogan. (1995a). "Effects of Gun Seizures on Gun Violence: 'Hot Spots' Patrol in Kansas City." *Justice Quarterly* 12: 673-694.

——— (1995b). "Deterrent Effects of Police Raids on Crack Houses: A Randomized Controlled Experiment." *Justice Quarterly* 12: 755-782.

Sherman, L., J. Schmidt and R. Velke. (1992). *High Crime Taverns: A RECAP Project in Problem-Oriented Policing*. (Final Report to the National Institute of Justice.) Washington, DC: Crime Control Institute.

Sherman, L., J. Shaw and D. Rogan. (1995). *The Kansas City Gun Experiment*. (National Institute of Justice, Research in Brief series.) Washington, DC: U.S. Department of Justice.

Sherman, L., and D. Weisburd. (1995). "General Deterrent Effects of Police Patrol in Crime Hot Spots: A Randomized Controlled Trial." *Justice Quarterly* 12: 625-648.

Silverman, E.B. (1999). *NYPD Battles Crime: Innovative Strategies in Policing*. Boston, MA: Northeastern University Press.

Skogan, W. (1990). *Disorder and Decline: Crime and the Spiral of Decay in American Neighborhoods*. New York, NY: Free Press.

References

——— (1999). "Measuring What Matters: Crime, Disorder, and Fear." In: R. Langworthy (ed.), *Measuring What Matters: Proceedings from the Policing Research Institute Meetings.* Washington, DC; National Institute of Justice, U.S. Department of Justice.

——— (2006). *Police and Community in Chicago: A Tale of Three Cities.* New York: Oxford University Press.

Skogan, W., and G. Antunes. (1979). "Information, Apprehension, and Deterrence: Exploring the Limits of Police Productivity." *Journal of Criminal Justice* 7: 217-242.

Skogan, W., and K. Frydl (eds.), (2004). *Fairness and Effectiveness in Policing: The Evidence.* Committee to Review Research on Police Policy and Practices. Committee on Law and Justice, Division of Behavioral and Social Sciences and Education. Washington, DC: The National Academies Press.

Skogan, W., and S. Hartnett. (1997). *Community Policing, Chicago Style.* New York, NY: Oxford University Press.

Skogan, W., S. Hartnett, J. DuBois, J. Comey, M. Kaiser, and J. Lovig. (1999). *On the Beat: Police and Community Problem Solving.* Boulder, CO: Westview Press.

Skolnick, J.H., and D. Bayley. (1986). *The New Blue Line: Police Innovations in American Cities.* New York: Free Press.

Sloan-Howitt, M.A., and G. L. Kelling. (1990). "Subway Graffiti in New York City: 'Getting Up' vs. 'Meanin' It and 'Cleanin' It'." *Security Journal* 1: 131-136.

Smith, C., and G. Patterson. (1980). "Cognitive Mapping and the Subjective Geography of Crime." In: D. Georges-Abeyie and K. Harries (eds.), *Crime: A Spatial Perspective.* New York, NY: Columbia University Press.

Smith, M. (2003). "Exploring Target Attractiveness in Vandalism: An Experimental Approach." In M. Smith and D. Cornish (eds.), *Theory for Practice in Situational Crime Prevention.* (Crime Prevention Studies, vol. 16.) Monsey, New York: Criminal Justice Press.

Smith, M., R.V. Clarke, and K. Pease. (2002). "Anticipatory Benefits in Crime Prevention." In: N. Tilley (ed.), *Analysis for Crime Prevention.* (Crime Prevention Studies, vol. 13.) Monsey, NY: Criminal Justice Press.

Sole Brito, C., and T. Allan (eds.), (1999). *Problem-Oriented Policing: Crime-Specific Problems, Critical Issues, and Making POP Work,* vol. 2. Washington, DC: Police Executive Research Forum.

Sole Brito, C., and E. Gratto (eds.), (2000). *Problem-Oriented Policing: Crime-Specific Problems, Critical Issues, and Making POP Work,* vol. 3. Washington, DC: Police Executive Research Forum.

Sousa, W., and G. L. Kelling. (2006). "Of 'Broken Windows,' Criminology, and Criminal Justice." In: D.L. Weisburd and A.A. Braga (eds.), *Police Innovation: Contrasting Perspectives.* New York: Cambridge University Press.

Sparrow, M. (1991). "The Application of Network Analysis to Criminal Intelligence: An Assessment of the Prospects." *Social Networks* 13: 251-274.

——— (2000). *License to Steal: How Fraud Bleeds America's Health Care System* (rev. ed.). Boulder, CO: Westview Press.

Sparrow, M., M.H. Moore and D.M. Kennedy. (1990). *Beyond 911: A New Era for Policing.* New York, NY: Basic Books.

Spelman, W. (1986). "The Depth of a Dangerous Temptation: Crime Control and the Dangerous Offender.". (Final Report to the National Institute of Justice.) Washington, DC: Police Executive Research Forum.

———— (1990). *Repeat Offender Programs*. Washington, DC: Police Executive Research Forum.

———— (1993). "Abandoned Buildings: Magnets for Crime?" *Journal of Criminal Justice* 21: 481-495.

———— (1995). "Criminal Careers of Public Places." In: J. Eck and D. Weisburd (eds.), *Crime and Place*. (Crime Prevention Studies, vol. 4.). Monsey, NY: Criminal Justice Press.

Spelman, W., and D. Brown. (1984). *Calling the Police: Citizen Reporting of Serious Crime*. Washington, DC: U.S. Government Printing Office.

Spelman, W., and J.E. Eck. (1989). "Sitting Ducks, Ravenous Wolves, and Helping Hands: New Approaches to Urban Policing." *Public Affairs Comment*, 35(2): 1-9.

Spergel, I. A. (1995). *The Youth Gang Problem: A Community Approach*. New York and London: Oxford University Press.

Spergel, I. A., and G. David Curry. (1990). "Strategies and Perceived Agency Effectiveness in Dealing with the Youth Gang Problem." In: C.R. Huff (ed.), *Gangs in America*. Newbury Park, CA: Sage Publications.

———— (1993). "The National Youth Gang Survey: A Research and Development Process." In: A. Goldstein and C.R. Huff (eds.), *Gang Intervention Handbook*. Champaign-Urbana: Research Press

Sutton, M. (1998). *Handling Stolen Goods and Theft: A Market Reduction Approach*. (Home Office Research and Statistic Directorate Research Findings No. 69.) London, UK: Home Office.

Sutton, M., J. Schneider and S. Hetherington. (2001). *Tackling Theft with the Market Reduction Approach*. (Crime Reduction Series Paper 8.) London, UK: Home Office

Taylor, R. (1997a). "Social Order and Disorder of Street-Blocks and Neighborhoods: Ecology, Micro-ecology, and the Systematic Model of Social Disorganization." *Journal of Research in Crime and Delinquency* 34: 113-155.

———— (1997b). "Crime, Grime, and Responses to Crime: Relative Impacts of Neighborhood Structure, Crime, and Physical Deterioration on Residents and Business Personnel in the Twin Cities." In: S.P. Lab (ed.), *Crime Prevention at a Crossroads*. Cincinnati, OH: Anderson.

———— (1999). "The Incivilities Thesis: Theory, Measurement, and Policy." In: R. Langworthy (ed.), *Measuring What Matters: Proceedings from the Policing Research Institute Meetings*. Washington, DC; National Institute of Justice, U.S. Department of Justice.

———— (2001). *Breaking Away from Broken Windows: Baltimore Neighborhoods and the Nationwide Fight Against Crime, Grime, Fear, and Decline*. Boulder, CO: Westview Press.

Taylor, R., and S. Gottfredson. (1986). "Environment Design, Crime, and Prevention: An Examination of Community Dynamics." In: A. Reiss and M. Tonry (eds.), *Communities and Crime.* (Crime and Justice series, vol. 8.) Chicago, IL: University of Chicago Press.

Tilley, N. (1992). *Safer Cities and Community Safety Strategies.* (Crime Prevention Paper No. 38.) London, UK: Home Office.

———— (1999). "The Relationship Between Crime Prevention and Problem-Oriented Policing." In: C. Sole Brito and T. Allan (eds.), *Problem-Oriented Policing: Crime-Specific Problems, Critical Issues, and Making POP Work* vol. 2. Washington, DC: Police Executive Research Forum.

———— (2002). "Introduction: Analysis for Crime Prevention." In: N. Tilley (ed.), *Analysis for Crime Prevention.* (Crime Prevention Studies, vol. 13.). Monsey, NY: Criminal Justice Press.

Tita, G., K.J. Riley, and P. Greenwood. (2003). "From Boston to Boyle Heights: The Process and Prospects of a 'Pulling Levers' Strategy in a Los Angeles Barrio." In S.H. Decker (ed.), *Policing Gangs and Youth Violence.* Belmont, CA: Wadsworth Publishing Company.

Tita, G., K.J. Riley, G. Ridgeway, C. Grammich, A. Abrahamse and P. Greenwood. (2004). *Reducing Gun Violence: Results from an Intervention in East Los Angeles.* Santa Monica, CA: Rand Corporation.

Titus, R., and A. Gover. (2001). "Personal Fraud: The Victims and the Scams." In: G. Farrell and K. Pease (eds.), *Repeat Victimization.* (Crime Prevention Studies, vol. 12.) Monsey, NY: Criminal Justice Press.

Titus, R., F. Heinzelmann and J. Boyle. (1995). "Victimization of Persons by Fraud." *Crime & Delinquency* 41: 54-72.

Toch, H., and J.D. Grant. (1991). *Police as Problem Solvers.* New York, NY: Plenum.

Townsley, M., R. Homel, and J. Chaseling. (2003). "Infectious Burglaries: A Test of the Near Repeat Hypothesis." *British Journal of Criminology* 43: 615-633.

Travis, Jeremy. 1998. "Crime, Justice, and Public Policy." Plenary presentation to the American Society of Criminology, Washington, DC, November 12. (http://www.ojp.usdoj.gov/nij/speeches/asc.htm).

Trojanowicz, R. (1983). "An Evaluation of a Neighborhood Foot Patrol Program." *Journal of Police Science and Administration* 11: 410-419.

Trojanowicz, R., and B. Bucqueroux. (1990). *Community Policing: A Contemporary Perspective.* Cincinnati, OH: Anderson Publishing Company.

———— and B. Bucqueroux. (1994). *Community Policing: How to Get Started.* Cincinnati, OH: Anderson Publishing Company.

Tyler, T.R. (1990). *Why People Obey the Law: Procedural Justice, Legitimacy, and Compliance.* New Haven, CT: Yale University Press.

———— (2000). "Social Justice: Outcomes and Procedures." *International Journal of Psychology* 35: 117-125.

———— (2001). "Public Trust and Confidence in Legal Authorities: What Do Majority and Minority Groups Members Want from the Law and Legal Institutions?" *Behavioral Sciences and the Law* 19: 215-235.

———— (2006). "Legitimacy and Legitimation." *Annual Review of Psychology* 57: 375-400.

Tyler, T.R., and C. Wakslak. (2004). "Profiling and the Legitimacy of the Police: Procedural Justice, Attributions of Motive, and the Acceptance of Social Authority." *Criminology* 42: 13-42.

U.S. Bureau of Alcohol, Tobacco, and Firearms. (ATF). (2000a). *Crime Gun Trace Reports. (1999): National Report.* Washington, DC: author.

——— (2000b). *Following the Gun: Enforcing Federal Laws Against Firearms Traffickers.* Washington, DC: author.

U.S. National Advisory Commission on Civil Disorders. (1968). *Report of the National Advisory Commission on Civil Disorders.* Washington, DC: U.S. Government Printing Office.

U.S. National Highway Traffic Safety Administration. (1995). *DWI Detection and Standard Field Sobriety Testing Student Manual.* Washington, DC: U.S. Department of Transportation.

U.S. President's Commission on Law Enforcement and Administration of Criminal Justice. (1967a). *The Challenge of Crime in a Free Society.* Washington, DC: US Government Printing Office.

——— (1967b). *Task Force Report: The Police.* Washington, DC: U.S. Government Printing Office.

van Djik, J. (2001). "Attitudes of Victims and Repeat Victims Towards the Police: Results from the International Crime Victims Survey." In: G. Farrell and K. Pease (eds.), *Repeat Victimization.* (Crime Prevention Studies, vol. 12.) Monsey, NY: Criminal Justice Press.

Visher, C., and D.L. Weisburd. (1998). "Identifying What Works: Recent Trends in Crime Prevention Strategies." *Crime, Law and Social Change* 28: 223-242.

Wakeling, S. (2003). *Ending Gang Homicide: Deterrence Can Work.* (Perspectives on Violence Prevention, No. 1.) Sacramento, CA: California Attorney General's Office/California Health and Human Services Agency.

Walker, S. (1992). *The Police in America.* (2nd ed.). New York, NY: McGraw-Hill.

Warr, M. (2002). *Companions in Crime: The Social Aspects of Criminal Conduct.* New York: Cambridge University Press.

Wartell, J., and N. La Vigne. (2004). *Prescription Fraud.* (Problem-Oriented Guides for Police Series, No. 24.) Washington, DC: U.S. Department of Justice, Office of Community Oriented Policing Services.

Weisburd, D.L. (1994). "Evaluating Community Policing: Role Tensions Between Practitioners and Evaluators." In: D. Rosenbaum (ed.), *The Challenge of Community Policing: Testing the Promises.* Thousand Oaks, CA: Sage Publications.

Weisburd, D.L. S. Bushway, C. Lum, and S. Yang. (2004). "Trajectories of Crime at Places: A Longitudinal Study of Street Segments in the City of Seattle." *Criminology* 42: 283-322.

Weisburd, D.L. and J. Eck. (2004). "What Can Police Do to Reduce Crime, Disorder, and Fear?" *Annals of the American Academy of Political and Social Science* 593: 42-65.

Weisburd, D.L. and L. Green. (1994). "Defining the Drug Market: The Case of the Jersey City DMAP System." In: D.L. MacKenzie and C. Uchida (eds.), *Drugs and Crime: Evaluating Public Policy Initiatives.* Newbury Park, CA: Sage Publications.

——— (1995a). "Policing Drug Hot Spots: The Jersey City DMA Experiment." *Justice Quarterly* 12(3): 711-736.

———— (1995b). "Measuring Immediate Spatial Displacement: Methodological Issues and Problems." In: J. Eck and D. Weisburd (eds.), *Crime and Place*. (Crime Prevention Studies, vol. 4.) Monsey, NY: Criminal Justice Press.

Weisburd, D.L. L. Maher and L. Sherman. (1992). "Contrasting Crime General and Crime Specific Theory: The Case of Hot Spots of Crime." *Advances in Criminological Theory* 4: 45-69.

Weisburd, D.L.S. Mastrofski and R. Greenspan. (2001). *Compstat and Organizational Change*. Washington, DC: Police Foundation.

Weisburd, D.L. S. Mastrofski, A.M. McNally, R. Greenspan, and J.Willis. (2003). "Reforming to Preserve: Compstat and Strategic Problem Solving inAmerican Policing." *Criminology and Public Policy* 2: 421-457.

Weisburd, D.L. and J. McElroy. (1988). "Enacting the CPO Role: Findings from the New York City Pilot Program in Community Policing." In: J. Greene and S. Mastrofski (eds.), *Community Policing: Rhetoric or Reality?* New York, NY: Praeger.

Weisburd, D.L. and J.T. McEwen (eds.), (1997). *Crime Mapping and Crime Prevention*. (Crime Prevention Studies, vol. 8.). Monsey, NY: Criminal Justice Press.

Weisburd, D.L. and C. Uchida. (1993). "Raising Questions of Law and Order." In: D. Weisburd and C. Uchida (eds.), *Police Innovation and Control of the Police: Problems of Law, Order, and Community*. New York, NY: Springer-Verlag.

Weisburd, D.L., E.J. Waring and E.F. Chayet. (1995). "Specific Deterrence in a Sample of Offenders Convicted of White Collar Crimes." *Criminology* 33: 587-607.

Weisburd, D.L.L. Wyckoff, J. Ready, J. Eck, J. Hinkle, and F. Gajewski. (2006). "Does Crime Just Move Around the Corner? A Controlled Study of Spatial Displacement and Diffusion of Crime Control Benefits." *Criminology* 44: 549-592.

Wellford, C., J. Pepper, and C.Petrie (eds.), (2005). *Firearms and Violence: A Critical Review*. (Committee to Improve Research Information and Data on Firearms. Committee on Law and Justice, Division of Behavioral and Social Sciences and Education.) Washington, DC: The National Academies Press.

Welsh, B.C., and D. Farrington. (2004). "Surveillance for Crime Prevention in Public Space: Results and Policy Choices in Britain and America." *Criminology and Public Policy* 3: 497-526.

Whyte, W.F. (1943). *Street Corner Society: The Social Structure of an Italian Slum*. Chicago: University of Chicago Press.

Willis, J.J., S.D. Mastrofski, and D.L. Weisburd. (2004). "Compstat and Bureaucracy: A Case Study of Challenges and Opportunities for Change." *Justice Quarterly* 21: 463-496.

Wilson, J.Q. (1993). "The Problem of Defining Agency Success." In: Princeton Study Group on Criminal Justice Performance Measures (ed.), *Performance Measures for the Criminal Justice System*. Washington, DC: Bureau of Justice Statistics.

Wilson, J.Q., and G. Kelling. (1982). "Broken Windows: The Police and Neighborhood Safety." *Atlantic Monthly*. (March): 29-38.

Wilson, O.W., and R. McLaren. (1977). *Police Administration*. (4th ed.). New York, NY: McGraw-Hill.

Winship, C., and J. Berrien. (1999). "Boston Cops and Black Churches." *The Public Interest.* Summer: 52-68.

Wolfgang, M., R. Figlio and T. Sellin. (1972). *Delinquency in a Birth Cohort.* Chicago, IL: University of Chicago Press.

Worrall, J. (2002). *Does "Broken Windows" Law Enforcement Reduce Serious Crime?.* (CICG Research Brief.) Sacramento, CA: California Institute for County Government.

Wright, J.D., and P.H. Rossi. (1994). *Armed and Considered Dangerous: A Survey of Felons and Their Firearms.* (2nd ed.). New York, NY: Aldine de Guyter.

Wright, J.D., J. Sheley and M.D Smith. (1992). "Kids, Guns, and Killing Fields." *Society* November/December: 84-89.

Zhang, S. (2002). "Chinese Gangs: Familial and Cultural Dynamics." In: C.R. Huff (ed.), *Gangs in America.* (3rd ed.). Newbury Park, CA: Sage Publications.

Zimring, F. (1981). "Kids, Groups, and Crime: Some Implications of a Well-Known Secret." *Journal of Criminal Law and Criminology* 72: 867-885.

Zimring, F., and G. Hawkins. (1973). *Deterrence: The Legal Threat in Crime Control.* Chicago, IL: University of Chicago Press.

Author Index

Subject Index

Churches, 43, 85, 180

Citizen satisfaction, 6, 7, 29, 174

City agencies, 39, 56, 182

Civil laws and remedies, 25, 49, 72, 178

Civil rights movement, 8

Classification of "problems," 17–18

Clergy, 95, 178, 179

Closed-circuit television, 45, 47, 70, 194 (see CCTV)

Clubs, 33, 64, 65, 116 (see also Bars; Pubs)

Coerced abstinence, 99, 101

Committee to Review Research on Police Policy and Practices), 33, 83

Community partnerships, 12, 174–179

Community patrol officer program (New York City), 176

Community policing, 12, 155, 168, 169, 177

Compstat, 53, 91, 151, 152, 153, 165, 166, 167, 168

Continuum of police strategies, 60

Controllers, 18

Convenience stores, 149, 161, 193

Co-offending, 75, 78, 79

Corruption, 6

Crack cocaine, 58

Crackdowns, 36, 57, 58, 89, 103, 149

Crime analysis, 22, 115, 145, 146, 147, 171, 185

Crime analysts, 18, 148, 149, 150, 174

Crime and Disorder Reduction Partnerships, 145

Crime facilitators, 75, 104, 118

Crime fighter model, 7–8

Crime habitats, 50, 51

Crime incident reviews, 156

Crime mapping, 148, 150, 151, 152, 154, 156

Crime pattern theory, 49 (see also Environmental criminology)

Crime places, 39–72

Crime prevention, 5–9 (see also Deterrence, Situational Crime Prevention, and specific projects)

Crime scripts, 47 (see also Script analytic approach)

CrimeStat III, 151

Crime triangle, 4, 28, 29, 48, 155

Criminal justice agencies, 84, 92, 96, 174, 184, 185

Criminal justice system, 5, 75, 78, 82, 89, 102, 103, 118, 119, 141, 146, 156, 179

Criminal network maps, 157

Criminology and criminological research, 4–6, 41–55, 185–187

Dangerous offenders, 75, 78, 80, 81, 83

Department of Justice (U.S.), 75, 90, 107

Detectives, 7, 8, 58, 76, 81, 82, 83, 122, 185

Deterrence, 5, 53, 71, 74, 75, 89, 92, 93, 94, 96, 100, 109, 119, 138, 139, 160, 180, 195

Diffusion (of benefits), 32, 40, 69, 133, 168, 171, 186, 190, 192, 194, 195, 196, 197

Directed patrol, 1, 20, 24, 56, 58, 153

Disorder, 9, 33, 40, 45, 46, 49, 52, 53, 54, 55, 56, 57, 58, 60, 61,